D1744840

Unexplored Dimensions of Discrimination

Reports for the Fondazione Rodolfo DeBenedetti

Unexplored Dimensions of Discrimination

Edited by

Tito Boeri, Eleonora Patacchini, and Giovanni Peri

OXFORD
UNIVERSITY PRESS

Great Clarendon Street, Oxford, OX2 6DP,
United Kingdom

Oxford University Press is a department of the University of Oxford.
It furthers the University's objective of excellence in research, scholarship,
and education by publishing worldwide. Oxford is a registered trade mark of
Oxford University Press in the UK and in certain other countries

© Fondazione Rodolfo Debenedetti 2015

The moral rights of the authors have been asserted

First Edition published in 2015

All rights reserved. No part of this publication may be reproduced, stored in
a retrieval system, or transmitted, in any form or by any means, without the
prior permission in writing of Oxford University Press, or as expressly permitted
by law, by licence or under terms agreed with the appropriate reprographics
rights organization. Enquiries concerning reproduction outside the scope of the
above should be sent to the Rights Department, Oxford University Press, at the
address above

You must not circulate this work in any other form
and you must impose this same condition on any acquirer

Published in the United States of America by Oxford University Press
198 Madison Avenue, New York, NY 10016, United States of America

British Library Cataloguing in Publication Data

Data available

Library of Congress Control Number: 2014957931

ISBN 978-0-19-872985-3

Cover image: © Digital Vision

Links to third party websites are provided by Oxford in good faith and
for information only. Oxford disclaims any responsibility for the materials
contained in any third party website referenced in this work.

Acknowledgments

Both parts of this book were originally prepared for the fourteenth European conference of the Fondazione Rodolfo Debenedetti, held in Trani in June 2012. This book draws much on the discussion in Trani, which involved a qualified audience of academicians, professional economists, representatives of unions and employers associations, lawyers, anti-discrimination associations, and policymakers. Needless to say, we are very much indebted to all those who attended that conference and contributed actively to the discussion.

In particular, we wish to express our gratitude to Daniela Del Boca, Sergio Briguglio, and Matteo Winckler, who provided very insightful remarks in the final panel. We are also indebted to Elena Gentile (Regional Councellor for Welfare, Work and Equal Opportunities) who opened the conference.

We are most grateful to Carlo De Benedetti, who enabled the Fondazione to exist and made possible this event, to which he also contributed with particularly insightful opening remarks.

Finally, special thanks go to Barbara Biasi, RachelePoggi, and Roberta Marcaletti who assisted me in the organization of the conference and worked hard and skillfully in preparing the background material for this volume.

Contents

List of Figures

List of Tables

List of Contributors

Massimo Anelli (University of California, Davis)

Tito Boeri (Bocconi University)

Luca Flabbi (IDB)

Christopher J. Flinn (New York University)

Ainara González de San Román (Universidad del País Vasco, Spain)

Daniel Hamermesh (University of Austin, Texas)

Sara de La Rica (Universidad del País Vasco, Spain)

Alan Manning (London School of Economics)

Jan C. van Ours (Tilburg University)

Eleonora Patacchini (Cornell University)

Giovanni Peri (University of California, Davis, NBER)

Giuseppe Ragusa (LUISS Guido Carli, Rome)

Mauricio Tejada (ILADES – Universidad Alberto Hurtado)

Yves Zenou (Stockholm University)

Introduction

Tito Boeri

Labor market discrimination is one of those allegations that is more difficult to prove before a jury of economists than before a judicial court. The issue is that the evidence typically being produced by the plaintiff in the trial period is more a measure of ignorance than truly a measure of discrimination. In many court rulings discrimination is identified in some residual, apparently unexplained, variation in the treatment (wage, hiring, layoff) of workers. For instance, differences in male and females wages not accounted for by differences in observed characteristics (age, education, previous work experience, etc.) between men and women are generally considered by lawyers as evidence of discrimination. The presumption is that, once account is made of age, education, work experience, and other observable characteristics of the worker, residual differences in the treatment of workers can only be attributed to prejudice and discriminatory practices of employers. This residual measure of discrimination seems to fit well into the economic definition of discrimination. The latter dates back to Kenneth Arrow and refers to "the valuation in the market place of personal characteristics of the worker that are unrelated to worker productivity" (Arrow 1973). In other words, discrimination occurs whenever the labor market position of individuals (the fact of having a job, the wage being received, the amount of hours worked) depends on characteristics that are unrelated to their productivity: a worker is treated differently than other workers simply because of her gender, race, age, sexual orientation, beauty, and so on, independently of her productivity.

Unfortunately this residual measure of discrimination may understate as well as overstate the actual extent of labor market discrimination (Altonji and Blank 1999). Some of the observed characteristics may be influenced by the existence of discrimination. Women, for instance, may invest less in education in anticipation of wage discrimination that reduces for them the returns to education. They may also devote more time to non-market, home-related, activities than their spouses and become the primary care-givers for children, giving up on career plans, because they expect a more favorable labor market treatment for their husbands. They may therefore become (desperate) housewives even if their performance in the university was way better than that of their not so much better half. When this self-selection of women into non-employment takes place, the true extent of discrimination is understated by gender differences in returns to education because also the differences in educational attainments are attributable to discrimination. In order to tackle these self-selection issues, one should ideally take into account of workers' histories well before labor market entry or at least make inferences as to the decisions made by individuals with respect to labor market participation.

It is also possible that some factors affecting individual productivity are not observed by researchers (and by the judges themselves). These omitted characteristics may be related to human capital characteristics and tastes and can be very important in affecting labor market outcomes. A large body of socio-psychological research, for instance, suggests that men and women differ quite systematically in psychological traits (including the so-called Big Five, that is, extroversion, agreeableness, conscientiousness, neuroticism, and openness to experience) and preferences. This makes some types of jobs more attractive to women and other jobs more attractive to men (Bertrand 2010). Thus, measures of discrimination not accounting for these unobserved differences in preferences may overstate the actual extent of discrimination.

The first part of this book is a major attempt to deal with these self-selection and unobservability issues in assessing the gender wage gap. A team of researchers led by Giovanni Peri, and including Massimo Anelli, Sara de La Rica, Ainara Gonzáles de San Román, Luca Flabbi, and Mauricio Tejada gathered a wealth of data on education and marriage choices of men and women, focusing in particular on the US, Spanish, and Italian labor markets. They developed quite sophisticated econometric models to estimate from these data the underlying and unobserved choice rules rather than confining themselves to characterize (reduced form) correlations between observed variables (pay, education, age, etc.). This enabled them also to consider at the same time gender wage and employment gaps. Last but not least, they made a major data collection effort, tracking individuals in Milan from their high school performance to major choice, to the labor market outcomes after tertiary education. To my knowledge, this is the first time that a similar "from paddle to the grave" tracking of potential determinants of wage gaps has been made.

The effort is well placed as the authors can address a number of substantial issues, which were left unexplored by most previous research on gender wage

1. How relevant is the different role played by men and women in rearing children on their labor market outcomes, and more general how do family needs affect differentially the working career of men and women?

2. How relevant is the choice of college major in determining the occupation and wage of individuals and how different is it between genders?

Some of the results among these unexplored dimensions of discrimination are quite striking. The authors find that the link between college major and occupational choice is very strong in all countries. There are two key dimensions along which women self-select themselves into less paid curricula. First, highly educated women, in spite of their better academic performance than men, tend to avoid math-intensive majors as Engineering and Mathematical sciences, preferring majors in the Humanities. Second, this major choice is coherent with an occupational choice giving priority to "teaching-type" jobs, as opposed to the engineering types of jobs, which are dominated by men. This double and interrelated difference (major and occupational choice) contributes significantly to explain gender gaps in career, wage, and earnings.

These findings are important in refining equal opportunity legislation and making it effective well before labor market entry of women takes place. For instance, a strategy to counteract women segregation into less paid jobs may also consider reducing the degree of tracking in school curricula. Allowing students to specialize later and postpone their major choice, it is possible that they would not follow stereotypes attributing to women talents generally outside the hard sciences, engineering and math. One may also argue in favor of a more balanced composition by gender of teachers in maternity schools as "teaching-type" of jobs may become popular among women on the basis of the example of pre-schools. Needless to say, the option to first enroll in the Humanities and then opt for teaching jobs may also be inspired by the choice of having more time for family responsibilities. In this respect, it is family policies inspired by equal opportunity principles (e.g., requiring a sizeable paternity leave) that may affect choices made well before entering the labor market.

While the first part of the book focuses on unexplored mechanisms generating labor market discrimination along the gender divide, the second part of the volume addresses unexplored outcomes. Discrimination has been typically addressed by the economic literature along the gender and the ethnic divide. There are, however, many other dimensions where prejudice may arise and affect labor market outcomes.

The second part of the book is on these unexplored dimension of discrimination, and a particular attention is placed on physical appearance, obesity, religion, and sexual orientation. One of the reasons why these dimensions have been less considered by empirical research is that it is extremely hard to gather information on these characteristics. The research team led by Eleonora Patacchini, and including Giuseppe Ragusa and Yves Zenou, tries to fill this gap. The first very useful thing they do is to offer an up to date literature review of the few studies devoted to these dimensions of discrimination. Next they draw on non-experimental data covering a number of European countries. Finally, they draw on a field experiment, carried out in the two largest Italian cities (Rome and Milan), by sending almost 2,500 "fake" CVs to real ads, where all curricula had pictures and some contained information about involvement in gay or lesbian friendly associations.

The results are quite striking in that they suggest that discrimination along these dimensions can be substantial. Muslims appear to be the most penalized religious minority in Europe in terms of labor-market outcomes, homosexuals have a lower chance of being employed and to participate to the labor market than their heterosexual counterparts, and obese women (identified on the basis of their Body Mass Index (BMI)) have significantly lower employment prospects that non-obese women. It is possible that part of the observed asymmetries in employment and wage outcomes is related to different attitudes towards work, but the size of these gaps is so large as to suggest that there is also a reluctance of employers to hire individuals with these characteristics. Moreover, the aforementioned "fake" CV experiment is concentrated on labor demand for workers having apparently the same characteristics, except sexual orientation or beauty. Its results, described in detail in Chapter 8 (Part II of this volume), indicate that male homosexuals have a 30 percent lower call-back rate than the average, while beauty significantly improves labor market prospects of women, notably low-skilled women, and not those of men. Notice that applications were not for positions of salesman or requiring a visual contact with clients, nor for traditionally female-dominated or male-dominated occupations, but were for the most related to jobs in call centers.

Although these types of experiments, in the tradition of correspondence study techniques, have not been undertaken in a large number of countries and, as most experiments, pose questions of external validity, it is nevertheless possible to compare them with those of previous studies in order to gauge their relevance. Most studies, including the pioneering by Bertrand and Mullainathan (2004) and a recent one on China by Zhou et al. (2013), have been looking either at race or gender discrimination. This book offers one of the first applications of the correspondence techniques to the study of discrimination along sexual orientation. The only previous study we are aware of is from Ahmed et al. (2011), who investigated whether homosexuals experienced discrimination in the hiring process in Sweden, found that, on average, gay men received 4 percent fewer callbacks than heterosexual men while lesbian women received 6 percent less callbacks than heterosexual women. This is a much smaller effect than that found by Patacchini, Ragusa, and Zenou.

Discrimination along the physical appearance dimension had been pre-viously investigated. For instance, Ruffle and Shtudiner (2010) sent out application letters to employers with and without a picture of either an attractive male/female or a plain-looking male/female. They found that attractive males are much more likely to receive callback than plain males while for females the difference in callback rates between attractive and plain applicants was small. This result goes just the other way round than the effect observed in Italy.

Taken together, the findings in the second part of the volume suggest that there is a large scope for a better enforcement of anti-discrimination laws in Europe. They are consistent with data on perceived discrimination (recalled also in the insightful discussion of the report by Alan Manning) indicating than more than 50 percent of Europeans believe that there is widespread discrimination by ethnic origin and sexual orientation. Unfortunately there is little tradition of jurisprudence counteracting labor market discrimination on this side of the Atlantic. Legislation is fairly strong—a 2000 EU Directive puts the burden of proof mostly on the employer—but apparently rarely enforced. Unions have for long underestimated the importance of anti-discrimination practices as they have been relying on employment protection legislation to defend workers against unfair layoffs. The problem is that in countries, like Italy, the law explicitly requires an involvement of unions in the suing of employers for discrimination practices. No role is given to other voluntary associations representing specifically some categories of workers potentially subject to discrimination, such as gay or lesbian associations.

Employers are typically not keen to embark on anti-discrimination cam-paigns as they reduce their monopsony power. The presence of market imperfections is also a factor that prevents competition to wash away discriminatory practices, by making firms led by prejudiced employers no longer viable.

As the report focuses on outcomes more than on the underlying mecha-nisms, it cannot identify specific policies that could tackle the sources of the observed asymmetries in labor market outcomes, which may not necessarily be related only to prejudice, but also to poor information about the quality of applicants, and hence so-called statistical discrimination, and self-selection of some categories of workers in occupational profiles offering lower wages and less stability than the average job.

One area where there is little doubt that policies could be improved is that of migration restrictions. Legislations requiring a frequent renewal of residence permits and conditioning these renewals upon the fact of having a job, put many migrant workers in a sort of limbo, conveying a very strong bargaining power to their employers. There are also restrictions for non-EU citizens in the access to public sector jobs, and rules that explicitly prevent them from having access to some cash transfers. Removing these asymmetries would be very useful also to promote a culture of equal opportunity and diversity at the workplace. Diversity is particularly important as employers may often favor their own kind rather than discriminating against specific minorities. Put it in the new terminology introduced by Daniel Hamermesh, they may be affected by endophilia—preferences for their own—rather than by exophilia, disliking others.

References

Ahmed, A., Andersson, L., and Hammarsted, M. (2011). "Are homosexuals discriminated against in the hiring process?", mimeo.

Altonji, J. and Blank, R. (1999). "Race and gender in the labor market." In: O. Ashenfelter and D. Card (Eds.), *Handbook of Labor Economics*, vol. 3. Amsterdam: Elsevier, pp. 3143–3259.

Arrow, K. J. (1973). "The theory of discrimination." In: O. Ashenfelter and A. Rees (Eds.), *Discrimination in Labor Markets*. Princeton: Princeton University Press, p. 3.

Bertrand, B. and Mullainathan, S. (2004). "Are Emily and Greg more employable than Lakisha and Jamal? A field experiment on labor market discrimination." *American Economic Review* 94: 991–1013.

Bertrand, M. (2010). "New perspectives on gender." In:O. Ashenfelter and D. Card (Eds.), *Handbook of Labor* Economics, vol. 4b. Amsterdam: Elsevier, pp. 1543–1590.

Ruffle, B. J. and Shtudiner, Z. (2010). "Are good-looking people more employable?", mimeo.

Zhou, X., Zhang, J., and Song, X. (2013). "Gender discrimination in hiring: Evidence from 19,130 Resumes in China," mimeo.

Part I
The Wage Gap in the Transition from School to Work

1

Gender Gap in Labor Market Outcomes: Less Explored Aspects and Dimensions

Giovanni Peri and Massimo Anelli

1.1 Introduction

Human talent is, by far, the most valuable economic factor available to a country. Giving women the same access to economic and political opportunities as men increases the growth potential of a country. Hence, a gap in women's economic and social opportunities and achievements is a net loss for the economy. Even setting social and human considerations aside, there are plenty of reasons, from an economic standpoint, to target the gender gap in wages and opportunities in order to understand it better, explore its less well-known dimensions and find mechanisms and policies to reduce it.

An example of the far-reaching implications of gender gap disparities can be seen in developing economies. Empowering women has become a key aspect of several development policies. Giving more opportunities and resources to women, it appears, increases the chances of economic success of families and communities in developing countries. The World Development Report of 2012 analyzes and dissects gender disparity in the world, with a special focus on developing countries, and proposes several policies to address it. The World Bank has developed a whole research agenda on "Gender and Development."[1] Developed countries are also monitoring their gender gap polices very carefully and the goal of gender equality is explicitly stated in several "Process and Strategy" statements of companies and countries. Since 2006, for instance, the World Economic Forum has produced a yearly Global Gender Gap report to monitor the progress that each country (rich and poor) is making in achieving gender equality in four key areas: health and

---

[1] See the website at <http://go.worldbank.org/A74GIZVFW0>.

survival, education, economic participation and opportunity, and political empowerment.

The first part of this book (Chapters 2–5) focuses on the difference in labor markets and income performances between men and women. The second part of the book will analyze other form of gap and potential discrimination on the labor markets driven by sexual orientation, physical aspects, and age. While the gender gap and its determinants have been widely studied, we focus on less-known aspects and we propose original approaches. First we combine structural, model-based methods in Chapter 2 with micro data to identify the role of discrimination and prejudice. Then we use less-explored (Chapter 3) or completely new data (Chapters 4 and 5) to make progress on less well-known issues such as the role of early schooling career and choices in college in determining the labor market gender gap. Moreover, we focus on the highly educated, and on three countries, Italy, Spain, and the United States, as representative of the whole range of variation in gender gap across developed economies. In the 2011 Global Gender Gap report the US was ranked 6th (from the top) in terms of gender inequality in earnings. Together with northern European countries, the US exhibits the smallest gender gap in earnings. Nevertheless, there is a very significant gender disparity in the US in access to highly paid and powerful positions both in the corporate world and in government (senior officers, CEOs, Board of Directors). Spain, on the other hand, has been a country with rapid economic growth in the last two decades and similarly fast progress on gender inequality. However, it was ranked 74th in the world in terms of its economic gender inequality, and so right in the middle of the distribution of 135 countries analyzed by the Global Gender Gap report. As we will document in Chapter 3, gender inequality in economic access and achievement is still significant in Spain, even when we focus only on the college educated. Finally, Italy was ranked 90th in terms of gender differences in economic achievement by the Global Gender Gap report. This is the country with the largest gender income differences among Organization for Economic Co-operation and Development (OECD) countries, except for Japan and Greece. There is a perception that even highly educated Italian women do not have access to the same occupations and opportunities that men have. We will analyze these issues in greater detail in Chapters 4 and 5.

In order to put the above countries into, further context, Italy and Spain are among the European countries with the higher wage and employment gap. Sweden, Norway, and Denmark are among those with smallest gaps. Differences in policies, in particular in the generosity of work–family reconciliation and maternity policies, may explain some of these differences within Europe (e.g. Christofides et al., 2010) and changes in policies are certainly in place in some of the countries analyzed (see Chapter 3). However, considering the US as reference—a country without generous policies and a low gender

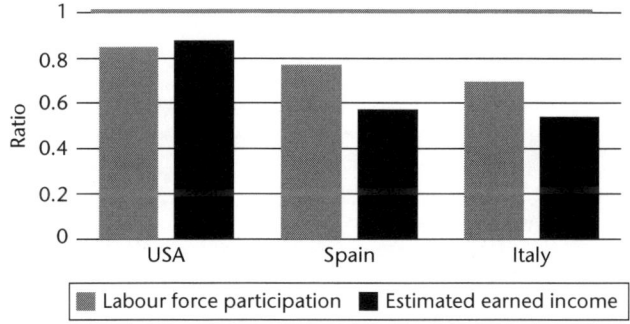

Figure 1.1. Labor force participation and income: female to male ratio, 2011.
Source: Global Gender Gap Report 2011.

gap—pushes us to look also for other explanations and to analyze less well-known aspects of the gender gap.

Figure 1.1 shows two measures of the gender gap that provide an idea of the range spanned by the countries considered. Italy exhibits a very substantial earning gap, showing that women earn 46% less than men (a number that we will confirm in our analysis in Chapters 4 and 5), while in the US the income gap is only 12%. Similarly, in the US women have a labour participation rate equal to 88% of the rate of men, while for Italy that figure is 70%. These countries, therefore, span a large part of the OECD range for many of the economic indicators of gender inequality. For instance, the female to male ratio in participation rate was 96% in Sweden, the OECD country closest to equality, and Italy was the OECD country with the lowest female to male ratio of participation rate. In terms of earned income, the US is the second country in the female to male ratio after Norway, (for which the ratio was equal to 1), and Italy is the second to last (before Japan, whose ratio was 0.51).

The recent trends for the gender gap in labor force participation, income and economic outcomes, show a decreasing gap in most countries. However, several rich countries, after some decades of progress in reducing such gaps, find themselves with an amount of gender inequality that is stubbornly persistent and hard to eliminate. One interesting regularity is that most OECD economies have completely eliminated disparity in the education gap between men and women. According to the Global Gender Gap report of 2011, the top 60 countries have a gender ratio in schooling achievement between women and men larger than or equal to 0.99. In the top 20 countries women outperform men in measures of schooling achievement. Figure 1.2 shows that for the three counties considered, Italy, Spain, and the US, women have clearly overtaken men in terms of tertiary school enrollment.[2]

[2] Other measures such as the proportion of young individuals with a college education show a similar advantage for women.

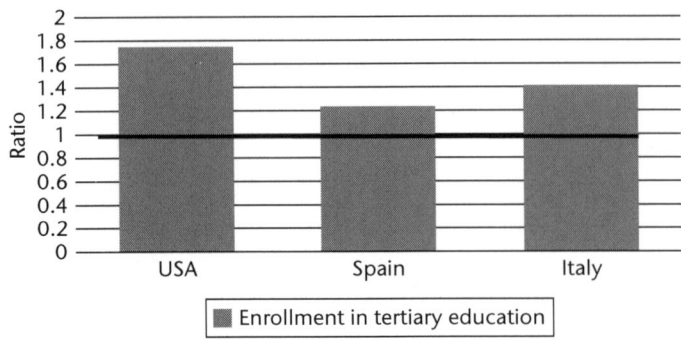

Figure 1.2. Tertiary education: female to male ratio, 2011.

Source: Global Gender Gap Report 2011.

In spite of these educational achievements, access to top-paid jobs, high wages, and equal opportunities at the top of the income distribution are still much harder for women. Women are underrepresented among senior officials, legislators, and managers and also among science, technology, and management professions. Hence most countries still exhibit a significant wage and income gender gap and, because men in those "high-power" positions have very high levels of education, the gender gap is substantial even among the highly educated.

In this book we analyze some potential explanations of the gender gap for highly educated individuals.[3] We apply a new model and estimation procedure (Chapter 2) and we provide an original perspective on the time evolution of the gap (Chapter 3). We also use novel, longitudinal data from high school to the labor market (Chapters 4 and 5). This allows us to identify interesting and still poorly known factors in determining the gender gap and its differences across countries. Our focus on the highly educated, and in particular on college-educated individuals, contributes to the novelty of this analysis.

In order to understand the gender gap among the college-educated and their labor market performance we need to go beyond the well-known fact (shown in Figure 1.2) that, in terms of college enrollment and schooling achievements, women have caught up and are leading men in most of the developed countries. Significant differences in the choice of field of study and in choices during their early career and in relation to the family and to children are highly relevant factors in determining the gap. Finally, there may still be a degree of discrimination, protected by friction and hysteresis,

---

[3] For a review of the gender gap literature see Bertrand (2010) and Blau, Kahn, and Lawrence (2008) and references therein.

in maintaining male privileges in some senior officer, director, and manager positions. Among the small network of highly educated and powerful corporate and political leaders, discrimination can still be an important part of the gender gap.

The three aspects that we will be focusing on are the role of prejudice and discrimination, the role of family and early career choice, and the role of the choice, of college major in determining the gender gap in labor market performances. Each of the three components will be studied using one of our chosen countries and our approach and data will bring novel understanding of the relevance of that aspect. Chapter 2 addresses the role of prejudice and discrimination looking at US data and developing a model that includes search frictions in the labor market, differences in productivity between men and women and "prejudiced" employers. The model is estimated on US data and it allows us to identify the effects of productivity and prejudice on wages and employment. Moreover, we consider high school-educated, college-educated, and graduate school-educated individuals separately, and we characterize the specific degree of gender prejudice in each group. In Chapter 3 we consider the role of family variables (marriage and children) and the early careers of women and their effect on the gender gap in wage and employment. In the chapter we use labor force survey data from Spain for the period 1994–2008 and we analyze how having children affects the employment and wage perspective of women and how much of the gender gap can be explained by childbearing combined with the evolution of family and maternity policies. Finally, in Chapters 4 and 5 we present and use a novel database on Italian high school graduates, their choice of college major, their academic qualities and their outcomes in terms of occupation, employment, and income, between 1 and 15 years after they have joined the labor force. This analysis reveals the crucial importance of college major choice in determining the gender gap; we analyze the determinants of choice of college majors considering academic ability, non-academic skills, family decisions, and the effects of peers and of teachers in high school, factors whose impact on major choice is still poorly understood.

1.2 The Role of Prejudice, Differential Productivity, and Labor Market Frictions on the Gender Gap

Chapter 2 of this book quantifies the impact of prejudice and discrimination on the gender gap in employment and wages. We will be careful to distinguish the two components and we will focus on one source of prejudice: the distaste experienced by prejudiced employers when hiring women.

While explicit prejudice has been a part of economic theory for a long time,[4] it is very difficult to directly observe and measure it. One way to estimate its presence and impact is to infer explicit prejudice from the observed behavior of labor market variables, using a specific model of the labor market. A good candidate for such a model, which we will apply to the US labor market, is a search-matching-bargaining model.

A search-matching-bargaining model is a good candidate for two main reasons. From a theoretical point of view, the presence of search frictions justifies the survival of prejudice employers in equilibrium, as suggested by Heckman (1998) and Altonji and Blank (1999). Namely, if prejudice is inefficient for the employers, because they hire an inefficiently low number of women, or they hire men instead, then in a perfectly competitive market with free entry it cannot survive in the long run. Market frictions are needed for prejudice to survive in equilibrium. Second, search models with matching and bargaining have been used in several empirical applications and have proved to be a good fit for the data (Eckstein and van den Berg, 2007). The applications performed in this chapter are based on Flabbi (2010a) and add Becker's taste discrimination to the framework of a search-matching-bargaining model, to separately identify the impact of explicit prejudice, of differential productivity and of gender-specific search frictions on labor market outcomes.

The separate identification of these three possible sources of gender differentials for different education groups is the first main contribution of the chapter that extends (2010a). The second main contribution of the chapter is to use the estimated model to build an innovative welfare measure to evaluate returns to schooling and to perform two policy experiments. Since the overall welfare of labor market participants depends on their current labor market state but also on the labor market dynamics related to the transitions between labor market states and job offers, we need a summary measure capable of taking into account all these components if we want to assess market returns and the impact of policy experiments. We use the welfare measure proposed by Flinn (2002), which assigns to each labor market state occupied by the workers in steady state the corresponding utility value weighted accordingly to the equilibrium steady state distribution. This allows a comparison of policies based on welfare.

---

[4] A theory of explicit prejudice ("taste discrimination") was first proposed by Becker in 1957 (see Becker, 1971) and has been very influential on the discrimination literature ever since (see Altonji and Blank, 1999).

1.3 The Role of Family Choice and Early Career in the Gender Gap

A second important component of the gender gap in the labor market performances is the different function of men and women in the family, with a specific role played in raising/educating children. In Chapter 3 we focus on this issue and we use data from Spain to analyze how family characteristics, in particular the presence of children, affected the labor supply decisions and the labor market performance of highly educated females in Spain and how this has evolved over the last 20 years.

Several important contributions in the literature have analyzed the evolution of the role of college-educated women in labor markets and their role within the family, especially focusing on the US. Goldin (2004a, 2004b), for instance, traces the demographic and labor force experiences of five cohorts of college graduates, from those born in 1900 to the last born in 1980, focusing on why career and family outcomes changed over time. She describes the path to the fast track that college graduate women have taken starting with the first cohort, born in 1900, and forced to choose between "family" and "career," to the latest group, born in 1980, which has achieved success in combining career and family.

In describing the trends that characterized some of the changes in women's performance in the US during the 20th century, Goldin (2004b) emphasizes the speed at which the various transformations took place, such as the one from jobs to careers and the one from early to later marriages. Moreover, most of these changes took place at the same time. The more likely factors to explain these rapid changes are, in Goldin's analysis: (1) government mandates, such as antidiscrimination policy in hiring and promotions, (2) change spurred by the resurgence of feminism that came on the heels of the Civil Rights movement in the 1960s, and (3) the contraceptive innovation, known as the pill, which gave young women freedom to plan their family and the ability to delay marriage and childbearing and plan for a career.

These transformations have produced a significant degree of women advancement in the US, and equality seems within reach. Nevertheless, family choices seem to penalize the labor market performance even of those among the most educated and highly skilled women. Goldin and Katz (2010) analyze the work and family choices among students graduating from one of the most elite institutions of higher US education (Harvard University). They explore the tradeoffs between family and career, particularly for college graduate women. They find that male earnings are strongly and positively related to the number of children in the family, whereas female earnings are negatively related, especially for those having three or more children. The negative impact of children on women's earnings is entirely accounted for by hours worked. In fact, a positive relationship between children and earnings exists for women working full-time full-year. This suggests higher reservation wages for those with more children and positive selection into the labor force based on the number of children.

Similarly, Bertrand et al. (2010) study the careers of MBAs from a top US business school to understand how career dynamics differ by gender between 1990 and 2006. Three proximate factors account for the large and rising gender gap in earnings: differences in training prior to graduation, differences in career interruptions, and differences in weekly hours. The greater career discontinuity and shorter working hours for females are largely associated with motherhood. They find that the presence of children is the main contributor to the lesser job experience, greater career discontinuity, and shorter work hours for female MBAs. Those mothers seem to actively choose jobs that are family friendly, and avoid jobs with long hours and greater career advancement possibilities.

In general, most of the existing literature, relative to industrialized countries, has found that the presence of children is particularly important to explain the gap in hours worked. Women in families with children work significantly less than women in families without (see for instance Waldfogel, 1998; Harkness and Waldfogel, 1999). Focusing specifically on Spain, the country considered in the analysis of Chapter 3, Molina and Montuenga (2009) use the Household Panel for 1994–2001 and find results confirming that there is clear evidence of a wage penalty for Spanish working women with children. Specifically, a birth in the family during a given year implies a wage loss of 9% of the woman's wage.

One interesting fact about the role of family on women's careers is that, possibly because of changing social norms, or because families have become much smaller, there seems to be a clear tendency to a reduction in the negative impact of children on the working hours of women. Considering Spain, and focusing on college-educated individuals (which will be the sample in our analysis), Figure 1.3 shows the profile of participation in the labor market in the early years of a person's career. We notice a negative female–male differential for all cohorts and ages, and especially for the cohort between 30 and 40, when the burden of raising children is highest. However, we also notice a drastic decrease in the gender gap moving from the older generations (born in 1960) to younger ones (born in 1975).

The role of family and children, therefore, while certainly changing in the recent decades, has usually penalized the labor participation of women. From the general evidence in industrialized countries it seems to have had a stronger role on labor supply than on wages. In Chapter 3 we will analyze more systematically its role in affecting employment, hours worked, and wages, focusing on the interesting case of Spain, where the participation of

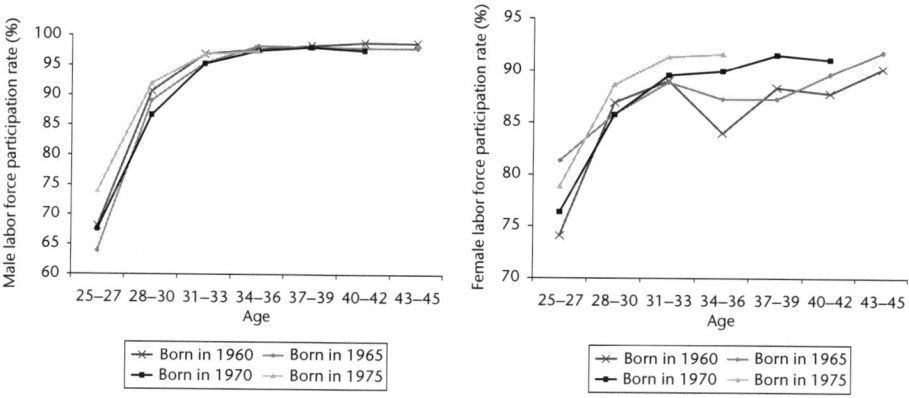

Figure 1.3. Life cycle of labor force participation rates, males and females.

educated women in the labor market seems to have increased substantially in the recent cohorts.

1.4 Gender Gap in the Choice of College Majors and Occupations

A third significant difference between men and women contributing to the gender gap in earnings and career is the difference in their fields of study while in college. This issue is tackled in Chapters 4 and 5. While the educational achievement gap has been eliminated, another gap persists and it has been the subject of studies by economists in several countries: the gender difference in the choice of college major and in the subsequent occupational choice. Women in many countries seem to shy away from majors in science, technology, engineering and management (STEM) and from related occupations. Some statistics on the general tendencies in the gender gap relative to the choice of major across OECD countries provides an idea of the extent of this phenomenon.[5]

We should emphasize that there is a substantial literature on the so-called math–science gender gap."[6] Economists, sociologists, and scholars of high education have noticed, across countries, that women tend to avoid math- and science-intensive majors in college. Most studies focus on the US and on the UK. There is also agreement that the science gap is an important component of the gender gap in earnings and differences in science education explain a large share of the gender earning gap, sometimes up to half of it (see for instance Paglin and Rufolo, 1990, and Brown and Corcoran, 1997).

[5] The figures are from Flabbi (2010a).
[6] See Xie and Shauman (2003) for an excellent overview of this topic.

In Chapters 4 and 5 we show new data from Italy and new analysis in this debate. The data are unique in that they contain detailed information on Italian students' high school and college career, following graduation from high school between 1985 and 2005, as well as measures of their labor market performance up to 15 years after they joined the labor force. We will explore how significant the gender differences are in the choice of college major and whether psychological, skill-based, or preference-based explanations are more consistent with the data. Italy is a representative case among OECD countries in terms of women's choice of college major.

To produce stylized facts we rely on the Flexible Professional in the Knowledge Society (REFLEX) dataset. The REFLEX dataset collects the results of a survey on graduates of tertiary education (equivalent to a College BA or a Master's in most countries) with about five years of experience since graduating in the academic year 1999/2000. The project covered 14 countries, all of them developed and most of them in Europe: Austria, Belgium (only Flanders), Finland, France, Germany, Italy, the Netherlands, Norway, Spain, UK, Czech Republic, Portugal, Japan, and Estonia.[7] The database is representative of the sampled cohort across countries. We will present only statistics relative to the aggregate of all countries.

The first fact emerging from the data is that over 50% of graduates with a tertiary degree in 1999/2000 were women in all countries, except for Germany and Japan, where the proportion was almost exactly 50%. Hence this database confirms that equality in tertiary graduation rates has been achieved in most developed countries and that education, as measured by years of schooling, cannot be a contributor to the gender gap. Figures 1.4 and 1.5 show, instead, prima facie evidence of the differences in choice of college majors. The aggregate categories used to classify college majors are constructed in order to keep the classification consistent across countries. Figure 1.4 shows how men and women who graduated in the year 2000 were distributed across college majors. Figure 1.5 shows the percentage of graduates of each of those college majors who are women.

Figure 1.4 clearly shows that engineering is the major that attracts the largest share of men (more than, 35%), while it attracts a very low share of women (barely above 10%). Conversely, health and humanities are among the most popular majors among women, while they attract a much lower percentage of men. Correspondingly, Figure 1.5 shows that while 75–80% of graduates in majors such as education, humanities and health are women, only 25% of graduates in engineering and 45% of graduates in mathematics and sciences are women. These tendencies are confirmed within each country.

---

[7] Luca Flabbi has made the data and the summary statistics relative to this database available for this book.

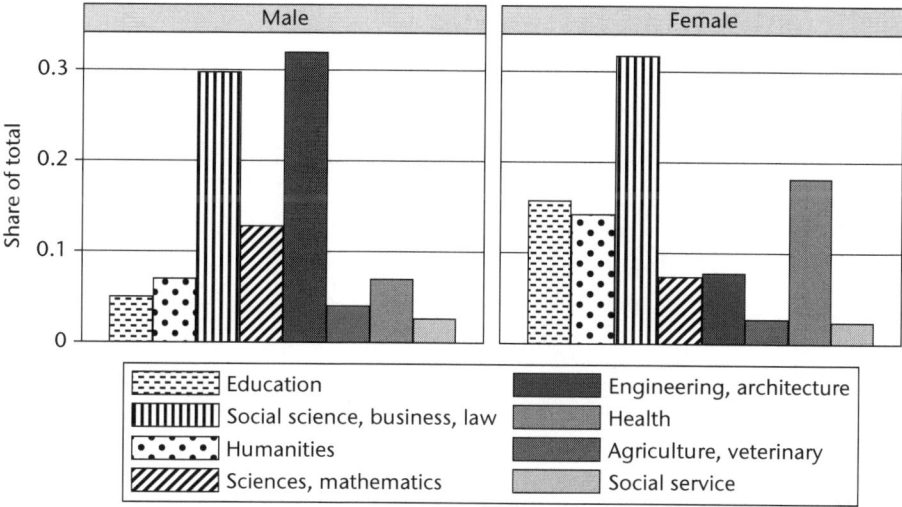

Figure 1.4. Field of study choice by gender. (Proportion of graduates in each field.)

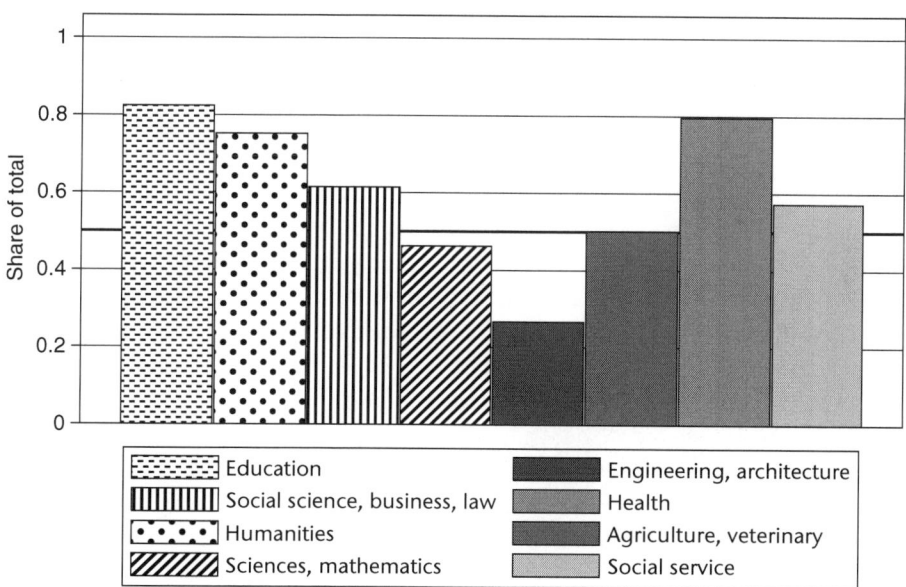

Figure 1.5. Proportion of women in field of study.

One possible reason for the gender gap in the choice of major is differential academic ability. If majors such as engineering and math and sciences are more demanding and men have a better academic performance than women, then a "vertical" differentiation of majors, according to the average quality of the student may generate this pattern. The fact that science majors are more

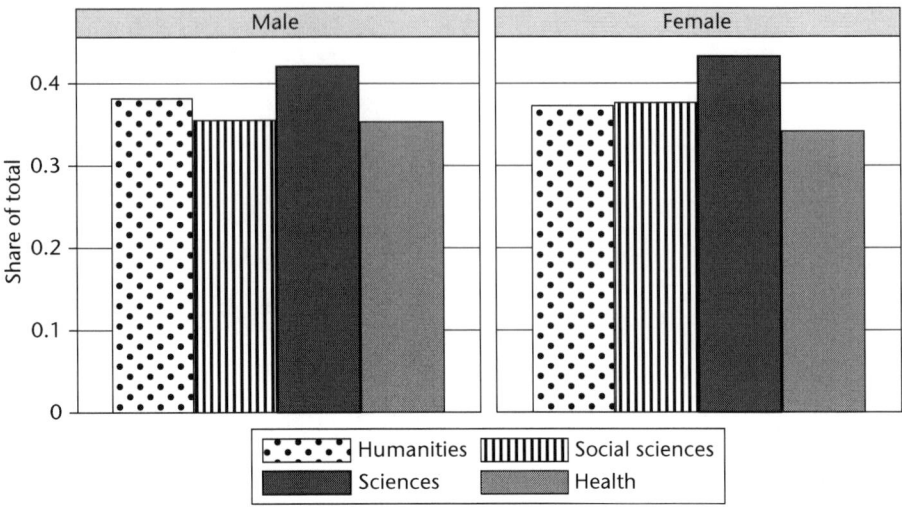

Figure 1.6. Top Grades secondary by field of study and gender. (Graduates with Top Grades in secondary school by tertiary school field.)

Note: Top Grades means top grades available or in the top 25% of country-specific distribution.

demanding than others is (partly) supported by Figure 1.6. This figure shows the percentage of students graduating from secondary school with a grade within the top quartile of the national grade distribution, attending college in each of four categories of majors and separated between men and women. The figure seems to support the idea that science majors are somewhat more selective and attract a higher percentage of top students. However, this selectivity is not very different for men and women. Hence to explain the much lower percentage of women in sciences it should be the case that the quality of women, as revealed by the grade in high school, is much lower than that of men. The two panels in Figure 1.7 dispel that explanation. They show the percentage of men and women in each quartile of the (aggregate) distribution of high school exit grades. In order to make the exit grades comparable across countries we consider only their relative distribution and we distinguish only between four quartiles within each country. The differences in distribution across grades are very small, with women being somewhat more concentrated in the third quartile relative to men and less in the first and fourth. We notice, overall, that high school grade distribution is similar between men and women and it does not show differences that would justify the large gap in enrollment in math-intensive majors observed in Figure 1.4. Hence, in general among the considered countries, women of high academic quality choose generally humanities and education, not engineering and science. As we will see in the in-depth analysis of Chapter 4, our micro-data from Italy fully confirm this tendency.

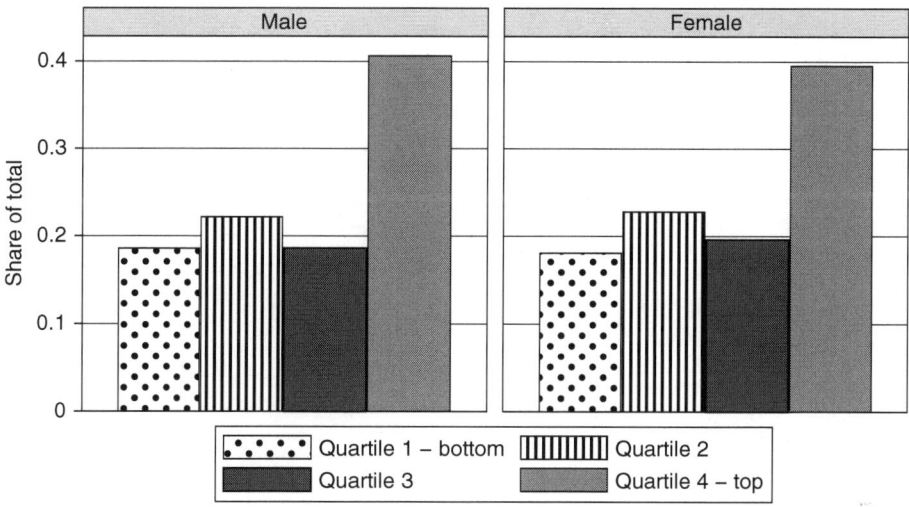

Figure 1.7. Secondary school grades distribution by gender. (Proportion of graduates in quartiles of grade distribution.)

Note: Grade distribution computed by country on the joint sample of males and females.

The persistent role of major choice in the labor market performance of individuals is due to the fact that different majors determine access to different occupations by providing students with different skills. If occupational differences are associated with different earning abilities and different career opportunities then this is a channel through which the choice of major will significantly affect income. All the individuals analyzed are highly educated and hence will have access to occupations classified as professionals and technicians (according to the ISCO code). In fact more than 80% of college-educated (men and women) are within this occupational group. Of the remaining college educated, around 5% are classified as clerks and another 5% as "senior officers." Within the category of "professionals and technicians," however, Figure 1.8 shows that more than 40% of men work in professions classified as physics, mathematics and engineering while only 12% of women do. On the other hand, almost 30% of women work in occupations classified as teaching while only 10% of men work in that group.

Summing up the stylized facts shown in this section, the link between college major and occupational choice seems very strong in all countries. This could be a crucial element to understand the gender gap. First, highly educated men and women, in spite of their equal educational attainment and comparable academic performance (in terms of grades), have a large and not decreasing gap in their choice of field of study and in the choice of occupation. Second, women exhibit systematically a negative gap in the probability

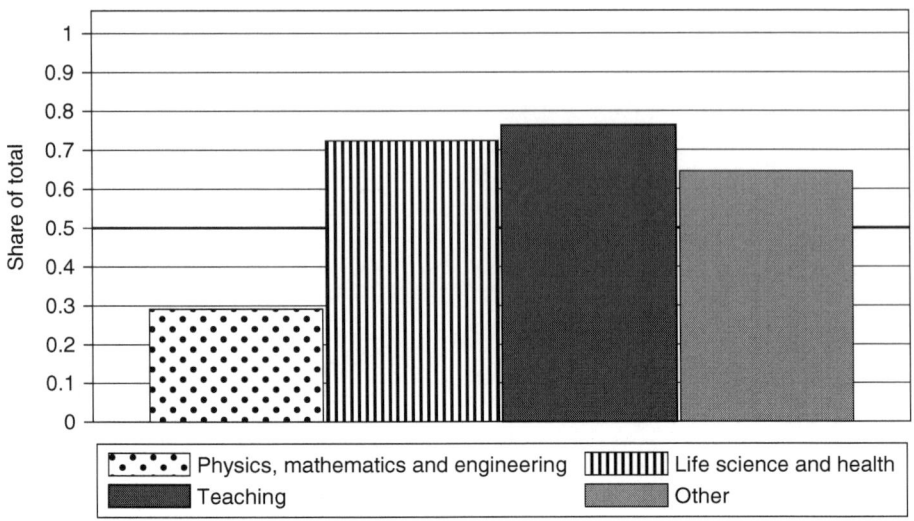

Figure 1.8. Proportion of women in occupation. (Professionals and technician.)
Note: First job after graduation.

of choosing math-intensive majors such as engineering and mathematical sciences, while they show a systematic positive gap in the choice of majors in the humanities. Third, the college major seems to be strongly correlated with the choice of occupation. In particular "teaching-type" jobs are dominated by women, while engineering-type jobs are dominated by men.

1.5 The Structure of Part I of the Book

The remaining chapters of the first part of this book follow the structure anticipated in this introduction. We tackle, in turn, the analysis of different determinants of the gender gap beginning, in Chapter 2, with the role of prejudice and market frictions on the wage and employment gap, measured using US data. Then, in Chapter 3, we analyze the role of family and children in causing a gender gap in employment and wages, and we use data from Spain to estimate those effects. In Chapters 4 and 5 we focus on the role of choice of college major in determining the gender gap and we analyze the causes of such different choices. We do this using a newly collected database of Italian high school graduates over the period 1985–2005 for which we have detailed information on high school performance, college career, and some labor market outcomes after up to 15 years from graduation. At the end of Chapter 5 we also distill and discuss some policy implications, with a special focus on the countries that we have considered and on the main results that we found in the empirical analysis.

2

Gender Gaps in Wages and Employment: The Role of Employers' Prejudice

Luca Flabbi and Mauricio Tejada

This chapter makes three contributions. First, we provide descriptive evidence on gender differentials by education in the US labor market over the last 20 years. Second, we use the structural estimation of a search model of the labor market to identify and quantify the impact of employers' prejudice on labor market gender differentials. Third, we connect the descriptive and analytical findings to recent policy interventions in the US labor market and we perform some policy experiments. While the US labor market has been studied extensively, the novelty of our approach is to use employment and wage data for highly educated men and women, and a search and friction model of the labor market to identify the role of employer prejudice in determining and maintaining the gender gap. The model is based on Flabbi (2010a) and the data are from the Annual Social and Economics Supplement (ASES or March Supplement) and the School Enrollment Supplement (October Supplement) of the Current Population Survey (CPS),[1] which is a representative household survey of the US population.

2.1 Descriptive Evidence

We organize the descriptive evidence following the decision process of an individual deciding to supply labor in the market. First, we look at the outcomes of education decisions. Second, we look at the decision to supply labor in the market both with respect to the *extensive* margin (the participation

[1] A detailed description of the data and the estimation sample is contained in the Appendix.

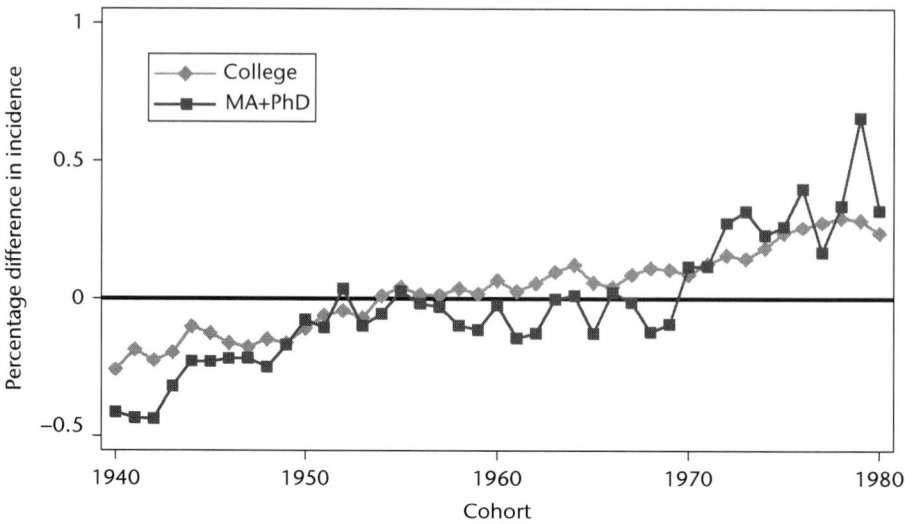

Figure 2.1. Gender gap in percentage of graduates by cohort.

decision) and to the *intensive* margin (the hours supply decision). We correlate this evidence with education and we look at the evolution over time. Third, we look at gender earnings differentials in the labor market. We compute both the raw differential and the differential conditional on standard human capital characteristics.

2.1.1 *Gender Differentials in Pre-Labor Market Characteristics*

Education decisions constitute the most important component of pre-labor market human capital. We will show in Chapter 3 (relative to Spain) and Chapter 4 (relative to Italy) that they influence not only future performance in the labor market but also the decision to participate in the labor market itself.

Figure 2.1 shows the male–female difference in the percentage of college graduates and Master's and PhDs for each cohort born between 1940 and 1980.

Confirming the evidence on school attainment presented in Chapter 1 we see that the difference has become positive, starting with the generation born in 1959 for college and with the generation born in 1971 for Master's and PhD. A positive gap means that women acquire more education than men. The fact is well known, but the explanation is less clear, especially in the light of the negative earning gap on the labor markets.[2]

---

[2] The most complete explanations proposed so far focus on the return to education on the marriage market: Chiappori et al., 2009; GE, 2011. For a different explanation based on job amenities, see Flabbi and Moro (2012). For international comparisons, see Becker et al. (2010).

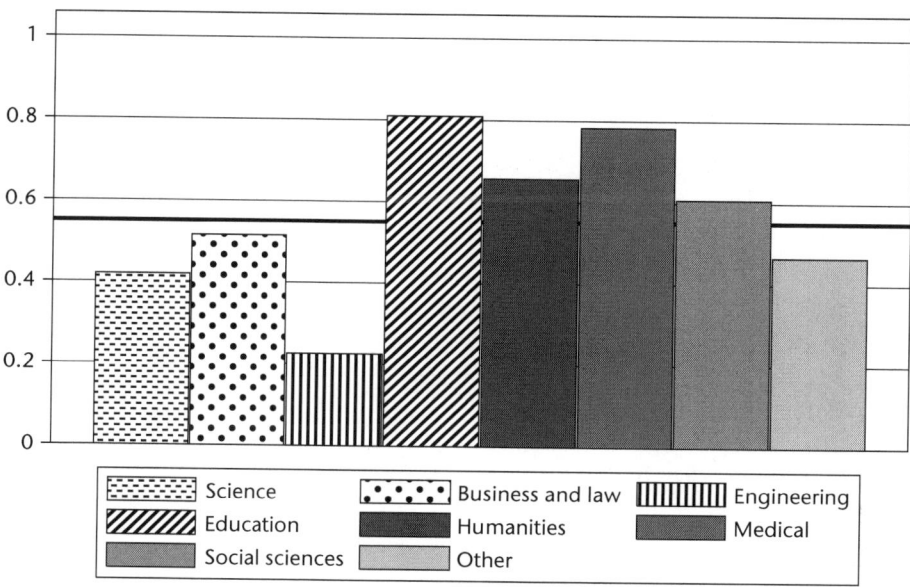

Figure 2.2. Proportion of women in field of study (2002).

Note: 30–45 years old.

In Figure 2.2 we look at one dimension of the quality of education: field of study. It shows that the asymmetries on fields of study choices are substantial. The proportion of women in the education and medical fields is much higher than the proportion of women in the population (the red horizontal line). The opposite is true for science and engineering. The red horizontal line reports the overall proportion of women in the population, providing a reference for which fields of study exhibit an over- or an under representation of women. This gender imbalance in the choice of college major is found in most OECD countries, as already discussed in Chapter 1.

Following Flabbi and Moro (2012),[3] Figure 2.3 reports the correlation between women's choice of college major and the degree of flexibility in the jobs associated with them. (In this figure flexibility simply means the possibility of working less than 30 hours a week.) It reveals a preference of women for majors leading to more flexible jobs.

2.1.2 Gender Differentials in Labor Supply

Figure 2.4 reports evidence on the decision to participate in the labor market by education level (college completed or more and less than college completed) and gender. Men systematically participate in the labor market more

---

[3] For some recent country-specific evidence on this correlation in European countries, see Beffy et al. (2009) and Chevalier (2011).

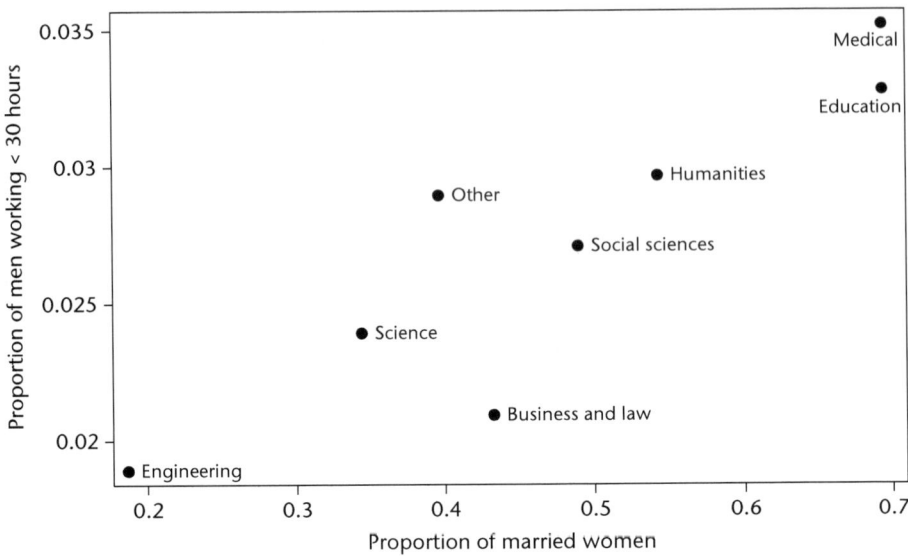

Figure 2.3. Majors with flexible jobs (2002).

Note: 30–45 years old.

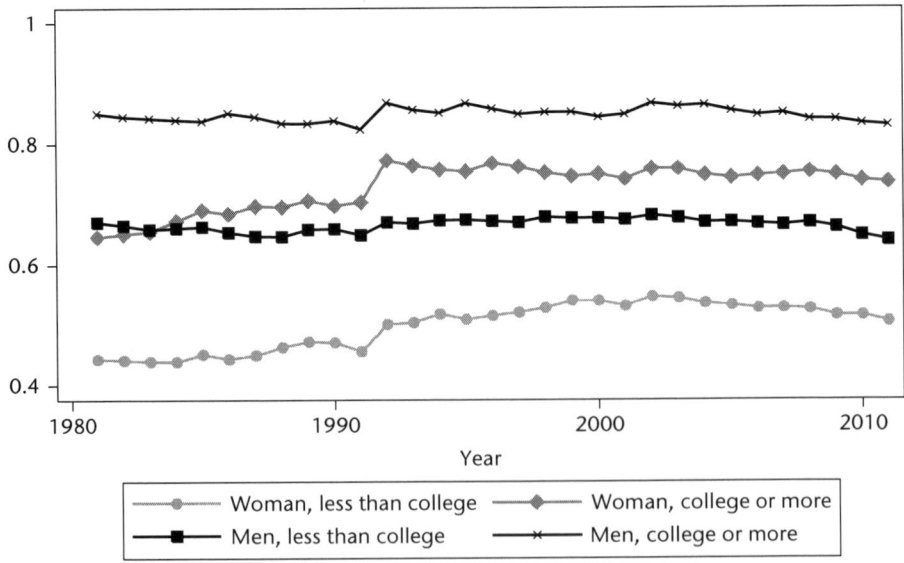

Figure 2.4. Participation rates by gender and education level. (Percentage of relevant group in adult civilian population.)

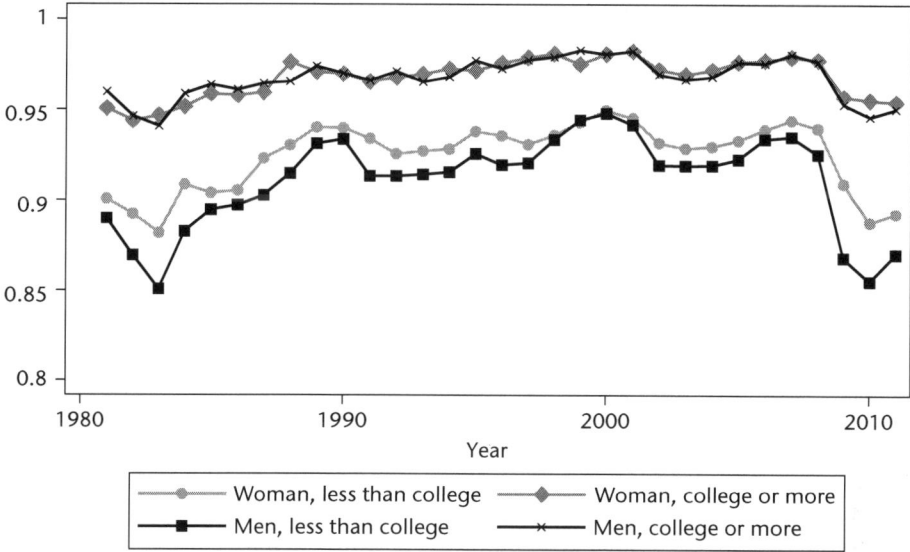

Figure 2.5. Employment rates by gender and education level. (Percentage of relevant group in labor force.)

than women both in the low education sample and in the high education sample, but the differential has been shrinking over time. Moreover the differential is smaller for the college sample and it has uniformly been smaller over the entire 20 year period under consideration.

Employment rates are reported in Figure 2.5 following the same structure used in Figure 2.4. We see no gender gap in employment rates among college graduates, while a small positive gap exists on the low education sample.[4] The lack of a gender gap in employment for the college graduates is quite an old phenomenon, involving cohorts going as far back as 1940.

We also look at the intensive margin of the labor supply. Figure 2.6 reports the incidence of part-time work. Results show a very large gender gap: women are twice (or more) as likely to work part time as men. The gap is not significantly reduced when focusing on college graduates. This is a feature that we will see confirmed in Chapter 3 with regard to Spanish data.

2.1.3 Gender Differentials in Earnings

Figure 2.7 reports estimates of the gender earnings gap from 1981 to 2011. We estimate the gap as the coefficient of a dummy =1 if the individual is a woman

---

[4] Employment rates are equal to the number of workers divided by workers plus those looking for a job.

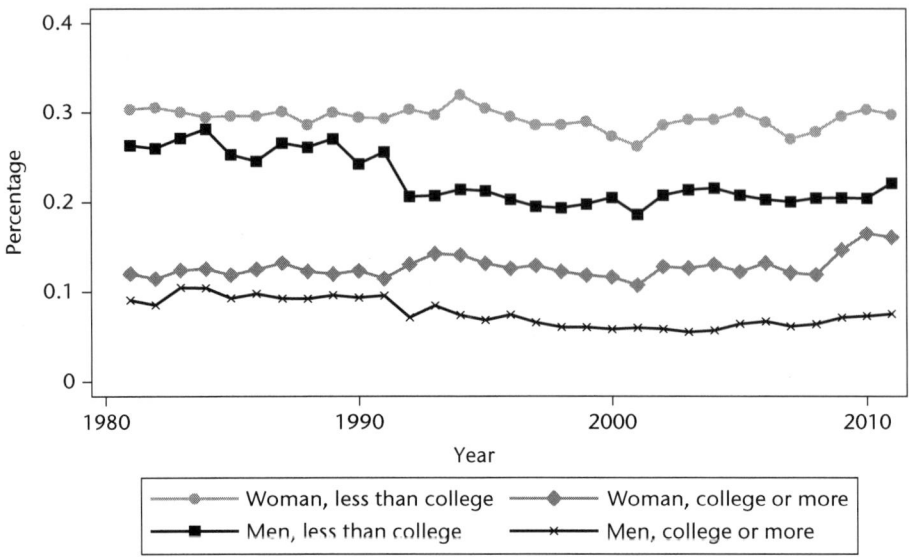

Figure 2.6. Gender gaps in part-time occupations. (Men vs. women with part-time jobs.)

in an ordinary least square (OLS) regression of log hourly earnings. The top panel (Figure 2.7a) reports results from a specification including a constant and the dummy woman: it is therefore an estimate of the raw differential at the mean, unconditional on any observables. The bottom panel (Figure 2.7b) reports results from a specification including a constant, the dummy woman, three educational dummies, age linear and squared, two race dummies, a dummy for marital status, and a dummy for presence of children younger than 18: it is therefore an estimate of the differential conditional on standard human capital and demographic characteristics. Dotted lines describe the 95% confidence interval.

The gender gap in wage and earnings has been persistent in the US labor market.[5] Figure 2.7a shows a significant convergence during the 1980s, following a trend started in the previous decade (not shown). In the following decade, however, the convergence slowed down and then stalled in the mid-1990s. The trend in the last ten years is less clear, with periods of minor convergence followed by a period of small divergence. The most recent year available (2011) reports the smallest gender earnings gap ever, breaking the 20% mark on the unconditional differential for the first time. Figure 2.7b (the conditional gender gap) shows a very similar evolution over time

---

[5] For over-time evidence in the US, see Eckstein and Nagypal (2004), Blau and Kahn (2006), Flabbi (2010b).

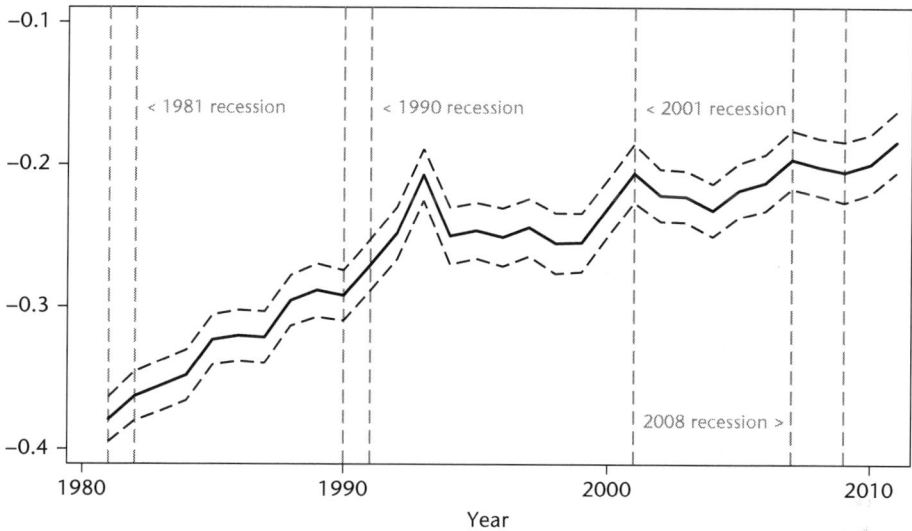

Figure 2.7a Gender earnings differential over time, unconditional case. (Points estimates and 95% confidence interval.)

Note: Dashed lines represent 95% confidence interval.

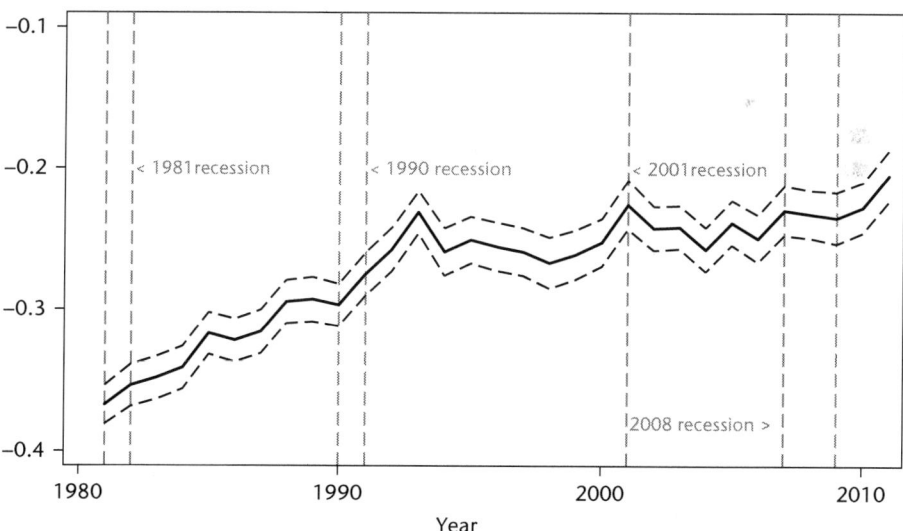

Figure 2.7b Gender earnings differential over time, conditional case. (Points estimates and 95% confidence interval.)

Note: Dashed lines represent 95% confidence interval.

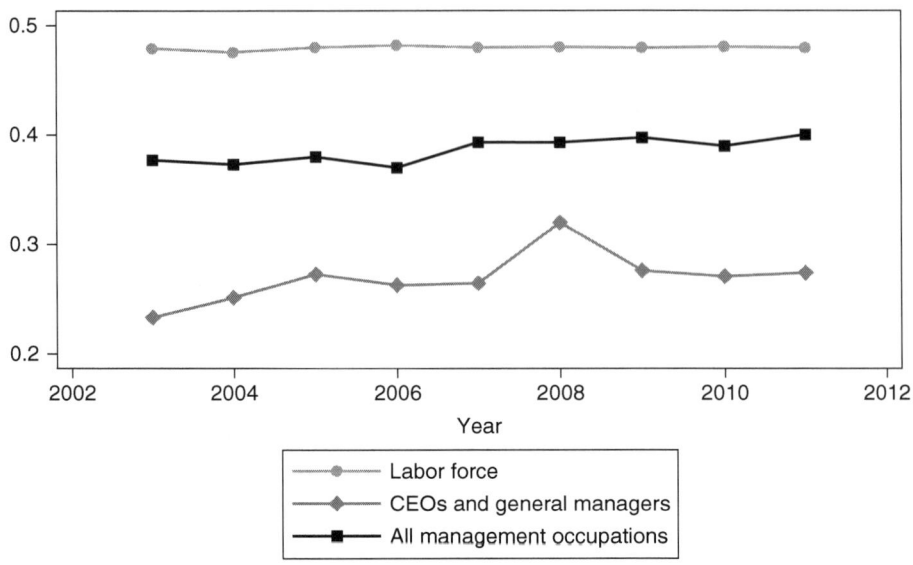

Figure 2.8. Gender composition of managerial occupations. (Proportion of women.)

but usually at a slighter lower level, implying that human capital differences do not explain the gender gap in earnings.

There is a large literature pointing out that the crucial sources of the gender gap in high-income economies may be concentrated at the top of the earnings distribution[6] and the top of the hierarchical ladder at the firm[7] (the so-called glass-ceiling hypothesis). Moreover several studies (e.g. Arulampalam et al., 2007; Christofides et al., 2010) have analyzed the gender wage differential in different parts of the wage distribution. Figure 2.8 reports some evidence on the gender asymmetries in the top hierarchical ladder at the firm. Among CEOs and general managers, only 20% are women, compared with a presence of women in the labor force which is very close to 50%. Overall, the proportion of men in management occupations is about 13% compared with about 8% for women. These differentials are essentially constant over time, even if the time span we are forced to consider is much smaller than in previous figures.[8] The data studied by Gayle et al. (2011) looks at the top executives in the Standard and Poor's Execucomp dataset.[9] Thanks to their

[6] See Albrecht et al. (2003); Blau and Kahn (2006); Bertrand, et al. (2010).

[7] See Bertrand and Hallock (2001); Albanesi and Olivetti (2006); Bertrand et al. (2010); Gayle et al. (2011).

[8] A change in the CPS definition of occupations means that the values we not comparable over the entire three decades we are considering in this study.

[9] Execucomp contains information on at least the top five executives in the S&P 500, S&P MidCap 400, S&P SmallCap 600 firms.

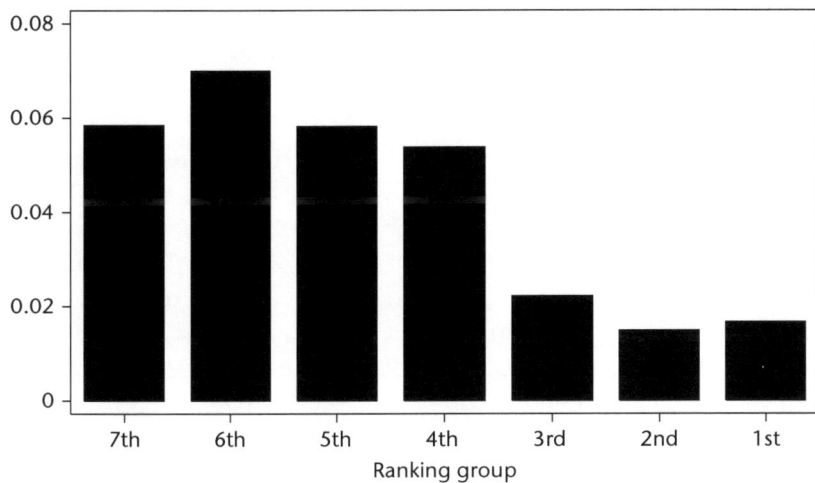

Figure 2.9. Positions within CEOs and general managers. (Proportion of women.)
Note: Gayl, Golan, and Miller (2009), Table 2.1.

data, they are able to look deeper into the still relatively large category of CEOs and general managers reported by the CPS. Based on job titles and transitions across occupations, they build seven rankings within the top executives rank (7th is the lowest and 1st the highest). Figure 2.9 reports the proportion of women in each of the ranks. Results show that the already very low presence of women among executives (no more than 6/7%) is becoming lower and lower as we move up the ranks.

2.2 The Impact of Employers' Prejudice

We now investigate the source of the observed gender differentials in the labor market – both in terms of wage differentials and of labor market dynamics. To do this we first present a model that helps us organize the main components that generate the gap.

2.2.1 The Search-Matching-Bargaining Model

Explicit prejudice may be present,[10] but it is hard to measure. While some empirical studies (e.g. Charles and Guryan 2008; Charles et al., 2010; Weber and Zulehner, 2010, 2012) attempt to identify employer discrimination by

[10] A theory of explicit prejudice ("taste discrimination") was first proposed by Becker in 1957 (see Becker, 1971) and has been very influential on the discrimination literature ever since (see Altonji and Blank, 1999).

using data on employers' hiring behavior, our strategy is to infer it from observable outcomes of labor market agents, which affect a parsimonious model of the labor market. We use a search-matching-bargaining model.

This model has merit both for theoretical and empirical reasons. From a theoretical point of view, the presence of search frictions justifies the survival of prejudice employers in equilibrium, as suggested by Heckman (1998) and Altonji and Blank (1999). From an empirical point of view, search models with matching and bargaining have been used in many empirical applications and have proved to have a good data fit (Eckstein and van den Berg, 2007). Flabbi (2010a) shows that when Becker's taste discrimination is added to the framework, the model is able to separately identify, under some assumptions, the impact of explicit prejudice, differential productivity, and gender-specific search frictions.

2.2.1.1 ENVIRONMENT

The model's environment is as follows.[11] The economy is populated by four types of agents infinitely lived: two types of workers (men and women) and two types of employers (prejudiced and unprejudiced). Unemployed workers are looking for jobs and employers are looking for workers to fill vacancies. Search frictions are present in the market so that it may take time before employers find a worker. Once an employer and a worker meet, they observe the productivity that their specific match will produce and agree upon a wage. Workers' utility depends on wages and there is no disutility from working. Employers' utility depends on profit and on the intensity of discrimination. The intensity of discrimination is defined as the disutility from hiring women that affects prejudiced employers (Becker, 1971).

While unemployed, workers enjoy unemployment and other benefits and costs correlated with the state of unemployment. While a position is vacant, employers sustain no cost and receive no benefit.

The technology used to produce the homogeneous good is constant returns to scale, with labor as the only factor of production. Therefore, the total output of an employer is the sum of the product of all his/her employees.

2.2.1.2 EQUILIBRIUM

Given this environment, workers have a very simple decision to make: accept or reject the match with a given employer. They make this decision by balancing the benefit of receiving a wage higher than the current utility of unemployment with the expected benefit of receiving a potentially better offer in the future. The *reservation wage is the lowest wage at which a worker would accept a job, and hence job offers associated with wages higher than the reservation wage will be accepted*. A similar argument holds for the employer.

---

[11] A formal description of the model is to be found in Chapter 2, Appendix B.

Wages are the result of a bargaining process between the worker and the employer upon observing types and match-specific productivity. We assume a Nash-Bargaining solution to this problem. Such a solution has the property that the worker and the employer will always agree to a match when the match is producing a surplus and they agree to share the surplus according to their respective bargaining weight and their outside options.[12] First, let us consider the wage of a man (subscript M) working for an employer (the employer's type has no impact on male workers) with a match-specific productivity equal to x:

$$w_M(x) = \rho U_M + \alpha(x - \rho U_M) \tag{2.1}$$

The expression states that the wage guarantees the worker his outside option (ρU_M) plus a portion of the surplus ($x - \rho U_M$) equal to the bargaining weight (α). The bargaining weight capture factors relate to the bargaining strength of workers with respect to employers: the higher the weight, the higher the wage at given productivity. The outside option of the worker is the present discounted value of being unemployed: the higher the outside option's utility, the higher the wage at given productivity because the worker will have a better state to go back to if the match is not realized. Finally, ($x - \rho U_M$) is the surplus generated by the match because it is the difference between what is produced in the match (x) and what would be received by the worker if the match is not realized (ρU_M). Notice that the employer does not lose anything if the match is not realized because the cost of keeping a vacancy open is zero.

Second, consider the wage of a woman (subscript W) working for an non-prejudiced employer with a match-specific productivity equal to x:

$$w_{WN}(x) = \rho U_W + \alpha(x - \rho U_W) \tag{2.2}$$

The expression is exactly equal to equation 2.1 with the difference that the outside option is allowed to be different. Notice also that the wage equation has two subscripts: W to denote women and N to denote non-prejudiced employers. Female wages vary by employer type.

Third, the wage of a woman with a match-specific productivity equal to x working for a prejudiced employer is:

$$w_{WP}(x) = \rho U_W + \alpha(x - d - \rho U_W) \tag{2.3}$$

The expression is different from equation 2.2 because the surplus is reduced by the disutility that prejudiced employers receive when hiring women (d): the higher the discrimination intensity d, the lower the wage for given productivity.

---

[12] See Chapter 2, Appendix C for analytical expressions of the surplus and the Nash-Bargaining product.

We are now ready to state the *equilibrium decision rules* resulting from the model:

1. The Optimal Decision rules are *reservation value rules*: both workers and employers agree on what these reservation values are. The reservation value rule in this case means that the match will be realized (i.e. both workers and employers agree to enter a job relationship governed by wage equations 2.1–2.3) if the match-specific productivity is higher than the *reservation productivity value*. The wages corresponding to these reservation productivity values are the *reservation wages*.

2. The reservation productivities are different between men and women and they are different between women accepting to work for a prejudiced employer and women accepting to work for an unprejudiced employer. We denote them with x^* and they are defined as follows:

$$x^*_M = \rho U_M \tag{2.4}$$

$$x^*_{WN} = \rho U_W \tag{2.5}$$

$$x^*_{WP} = \rho U_W + d \tag{2.6}$$

3. The reservation wages, on the other hand, are worker type specific but not employer type specific. We denote them with $w*$ and they are defined as follows:

$$w^*_M = \rho U_M \tag{2.7}$$

$$w^*_W = \rho U_W \tag{2.8}$$

The structure of the equilibrium has some interesting implications about the impact of prejudice on labor market outcomes:

1. The presence of prejudiced employers makes the present discounted value of participating in the market (U) lower for women than men (see Proposition 1 in Flabbi, 2010a).

2. Wage discrimination is present in prejudiced employers. Women working for prejudiced employers receive lower wages than men working for prejudiced employers with the same level of productivity. This is easy to see by comparing wage equation 2.1 with wage equation 2.3: for given x, women earn lower wages because of the negative impact of d (the direct effect of prejudice) and because the women's outside option is lower than the men's outside option (the equilibrium or "spillover"[13] effect of prejudice).

3. Wage discrimination is also present in unprejudiced employers. Women working for unprejudiced employers are also receiving lower wages for the same productivity. The effect results from comparing equations

---

[13] For a formal definition of this spillover effect, see Definition 4 in Flabbi (2010a).

2.1 and 2.2: if women's outside option is lower (as stated in the first equilibrium) then unprejudiced employers also discriminate. This is an important result that allows us to make a clear distinction between explicit prejudice (applicable only to some employers) and wage discrimination (extending to all women).

4. Partial segregation arises in equilibrium: women are overrepresented in unprejudiced employers and underrepresented in prejudiced employers. The model predicts partial segregation as opposed to complete segregation. Complete segregation is a starker result which is at odds with the recent empirical evidence.

2.2.2 Estimation and Identification

Search and matching models have been extensively studied and implemented. The identification theory is laid out by Flinn and Heckman (1982): they show that under an appropriate parametric assumption the crucial structural parameters of the model are identified from data on unemployment durations and accepted wages.

To Flinn and Heckman's result, we have to add the identification of the prejudiced parameters. Flabbi (2010a) shows that, under the same parametric assumptions imposed by Flinn and Heckman (1982),[14] the proportion of prejudiced employers and the disutility they receive from hiring women are identified. This is a useful result because it allows for the separate identification of the prejudiced parameters, the gender-specific productivity parameters, and the gender-specific search frictions parameters.

Estimation is performed by maximum likelihood: after a first stage in which an order statistic (the minimum observed wage) is used to obtain a strongly consistent estimator of the reservation wages, the maximization of the resulting concentrated likelihood delivers estimates of all the remaining structural parameters. The analytical expression for the maximum likelihood estimator is provided in Appendix 2C in Chapter 2.

2.2.3 Results

2.2.3.1 ESTIMATION RESULTS

Tables 2.1 and 2.2 show the relevant predicted values obtained from our estimation results. The Maximum Likelihood Estimates of the structural parameters are reported in Table 2A.2 of Appendix 2. Table 2.1 focuses on the cross-sectional distribution of productivity and wages. The Accepted Wages distribution corresponds to the observed wage data and it is the

---

[14] On top of showing that a distributional assumption is essential to obtain identification, they also show that estimation results may be sensitive to the distributional assumption used. In Chapter 2, Appendix C, we discuss some sensitivity analysis we performed in this respect.

Table 2.1. Estimation results – predicted productivity and wages

	Master and PhD		College		High School	
	1995	2005	1995	2005	1995	2005
Men						
Productivity						
Average	49.88	58.48	43.12	45.20	28.81	28.73
	(1.509)	(2.052)	(0.828)	(0.876)	(0.393)	(0.422)
Variance	911.33	1748.68	800.26	1074.05	290.35	345.02
	(113.068)	(241.048)	(61.566)	(82.764)	(16.632)	(20.879)
Offered Earnings						
Average	30.36	34.68	25.85	27.60	18.24	18.36
	(0.754)	(1.026)	(0.414)	(0.438)	(0.196)	(0.211)
Accepted Earnings						
Average	30.50	34.95	26.00	28.04	18.42	18.72
	(0.753)	(1.028)	(0.414)	(0.437)	(0.194)	(0.207)
Women						
Productivity						
Average	42.68	45.39	40.21	36.42	23.35	22.70
	(1.485)	(2.210)	(3.587)	(1.091)	(1.916)	(0.796)
Variance	367.94	567.13	382.25	610.60	146.42	186.91
	(50.505)	(113.378)	(33.931)	(49.093)	(8.280)	(11.983)
Offered Earnings						
Average	25.03	25.92	20.20	21.75	12.42	14.19
	(2.600)	(5.538)	(0.777)	(1.202)	(0.213)	(0.817)
Average at Prejudiced	20.63	19.19	19.21	21.14	12.42	13.78
	(15.127)	(24.569)	(0.378)	(0.702)	(0.213)	(0.600)
Average at Unprejudiced	25.81	27.73	23.31	21.84	14.44	14.35
	(0.742)	(1.105)	(1.794)	(0.546)	(0.958)	(0.398)
Accepted Earnings						
Average	24.53	26.44	19.77	21.66	12.88	14.17
	(1.711)	(3.453)	(0.369)	(0.325)	(0.204)	(0.162)
Average at Prejudiced	17.32	21.46	18.64	19.31	12.88	13.32
	(9.401)	(16.124)	(1.169)	(0.503)	(0.204)	(0.503)
Average at Unprejudiced	25.81	27.78	23.32	21.99	14.47	14.51
	(0.740)	(1.092)	(1.790)	(0.493)	(0.913)	(0.332)

Notes: The table reported predicted values based on the maximum likelihood estimated structural parameters. Estimated parameters are reported in Table 2A.2 in the Appendix. Asymptotic standard errors by Delta method in parentheses.

measure conventionally used to compute the gender wage gap. The wage offers distribution is not directly observed and we are able to predict it thanks to the model structure. It indicates the wage offers actually received by men and women before they decide whether to accept them. In many respects, the wage offer distribution represents a better measure for capturing the actual disadvantage experienced by women because it avoids the selection bias due to gender differences in reservation wages.[15] The productivity distribution is

---

[15] This is one of the advantages of obtaining structural parameters estimates. The first paper estimating a search-matching-bargaining model (Eckstein and Wolpin, 1995) makes a similar argument in the context of returns to schooling estimation.

Table 2.2. Estimation results – predicted labor market dynamics

	Master and PhD		College		High School	
	1995	2005	1995	2005	1995	2005
			Men			
Hazard Rate out of Unemployment						
Overall	0.1111	0.2751	0.1948	0.1757	0.2261	0.2228
	(0.0454)	(0.0794)	(0.0339)	(0.0237)	(0.0201)	(0.0195)
To a Prejudiced Empl.	0.0167	0.0582	0.1478	0.0216	0.2261	0.0626
	(0.0086)	(0.0341)	(0.0601)	(0.0246)	(0.0201)	(0.0584)
To an Unprejudiced Empl.	0.0943	0.2169	0.0471	0.1541	0.00001	0.1602
	(0.0389)	(0.0693)	(0.0550)	(0.0321)	(0.0009)	(0.0598)
Hazard Rate out of Employment						
Overall	0.0017	0.0082	0.0056	0.0071	0.0154	0.0150
	(0.0010)	(0.0034)	(0.0014)	(0.0014)	(0.0020)	(0.0019)
Labor Market Status						
Emp. Rate at Prejudiced	0.1483	0.2056	0.7371	0.1183	0.9362	0.2634
	(0.0462)	(0.1048)	(0.2712)	(0.1337)	(0.0066)	(0.2445)
Emp. Rate at Unprejudiced	0.8367	0.7655	0.2348	0.8429	0.0001	0.6736
	(0.0465)	(0.1050)	(0.2712)	(0.1338)	(0.0036)	(0.2445)
Unemployment Rate	0.0150	0.0289	0.0281	0.0388	0.0637	0.0630
	(0.0061)	(0.0082)	(0.0048)	(0.0051)	(0.0055)	(0.0053)
			Women			
Hazard Rate out of Unemployment						
Overall	0.2491	0.2393	0.2619	0.2261	0.2709	0.2380
	(0.1114)	(0.0798)	(0.0390)	(0.0308)	(0.0282)	(0.0231)
To a Prejudiced Empl.	0.0023	0.0031	0.1959	0.0226	0.2709	0.0619
	(0.0271)	(0.0315)	(0.0823)	(0.0273)	(0.0283)	(0.0620)
To an Unprejudiced Empl.	0.2468	0.2361	0.0660	0.2035	0.00002	0.1761
	(0.1136)	(0.0848)	(0.0776)	(0.0388)	(0.0011)	(0.0640)
Hazard Rate out of Employment						
Overall	0.0041	0.0049	0.0110	0.0086	0.0134	0.0136
	(0.0026)	(0.0023)	(0.0023)	(0.0017)	(0.0020)	(0.0019)
Labor Market Status						
Emp. Rate at Prejudiced	0.0092	0.0128	0.7179	0.0963	0.9527	0.2459
	(0.1070)	(0.1287)	(0.2821)	(0.1157)	(0.0062)	(0.2451)
Emp. Rate at Unprejudiced	0.9747	0.9670	0.2418	0.8671	0.0001	0.6999
	(0.1072)	(0.1294)	(0.2821)	(0.1161)	(0.0039)	(0.2452)
Unemployment Rate	0.0161	0.0202	0.0403	0.0366	0.0472	0.0542
	(0.0071)	(0.0123)	(0.0059)	(0.0108)	(0.0048)	(0.0090)

Notes: The table reported predicted values based on the maximum likelihood estimated structural parameters. Estimated parameters are reported in Table 2A.2 in the Appendix. Asymptotic standard errors by Delta method in parentheses.

also unobserved and it is the true primitive distribution in the model. Finally, another unobserved component that we are able to recover is the assignment of women to prejudiced and unprejudiced employers.

The gender gap in accepted wages is in line with the descriptive evidence, ranging from 26% to 20% overall. The gap is decreasing over time for the high school sample, it is stable for the college sample, and actually increasing for the Master and PhD sample. The evidence of the gender wage gap over time – for example Eckstein and Nagypal (2004), Blau and Kahn (2006), and Flabbi (2010b) – report a stable or decreasing gap, but they do not focus on schooling level as high as Master's and PhD. This relative disadvantage of very high-skilled women is a robust finding throughout this chapter.

The gender gap in wage offers is smaller than the gender gap in accepted wages at high education levels and larger at low education levels. This evidence is consistent with high-skilled women being relatively more selective than similarly educated men. Two possible sources of this behavior are: 1) gender- and education-specific preferences for job amenities and 2) gender asymmetries in household-level decisions. An example of the first is illustrated in Flabbi and Moro (2012): women with a college degree value work flexibility more than women with a high school degree. An example of the second is analyzed in Flabbi and Mabli (2012): once we take into account that labor market decisions arc taken at the household level, gender differentials in wage offers are estimated to be smaller than in an individual search model. Both elements are ignored in the version of the model we estimate. We will comment on the results starting from the earnings decomposition in Table 2.3. The full results are in the Appendix 2C of this chapter.

The gender gap in productivity is relatively small, but increasing over time, for the college and high school sample. The gender productivity gap for Master's and PhD holders is quite large and increasing over time. As a result, and as we will see in the next section, differentials in productivity are responsible for most of the gap we observe in the highest education group.

The gender gap between workers employed by prejudiced employers and workers employed by unprejudiced employers is larger the higher the education level. For example, the gender gap in wage offers at prejudiced employers on the Master's and PhD sample in 2005 is equal to 55% while at unprejudiced employers is equal to 80%. This corresponding difference for lower education levels is about two percentage points. This result shows that even if the overall impact of prejudice on the high-skilled sample is smaller than the impact of gender-specific productivity, it still has a major impact in generating wage discrimination.

Table 2.2 shows some evidence of labor market dynamics: the hazard rates out of a given labor market state and the proportion of workers in each labor market state in equilibrium. The overall hazard rate out of unemployment is higher for women, a result explained both by higher arrival rates of offers and by lower reservation wages (see Table 2A.2 in the Appendix 2C of this Chapter). The gender gap in unemployment rates is relatively small. Larger differences are observed in the distribution of men and women between prejudiced and unprejudiced employers. Notice that we report the overall employment by employer type, so when the proportion of prejudiced employers is extremely high (as in the high school sample in 1995) most employed workers must work for them.

2.2.3.2 GENDER WAGE GAP DECOMPOSITION

Table 2.3a reports a decomposition of the gender wage gap at different points of the accepted wages distribution. The gap is decomposed in the three sources of gender differentials assumed in the model: productivity, search frictions, and prejudice. We perform the decomposition by taking into account equilibrium effects, in other words by taking into account that changing the labor market environment induces individual agents to adjust their behavior.

The procedure we implement is the following. To isolate the impact of productivity, we assume that all the other differences between men and women do not exist: there are no prejudiced employers in the economy and men and women face the same search frictions. Given this new environment, we compute the optimal decision rules and we obtain new accepted wages distributions. For these counterfactual distributions we compute average accepted wages for men and women and we take the ratio of women's values over men's values. These ratios are reported in Table 2.3a. For example, the first row relative to college graduates states that if the only difference between men and women was the differential productivity, then the observed wage differential at the mean of the entire distribution would be much smaller than the one observed in the data: 8.9% as opposed to 22.1%. To isolate the impact of prejudice, we follow the same procedure: we fix productivity and search frictions of women equal to those of men but we allow the proportion of prejudiced employers and their disutility to be equal to the one we estimate. We recomputed the equilibrium and we obtained the statistics on the counterfactual wage distribution. The same exercise is done to isolate the impact of search frictions: the only parameters allowed to be different are the arrival rate of offers and the job termination rate.

Differences in productivity are the most important factor in explaining the wage gap for the top education level in 1995: productivity differentials alone will generate the entire differential we observe at the mean. This strong impact becomes smaller in 2005 and it is significantly smaller in the college sample but similar in the high school sample. The impact of search frictions always plays in favor of women: we would actually observe a reverse gender wage gap if the only differences between men and women in the labor market were due to search frictions.[16] Finally, the impact of prejudiced employers is very strong for college graduates in 1995: prejudice is the most important factor in

---

[16] The positive impact of search frictions is mainly driven by the higher arrival rate of job offers to women (see Table 2.A2 in the Appendix).

Table 2.3a. Wage gap decomposition – woman/men ratio on average accepted wage

Gap	1995				2005			
Generated by:	Overall	Top 50%	Top 25%	Top 10%	Overall	Top 50%	Top 25%	Top 10%
				Master and PhD				
Productivity	0.835	0.883	0.865	0.857	0.699	1.628	1.344	1.130
Prejudiced	0.935	0.958	0.971	0.982	0.881	0.923	0.950	0.974
Search Frictions	1.337	1.195	1.139	1.088	1.052	1.031	1.021	1.013
All Parameters	0.804	0.867	0.853	0.849	0.756	0.857	0.841	0.834
Sample	0.823	0.791	0.793	0.812	0.728	0.682	0.638	0.568
				College				
Productivity	0.911	0.937	0.911	0.892	0.758	0.827	0.838	0.857
Prejudiced	0.801	0.862	0.898	0.931	0.976	0.984	0.988	0.993
Search Frictions	1.116	1.073	1.054	1.036	1.106	1.066	1.047	1.030
All Parameters	0.760	0.824	0.824	0.828	0.773	0.837	0.846	0.862
Sample	0.779	0.779	0.775	0.797	0.794	0.793	0.806	0.869
				High School				
Productivity	0.769	0.777	0.772	0.770	0.742	0.766	0.771	0.780
Prejudiced	0.853	0.888	0.910	0.932	0.964	0.974	0.980	0.985
Search Frictions	1.091	1.063	1.050	1.038	1.036	1.025	1.019	1.014
All Parameters	0.699	0.718	0.723	0.731	0.757	0.776	0.779	0.787
Sample	0.701	0.711	0.724	0.745	0.763	0.763	0.778	0.793

Notes: Women/men ratio on average accepted earnings computed over the entire distribution and over the top 50%, the top 75% and the top 10%. All counterfactuals are generated taking into account equilibrium effects.

explaining the wage gap for this year and education group. The impact of prejudice becomes smaller over time, becoming less important than the impact of productivity in 2005. Instead, the top education group (Master's and PhD) shows the opposite trend: smaller impact in 1995 and stronger impact in 2005.

We also find that Master's and PhD graduates in 2005 are the only group exhibiting evidence of a glass ceiling, that is a wage gap increasing as we move toward the top of the accepted wages distribution. This increasing wage gap is captured by the model but with a much smaller magnitude than in the data.

Table 2.3b reports the wage gap decomposition conditioning on marital status and the presence of children. As we compare the overall sample the sample of married individuals and the sample of married individuals with children, the decomposition changes but the magnitudes are similar. The most striking result is in the sample of Master's and PhDs in 2005: as we move from the entire sample to the sample of married with children, productivity becomes less important while prejudice becomes more important in explaining the wage gap. This result is present but less strong in 1995 and it is not present in the other education groups.

Overall the wage decomposition exercise shows the following features. Prejudice has a significant impact in the wage gap but the impact is decreasing over time, reaching a level smaller than the impact of differential productivity

Table 2.3b. Wage gap decomposition – conditioning on marital status and children – woman/men ratio on average accepted wage

Gap	1995			2005		
Generated by:	Entire Sample	Married	Married with Children	Entire Sample	Married	Married with Children
			Master and PhD			
Productivity	0.835	0.835	0.884	0.699	0.698	0.874
Prejudiced	0.935	0.964	0.960	0.881	0.878	0.812
Search Frictions	1.337	1.387	1.373	1.052	0.895	1.064
All Parameters	0.804	0.793	0.778	0.756	0.727	0.729
Sample	0.823	0.820	0.809	0.728	0.700	0.752
			College			
Productivity	0.911	0.872	0.754	0.758	0.719	0.735
Prejudiced	0.801	0.795	0.877	0.976	0.976	0.984
Search Frictions	1.116	1.135	1.072	1.106	1.051	1.070
All Parameters	0.760	0.737	0.736	0.773	0.753	0.751
Sample	0.779	0.758	0.753	0.794	0.774	0.775
			High School			
Productivity	0.769	0.697	0.628	0.742	0.701	0.666
Prejudiced	0.853	0.933	0.794	0.964	1.000	0.937
Search Frictions	1.091	1.049	1.126	1.036	0.982	0.941
All Parameters	0.699	0.744	0.646	0.757	0.818	0.721
Sample	0.701	0.683	0.652	0.763	0.748	0.727

Notes: Women/men ratio on average accepted earnings computed over the entire distribution. All counterfactuals are generated taking into account equilibrium effects. Married means married at least once. Married with Children means married and with children younger than 18 years old.

on all education groups in 2005. The exception is the top education group: Master's and PhD graduates experience a stronger impact of prejudice in 2005 than 1995. By estimating the model for individuals married and with children, we find that a good portion of the impact is driven by this group. This result would imply that the impact of prejudice is one of the possible channels of the impact of fertility decisions on labor market outcomes. Master's and PhD graduates also Makeup the education group that shows evidence of a glass ceiling in 2005, confirming the view that considers the glass ceiling as the remaining obstacle to gender equality in the labor market.[17]

2.3 Policy Implications and Policy Experiments

Thanks to the estimates and to the structural model we are able to compute the welfare effect of discrimination. In particular, we first compute a "welfare return" to schooling for men and women, in other words the

---

[17] One possible reason for this poor fit is the imprecise estimates of the prejudiced parameters: probably because of the small sample size, the estimate of the disutility suffered by the prejudiced employers hiring Masters and PhDs is very imprecise. See Table A2 in the Appendix, parameter k.

Table 2.4. Welfare returns to schooling – ratio of average welfare measures

	1995			2005		
	MA and PhD / College	MA and PhD / High School	College / High School	MA and PhD / College	MA and PhD / High School	College / High School
Entire Sample						
Overall						
All Parameters	1.268	1.925	1.518	1.238	1.926	1.555
Without Prejudiced	1.177	1.840	1.564	1.314	2.032	1.547
Men						
All Parameters	1.215	1.824	1.501	1.240	1.941	1.565
Without Prejudiced	..	..	..	..	..	..
Women						
All Parameters	1.307	2.007	1.535	1.242	1.944	1.565
Without Prejudiced	1.120	1.832	1.635	1.406	2.167	1.541
Married with Children						
Overall						
All Parameters	1.311	2.026	1.545	1.242	1.999	1.609
Without Prejudiced	1.259	1.863	1.480	1.379	2.168	1.572
Men						
All Parameters	1.224	1.812	1.481	1.201	1.930	1.606
Without Prejudiced	..	..	..	..	..	..
Women						
All Parameters	1.372	2.219	1.617	1.274	2.079	1.632
Without Prejudiced	1.261	1.849	1.466	1.608	2.481	1.543

Notes: The table presents ratio of the average welfare measures of the corresponding education levels. Welfare measures are computed using the estimated structural parameters. See main text for the complete definition. Married with Children means married and with children younger than 18 years old.

welfare differentials enjoyed by labor market participants at different levels of schooling.

Second, we perform policy experiments that mimic some policies implemented in the US labor market: equal pay policies and affirmative action policies. In equal pay policy, we impose that wage schedules cannot be set according to gender. In the affirmative action policy, we implement an employer subsidy to hire women. The equal pay policy is effective in redistributing welfare from men to women but it is never enough to completely close the gender gap.

2.3.1 *Welfare Measure and Returns to Schooling*

The overall welfare of labor market participants depends on their whole labor market history. A summary measure of overall workers' welfare should then go beyond the comparison of wage gaps that we presented in Section 2.3.2.

One relatively straightforward way in which to proceed is assigning to each labor market state the corresponding utility value (corresponding to the wage if the worker is employed and to the flow utility of unemployment if the worker is unemployed) and then averaging these utility values according to the equilibrium steady state distribution. This summary measure takes into account both the cross-sectional and the expected dynamics components of the labor market.[18]

We use this welfare measure to compare schooling decisions. We have seen that women acquire more education than men even if the usual returns to schooling do not seem to suggest a higher return for women than men in the labor market. We contribute to the debate by computing the returns based on our welfare measure. We also perform the counterfactual experiments of computing what the returns would be if there were no prejudiced employers in the labor market. The results are reported in Table 2.4, where we compute for each year the gender-specific return of each schooling level. The first column states that completing Master's or PhD increases welfare on average by about 26.8% with respect to simply completing college. The returns increase to 92.5 with respect to completing only high school and they are about 51.8% when comparing college with high school.

The comparison of men and women is even more interesting. In 1995, female returns to education are higher than male returns. This provides an explanation reconciling the observed higher levels of education and lower hourly wages for women than for men. By simply looking at cross-sectional wages, we are ignoring that women may have more to gain in terms of the overall labor market dynamic by acquiring additional education. In 1995 women completing Master's and PhDs received a 30.7% higher return relative to college graduates and a 100.7% higher return relative to high school graduates; men received, respectively, a 21.5% return and a 82.4% return. However, in 2005 there was essentially no difference in the returns between men and women, implying that those incentives may be coming to an end. Finally, from a simulation we see that if prejudice were to be eliminated in a market similar to the one we estimate in 2005, then the welfare returns for Master's and PhD would be higher for women than men.

2.3.2 Equal Employment Opportunity Policies

Equal Employment Opportunity policy interventions date back at least to the Civil Rights Act of 1964 which made it unlawful for an employer to "fail or refuse to hire or to discharge any individual, or otherwise to discriminate against any individual with respect to his compensation, terms, conditions

---

[18] An in-depth discussion of this and similar welfare measures is in Flinn (2002). For the analytical expression of the welfare measure we use here, see Flabbi (2010a), Appendix A.5, Definition 5.

or privileges or employment, because of such individuals race, color, religion, sex, or national origin". [Section 703 (a)].[19]

Equal Pay policies – those that we specifically aimed at eliminating pay discrimination – are an active part of the equal employment opportunity policy agenda. The first Act signed by President Obama into law after his inauguration is an example of equal pay policy. The Lilly Ledbetter Fair Pay Act of 2009 is a federal statue amending the Civil Rights Act of 1964, stating that the 180-day statute of limitation for filing an equal pay lawsuit regarding pay discrimination resets with each new discriminatory paycheck.[20]

A simple implementation of an equal pay policy within the search-matching bargaining model of the previous section would be to require each employer to pay the same wage to workers with identical productivity. Enforcement of such a policy assumes that the authority observes productivity, a very strong assumption. An alternative way to think of this equal pay policy is that it requires that gender cannot be observed when wages and hiring are decided.[21]

We impose the requirement that each employer has to pay the same wage to workers with identical productivity. As a result, offered wages are the average between the wages that would have been offered without the policy, where the average is over the respective proportions of men and women in the population. The new wage equations are reported in Appendix 2B of this chapter.

Results of the policy are summarized in Table 2.5. For each year, the first column of Table 2.5 reports the benchmark model, the second reports the equilibrium under the equal pay policy experiment and the third under the affirmative action policy experiment that we will discuss in the next section. The benchmark model is the model simulated using the point obtained by our estimation procedure. The table reports average welfare values by gender, year, and education normalized with respect to men's average welfare value in the appropriate year education cell. The top panel reports values obtained from the entire sample estimates; the bottom panel reports values obtained from the married with children sample estimates. For example, looking at the first column in 2005 we observe that the average welfare of Master's and PhD

---

[19] The Act also established a specific institutional body to implement the law: the Equal Employment Opportunity Commission (EEOC). The role of the EEOC was progressively expanded by subsequent legislation and the Commission is now responsible for enforcing all the federal statutes prohibiting discrimination.

[20] The Paycheck Fairness Act was recently reintroduced in the 112th Congress after having twice passed the US House of Representatives but falling two votes short of a Senate vote on its merits in the 111th Congress.

[21] Very limited examples of such a policy have been implemented in practice. Blind auditions to hire musicians implemented by some of the major US orchestras are probably the most well known (Goldin and Rouse, 2000).

Table 2.5. Policy experiments – relative average welfare measures

	1995			2005		
	All Parameters	Equal Pay	Affirmative Action	All Parameters	Equal Pay	Affirmative Action
Entire Sample						
Master and PhD						
Men	1.0000	0.9459	0.9861	1.0000	0.9149	0.9799
Women	0.7857	0.8088	0.8067	0.7659	0.7656	0.7841
Overall	0.9063	0.8860	0.9076	0.8787	0.8376	0.8785
College						
Men	1.0000	0.9111	0.9826	1.0000	0.9678	0.9830
Women	0.7299	0.8250	0.7487	0.7650	0.7950	0.7827
Overall	0.8684	0.8691	0.8686	0.8802	0.8797	0.8809
High School						
Men	1.0000	0.9202	0.9816	1.0000	0.9624	0.9827
Women	0.7138	0.7985	0.7327	0.7650	0.8040	0.7837
Overall	0.8586	0.8601	0.8586	0.8856	0.8853	0.8858
Married with Children						
Master and PhD						
Men	1.0000	0.9653	0.9900	1.0000	0.9108	0.9825
Women	0.7618	0.8401	0.7836	0.7703	0.8737	0.7896
Overall	0.9035	0.9146	0.9064	0.8895	0.8929	0.8897
College						
Men	1.0000	0.9360	0.9816	1.0000	0.9669	0.9834
Women	0.6794	0.7337	0.6984	0.7265	0.7570	0.7435
Overall	0.8432	0.8371	0.8431	0.8604	0.8598	0.8610
High School						
Men	1.0000	0.8605	0.9797	1.0000	0.9323	0.9806
Women	0.6222	0.6696	0.6409	0.7151	0.7495	0.7332
Overall	0.8084	0.7637	0.8079	0.8588	0.8417	0.8580

Notes: The table reports average welfare normalized with respect to men in the benchmark model. Benchmark Model is the model at the estimated parameters. Equal pay means each employer must pay one wage at same productivity. Affirmative action means employers receive a flow subsidy equal to 5% of the men's average accepted wage when hiring a woman and the subsidy is financed by a lump-sum tax on all workers. Married with children means married and with children younger than 18 years old.

women is 76% of the average welfare of Master's and PhD men. The value increases as education decreases, reaching about 80% on the high school graduates sample.

The equal pay experiment is effective in redistributing welfare from men to women but it is never enough to completely close the gender gap. In general, the equal pay policy is more effective in reducing the gap at low education levels than at high education levels. By looking at the overall average welfare values, we observe that for Master's and PhDs in the married with children sample there is a positive effect for the policy in aggregate. This is also marginally true for the entire sample of college and high school graduates in 1995. Overall, the policy imposes a very strong requirement in terms of wage determination but it does not seem to generate very large effects, with the possible exception of very high-skilled individuals who are married and have young children.

2.3.3 *Affirmative Action Policies*

Affirmative Action policies in the labor market officially started in the US with the 1961 Kennedy Executive Order #10925 that mandates "affirmative action" to avoid discrimination by race in the labor market. The 1967 Johnson Executive Order #11375 extends its application to cover women. In the legislative and policy debate an affirmative action policy is any anti-discrimination policy that requires proactive steps (Holzer and Neumark, 2000). In the economic literature, an affirmative action policy is frequently described as a "quota" policy, in other words a system of exogenously imposed numerical yardsticks for minority in hiring, federal contracting, or school enrollments.

The difference between proactive steps and exogenously imposed quotas seems to inform a lot of the debate on affirmative action in the labor market and in education. Donohue and Heckman (1991) focus on the impact of the Civil Rights legislation on labor market outcomes of African Americans. They also broaden the definition of affirmative action beyond a simple quota system and conclude that the policies had a significant role in improving labor market outcomes. The two most recent Supreme Court opinions about affirmative action – Grutter vs. Bollinger and Gratz vs. Bollinger – were delivered on June 24, 2003 and stress the unconstitutionality of explicit quota policies but the admissibility of proactive policies. The tendency of the legislation and the public policy debate has been to push affirmative action policies away from rigid and exogenous quota targets toward other proactive steps that could endogenously generate similar outcomes.

In line with this debate, we propose an affirmative action policy which is not a quota policy but a proactive step in the form of a subsidy. The policy is defined as a subsidy paid by a lump-sum tax on workers received by an employer for each woman hired. The impact of the policy is magnified by the spillover effects: not only does the presence of a flow subsidy have a direct positive impact on women's wages because firms receive additional revenue from hiring them, but it also has an indirect positive impact because it increases women's outside options. We fix the subsidy to be equal to 5% of men's average wages in the corresponding year and education group.

The results of the subsidy policy are reported in the third column of each year in Table 2.5. The policy is less effective in closing the gap than the equal pay policy, but at the same time it is generating more net gains. Net gains are realized in both 1995 and 2005 on the college sample and in 1995 on the Master's and PHD sample. Another advantage of the policy is that it can be calibrated more precisely by increasing or decreasing the subsidy, and its costs can be distributed in a variety of ways by changing the structure of the tax necessary to support it. In this respect, the lump-sum tax implemented here is the least distortionary for the economy but it is also the most costly for men. More than half of the education year combinations generate positive gains. This is also the policy that generates the largest impact on the group that previous evidence has shown to be the most problematic: women with top education skills, supplying labor in the most recent years.

2.4 Summary and Conclusions

2.4.1 *Summary of Results*

Three main results emerge from the descriptive evidence on gender differentials by education in the US labor market over the last 20 years.

1. Women acquire more college education than men. The proportion of women with a Master's or PhD degree is still smaller than the proportion of men but the differential is shrinking. For all OECD countries (Chapter 1) and for Italy (Chapter 4), there is a large gender asymmetry in the choice of field of study.

2. Women participate less than men in the labor market but when they do, they obtain similar employment rates. The intensive margin of the labor supply shows a large gender gap, mainly as a result of the larger incidence of part-time work among female workers. The gender gap in labor supply is not reduced but actually magnified by additional education. This result is in line with the evidence for Spain presented in Chapter 3.

3. The gender earnings gap is about 20%, even after controlling for standard human capital and demographics characteristics. The gap shows a significant reduction over time (it was about 35% in the early 1980s) but has remained fairly stable in the last 10–15 years.

We have used a search-matching-bargaining model to investigate some of the sources of the observed gender differentials. We focus on gender differentials with the objective of isolating the impact of three determinants of gender gaps: productivity differences, employers' prejudice, and search frictions. Four main results emerge from this analysis.

1. Prejudice has a significant impact in explaining the wage gap, but the impact is decreasing over time and it becomes smaller than the impact of productivity on all education groups in 2005.

2. Search frictions favor women because of the higher frequency with which they receive job offers.

3. Master's and PhD graduates are an exception to the decreasing impact of prejudice over time: they experience a stronger impact of prejudice in explaining the wage gap in 2005 than in 1995. We find that a good portion of this result is due to the sample of married individuals with young children.

4. We also decompose the impact of the three sources of the gender wage gap at different points of the distribution: the data show evidence of glass-ceiling effects on the Master's and PhD sample in 2005, a result that the equilibrium effects of all three factors together is able to only partially explain.

We use the structural estimates of the model to build a welfare measure to evaluate returns to education for men and women and two policy interventions. The first policy imposes the same wage for the same productivity between men and women. The second is an affirmative action policy providing incentives to hire women. Three main results emerge from the exercise:

1. In 1995, female returns to schooling in terms of welfare are higher than male returns. This result provides a rationale for the apparent empirical puzzle of women acquiring more education than men even if they are paid less for these skills in the labor market. In 2005, however, female returns were estimated to be lower than male returns, implying that women's attitudes toward education could change, reversing the positive education gap.

2. The equal pay policy redistributes welfare from men to women but it is not able to fully close the gender gap. Given the strong requirement in terms of wage determination imposed by the policy, we judge it not very effective.

3. The affirmative action policy has a smaller impact on closing the gender gap than the equal pay policy but it is more likely to generate net welfare gains. The impact of the policy is increasing in worker's education levels and it seems to target well the most problematic education and demographic group: Master's and PhD graduates who are married and with young children, observed in 2005.

2.4.2 Conclusions

The evidence provided in this chapter has uncovered important determinants of the gender gap, by identifying the impact of prejudice in labor markets with friction. On top of the traditional issues of lower participation rates and gender gaps in wages, new issues that are likely to become more relevant in the future include:

1. Convergence in education levels is not enough to close gender gaps in the labor market.
2. There is evidence of glass-ceiling effects. The evidence includes a marked underrepresentation of women in top positions at firms and a larger gender wage gap at the top of the wage distribution.

The conclusion of our analytical contribution is that prejudice may still have a role in explaining the evidence. Even if the magnitude of our effects is conditional on a highly stylized model, we characterize in some detail at least one scenario where the presence of prejudiced employers in the labor market has substantial effects. In particular, it is responsible for the reversal of the return to school ranking in recent years, and it may explain up to 44% of the gender wage gap of the top education group (Master's and PhD) in 2005.

If prejudice is still important, then policy interventions may be effective in attaining both efficiency and welfare gains. We use our model to evaluate an equal pay policy and an affirmative action policy. Among the policies we consider, we favor an affirmative action policy structured as a relatively modest subsidy provided to employers for hiring women. We favor this policy because it is frequently able to close the gender gap without reducing overall welfare and because it is effective in targeting the group that should take center stage in the future debate about gender differentials: high-skilled, high-earning workers who also have family responsibilities.

Appendix to Chapter 2

Luca Flabbi and Mauricio Tejada

2A Data Sources and Definitions

2A.1 *Data used in the Descriptive Evidence Section*

The data used in the descriptive evidence section are extracted from the Annual Social and Economics supplement (ASES or March Supplement) and the School Enrollment Supplement (October supplement) of the Current Population Survey (CPS). The first supplement contains data on family characteristics, household composition, marital status, education attainment, earnings, labor market status, work experience, job characteristics. The second focuses on school enrollment, college attendance, fields of study, major choices. Both supplements are conducted annually. We use the March yearly supplement from 1981 to 2011 and the October supplement in 2002. We use only the 2002 supplement because it is the only one reporting field of study choices.

2A.1.1 INDIVIDUAL CHARACTERISTICS
The individual characteristics are obtained from the CPS questions on gender, race, age, marital status, and presence of children under 18 years of age in the household. The year of birth, for the analysis by cohort, was inferred from the year of the survey and the age.

2A.1.2 EDUCATION LEVEL AND FIELDS OF STUDY
The education levels and fields of study choices are obtained from the set of questions related to education attainment in the March supplement and with school enrolment in the October supplement. We classify education level in three groups according to the highest degree obtained: (1) Master's and Doctorate, (2) college degree and (3) high school degree. It is important to mention that this classification is used from 1992 onward, because in that year there was a major change in the coding of the CPS data to classify education attainment. For the survey years before 1992, we simply define college graduates as persons with 14 years or more of education.

The gap in Figures 2.1 and 2.2 is calculated as a percentage difference with respect to men, namely it is $(x_W - x_M) / x_M$ where x is percentage of college graduates.

The field of study choice variable is only collected in the October supplement of 2002 and this is why Figures 2.4 and 2.5 report the distribution only in 2002.

2A.1.3 LABOR MARKET STATUS
The labor market status (employment, unemployment, and nonparticipation) is obtained by a set of questions organized by the CPS team in the monthly labor force recode variable which directly assigns each individual in the sample to employment, unemployment, or not in the labor force status. Excluded from the universe are children and members of the armed forces.

2A.1.4 EARNINGS AND HOURS WORKED
Hourly earnings are obtained either by using the value directly reported in the CPS survey or by computing the value (by dividing weekly earnings by the usual hours worked per week). Earnings are measured in real terms. We express earnings in 2005 US dollars by deflating them by the Consumer Price Index for All Urban Consumers. For hours worked we use, as before, the usual hours worked per week directly reported in the survey.

2A.1.5 UNEMPLOYMENT DURATIONS
Unemployment durations are measured in months and they are obtained by rescaling the original weekly unemployment durations reported in the CPS.

2A.1.6 JOB CHARACTERISTICS
The job characteristics are obtained from the set of questions related to full/part-time job and occupational classification. The codes in this last variable are the 2002 NAICS equivalent. It is important to mention that all the descriptive analysis related to occupations is done from 2002 onwards, because in that year there was a major change in the coding used in the CPS to classify occupations.

2A.2 Data used in the Impact of Employer's Prejudice Section

The data used in the structural estimation of the search-matching-bargaining model with employers' taste discrimination are extracted from the March supplement of the CPS for 1995 and 2005. These years were chosen because they satisfy two criteria. First, these are neither boom years nor recession years, and therefore they seem appropriate to describe a model under the steady state assumption. Second, they are equally spaced over time and far away enough to potentially describe different steady states.

Table 2A.1. Descriptive statistics – estimation sample

	Master and PhD		College		High School	
	1995	2005	1995	2005	1995	2005
Observations						
N	711	861	2290	2891	3942	4019
N (Wages, Women)	306	437	1071	1420	1856	1850
N (Duration, Women)	5	9	45	54	92	106
N (Wages, Men)	394	403	1141	1362	1867	1933
N (Duration, Men)	6	12	33	55	127	130
Hourly Earnings in Dollars						
Overall						
Average	27.79	31.26	22.86	24.74	15.60	16.46
Std. Dev.	12.89	36.74	11.73	15.44	7.35	8.22
Women						
Average	24.55	26.43	19.79	21.83	12.88	14.20
Std. Dev.	10.10	12.04	10.19	15.97	5.92	7.11
Men						
Average	30.30	36.49	25.74	27.78	18.30	18.63
Std. Dev.	14.20	51.06	12.34	14.24	7.63	8.62
Diff (%)						
Average	−18.97	−27.56	−23.11	−21.41	−29.64	−23.81
Monthly Unemployment Duration						
Overall						
Average	6.73	3.87	4.38	5.06	4.12	4.36
Std. Dev.	7.07	4.19	5.15	5.79	5.12	5.15
Women						
Average	4.02	4.18	3.82	4.42	3.69	4.20
Std. Dev.	4.14	4.40	4.39	5.16	3.97	5.37
Men						
Average	9.00	3.63	5.13	5.69	4.42	4.49
Std. Dev.	8.52	4.21	6.04	6.33	5.81	4.98
Diff (%)						
Average	−55.38	14.99	−25.57	−22.26	−16.52	−6.37

Note: Data extracted from the Annual Social and Economic Supplement (March Supplement) of the CPS for the years 1995 and 2005. In each education label the sample includes individuals who are white and 30 to 55 years old.

An important assumption in the model is ex ante agents' homogeneity. To obtain the estimation sample, we extract individuals' homogeneous sample with respect to the following characteristics: race (white), age (30 to 55 years old), and education (Master's and PhD; college; high school).

The variables used in the estimation are: real hourly wages, unemployment duration in month, gender, education level, and labor market status. Wages are available only for individuals currently employed and unemployed duration only for individuals currently unemployed. As a result unemployment durations are not complete spells but ongoing spells.

Table 2A.1 presents number of observations and descriptive statistics, by education level and year, of the sample used in the Maximum Likelihood Estimation procedure.

2B The Formal Model

2B.1 *The Search-Matching-Bargaining Model*

2B.1.1 THEORY
Environment: The model is developed in continuous time and it is populated by four types of agents infinitely lived: two types of workers – Men (M) and Women (W) – and two types of employers – Prejudiced (P) and Unprejudiced (N). The workers' type is defined by gender. The employers' type is defined by a difference in preferences: prejudiced employers receive a disutility flow (d) from hiring women.

There is random matching and there is not on-the-job search. Workers meet employers following a Poisson process with an instantaneous rate of arrival λ. Once an employer and a worker meet, they observe a match-specific productivity value (x), which is drawn from an exogenous distribution denoted by the cumulative density function (CDF), G. Once a match is formed, it can be terminated following a Poisson process at an instantaneous rate η.

Workers' utility functions are linear in wages and no disutility from working is assumed. While unemployed, workers receive an instantaneous utility flow b. Time is discounted by a constant and common rate ρ. All the model's parameters are common knowledge. Markets are fully segmented along gender education year cells. We denote gender with g, employer's type with t, year with y, and education with e.

Value Functions: The value of employment for a worker of type g working at an employer of type t, producing x, in year y, with an education e is:

$$(\rho + \eta_{gye}) V_{gye} \left[w_{gtye}(x) \right] = w_{gtye}(x) + \eta_{gye} U_{gye} \tag{A.1}$$

where w(x) denotes the wage, which is determined by Nash-bargaining.

The value of unemployment conditioning on type, education, and year is

$$\rho U_{gye} = b_{gye} + \lambda_{gye} \left\{ \begin{array}{l} p_{ye} \int \max \left[V_{gye} \left[w_{gPye}(x) \right] - U_{gye}, 0 \right] dG_{gye}(x) + \\ (1 - p_{ye}) \int \max \left[V_{gye} \left[w_{gNye}(x) \right] - U_{gye}, 0 \right] dG_{gye}(x) \end{array} \right\}$$

$$\tag{A.2}$$

Wages: We assume the axiomatic Nash-bargaining solution to the bargaining problem faced by workers and employers bargaining over the wage, given the match-specific productivity x and their types. The solution corresponds to maximizing the product of the worker's and employer's surpluses, weighted by their bargaining power α:

$$w_{\text{gtye}}(x) = \text{argmax}_w \left\{ V_{\text{gye}}[w] - U_{\text{gye}} \right\}^\alpha \left\{ \frac{x - d_{\text{ye}} \mathbf{1}_{\{g=W\}} - w}{(\rho + \eta_{\text{gye}})} \right\}^{(1-\alpha)} \quad (A.3)$$

The wages schedules reported in the main text as equations 1–3 are simply specializations of equation A.3.

Equilibrium: Optimal decision rules are characterized by the reservation value property; that is the match is mutually accepted if the match-specific productivity value is higher than an appropriate reservation value. The reservation value is determined as the value at which the agents are indifferent between accepting and rejecting the match. The reservation values are reported in equations 4–6 in the main text. By adding the optimal decision rules to the value functions, we obtain an equation that implicitly defines the only necessary equilibrium object, the value of unemployment U:

$$\rho U_{\text{gye}} = b_{\text{gye}} + \lambda_{\text{gye}} \left\{ \begin{array}{l} p_{\text{ye}} \int_{\rho U_{\text{gye}} + d\mathbf{1}_{\{g=W\}}}^\infty \left[x - d_{\text{ye}} \mathbf{1}_{\{g=W\}} - \rho U_{\text{gye}} \right] dG_{\text{gye}}(x) + \\ (1 - p_{\text{ye}}) \int_{\rho U_{\text{gye}}}^\infty \left[x - \rho U_{\text{gye}} \right] dG_{\text{gye}}(x) \end{array} \right\}$$

$$(A.4)$$

We are now ready to propose the following:

Definition 1: In each market defined by year and education group, given the vector of parameters $\{\lambda_{\text{gye}}, \eta_{\text{gye}}, \rho, b_{\text{gye}}, \alpha, d_{\text{ye}}, p_{\text{ye}}\}$ and the CDF of match-specific productivity values $G_{\text{gye}}(x)$, the equilibrium is defined by the vectors of values of unemployment U^*_{gye} that solves equation A.4, which in turn determines the reservation values characterizing the optimal decision rules.

2B.1.2 ESTIMATION RESULTS

The estimates of the structural parameters are reported in Table 2A.2. The estimation is performed jointly for 1995 and 2005 but separately by education level. The joint estimation is done to constrain the relative prejudiced preferences to be the same over the ten year period. Following Flabbi (2010b), we assume that the proportion of prejudiced employers is quicker to adjust than preferences; therefore we leave the first one free to change over time while we constrain the second to be the same over the two periods. In estimation, we re-parameterize the model and we estimate the disutility of prejudiced employers relative to the average male productivity. This ratio is the parameter *k* reported in Table 2A.2.

Table 2A.2. Maximum likelihood estimation results (entire sample) — structural parameters

	Master and PhD		College		High School	
	1995	2005	1995	2005	1995	2005
λ_M	0.1119	0.2781	0.1965	0.1798	0.2298	0.2299
	(0.0457)	(0.0803)	(0.0342)	(0.0243)	(0.0204)	(0.0202)
λ_W	0.2906	0.3003	0.2731	0.2345	0.2869	0.2493
	(0.1355)	(0.1249)	(0.0410)	(0.0324)	(0.0304)	(0.0246)
η_M	0.0017	0.0082	0.0056	0.0071	0.0154	0.0150
	(0.0010)	(0.0034)	(0.0014)	(0.0014)	(0.0020)	(0.0019)
η_W	0.0041	0.0049	0.0110	0.0086	0.0134	0.0136
	(0.0026)	(0.0023)	(0.0023)	(0.0017)	(0.0020)	(0.0019)
μ_M	3.7536	3.8622	3.5851	3.6000	3.2107	3.1833
	(0.0290)	(0.0335)	(0.0184)	(0.0193)	(0.0135)	(0.0152)
σ_M	0.5587	0.6426	0.5983	0.6499	0.5477	0.5910
	(0.0220)	(0.0258)	(0.0140)	(0.0152)	(0.0105)	(0.0120)
μ_W	3.6618	3.6937	3.5879	3.4058	3.0319	2.9675
	(0.0374)	(0.0518)	(0.1058)	(0.0411)	(0.1003)	(0.0459)
σ_W	0.4289	0.4931	0.4607	0.6153	0.4876	0.5563
	(0.0246)	(0.0378)	(0.0398)	(0.0253)	(0.0390)	(0.0236)
p	0.1506	0.2117	0.7584	0.1231	0.9999	0.2811
	(0.0469)	(0.1079)	(0.2790)	(0.1391)	(0.0039)	(0.2609)
k	1.3796	1.3796	0.2513	0.2513	0.1399	0.1399
	(3.8471)	(3.8471)	(0.0679)	(0.0679)	(0.0763)	(0.0763)
w_M^*	10.8382	10.8800	8.5801	10.0000	7.6605	8.0000
w_W^*	8.9373	10.0713	6.4249	7.2500	5.5156	6.0000
lnL	−6142	−19721	−26548			
N	1572		5181		7961	

Note: Asymptotic standard errors in parentheses. Joint estimation on all years by education level.

The estimates of the structural parameters are in line with previous literature (Flabbi, 2010a, b; Flinn, 2006; Bowlus and Eckstein, 2002): women usually have higher arrival rates of offers and lower average productivity. The proportion of prejudiced employers and the relative disutility of discrimination are consistent with the result of Flabbi (2010b): the labor market for college graduates sees a decrease in the proportion of prejudiced employers and a disutility value equal to about 30% of average male productivity. If high school graduates also experience a decrease in the proportion of prejudiced employers, this is not the case for the sample of Master's and PhD. However, the estimates of the prejudiced parameters are much more imprecise in this sample, probably because of the smaller sample size.

2B.2 *Policy Implications and Policy Experiments*

We report here the wage schedule used in performing the policy experiments. In the equal pay policy, we impose the requirement that each employer has to pay the same wage to workers with identical productivity by interpreting the Nash-bargaining wage schedules defined before as reduced form-sharing rules. Defining the proportion of men in the population with m, the new wage equations become:

$$w_N(x) = \rho U + \alpha [x - \rho U] \tag{A.5}$$

$$w_P(x) = \rho U + \alpha [x - (1 - m)d + \rho U] \tag{A.6}$$

where:

$$\rho U = m \rho U_M + (1 - m) \rho U_W \tag{A.7}$$

Notice that by definition the wage equations are not gender-specific. However, they remain employer-specific, as indicated by the subscripts P and N.

The affirmative action policy is defined as a flow subsidy received by each employer for each woman hired. The subsidy is paid by a lump-sum tax on workers. Defining with γ the subsidy and with t the endogenous tax rate necessary to finance it, the new wage equations become:

$$w_M(x, \gamma) = \rho U_M(\gamma) + t(\gamma) + \alpha [x - t(\gamma) - \rho U_M(\gamma)] \tag{A.8}$$

$$w_{WN}(x, \gamma) = \rho U_W(\gamma) + t(\gamma) + \alpha [x + \gamma - t(\gamma) - \rho U_W(\gamma)] \tag{A.9}$$

$$w_{WP}(x, \gamma) = \rho U_W(\gamma) + t(\gamma) + \alpha [x + \gamma - d - t(\gamma) - \rho U_W(\gamma)] \tag{A.10}$$

The first equation states that men receive a wage that should compensate for the tax they pay but takes into account the reduced surplus implied by the tax. The second equation states that women working for unprejudiced employers receive the same tax effects but at the same time see the surplus increased by the subsidy γ. Finally, the third equation states that women working at prejudiced employers receive similar impacts from the presence of the tax and the subsidy but still share the cost of the disutility implied by prejudice. We denote the tax rate and the value of unemployment as a function of γ to emphasize that they are endogenous objects changing with the subsidy.

2C Complete Results

The maximum likelihood estimates of the structural parameters are reported in Tables 2A.2–2A.4.

The model estimation is performed assuming that productivity, for both males and females, follows a log-normal distribution or $\ln(x) \sim N(\mu, \sigma^2)$. Under this assumption the average productivity and its variance are $\exp(\mu + 0.5\sigma^2)$ and $(\exp(\sigma^2) - 1)\exp(2\mu + \sigma^2)$. Therefore, μ and σ reported in Table 2A.2–2A.4 refer to the location and scale parameters of the log-normal

Table 2A.3. Maximum likelihood estimation results (married) – structural parameters

	Master and PhD		College		High School	
	1995	2005	1995	2005	1995	2005
λ_M	0.0534	0.2798	0.2062	0.1975	0.2539	0.2649
	(0.0378)	(0.0885)	(0.0404)	(0.0305)	(0.0251)	(0.0269)
λ_W	0.2312	0.2082	0.3018	0.2256	0.2873	0.2503
	(0.1220)	(0.1275)	(0.0477)	(0.0347)	(0.0316)	(0.0256)
η_M	0.0003	0.0077	0.0054	0.0068	0.0155	0.0150
	(0.0003)	(0.0034)	(0.0015)	(0.0015)	(0.0022)	(0.0022)
η_W	0.0031	0.0021	0.0126	0.0076	0.0135	0.0141
	(0.0022)	(0.0013)	(0.0028)	(0.0016)	(0.0021)	(0.0021)
μ_M	3.7581	3.8349	3.6079	3.6389	3.2447	3.2280
	(0.0314)	(0.0396)	(0.0196)	(0.0197)	(0.0136)	(0.0153)
σ_M	0.5557	0.6734	0.5932	0.6303	0.5251	0.5719
	(0.0241)	(0.0312)	(0.0149)	(0.0154)	(0.0106)	(0.0120)
μ_W	3.6321	3.6891	3.5690	3.3913	2.9446	2.9363
	(0.0423)	(0.0598)	(0.1208)	(0.0450)	(0.0950)	(0.0154)
σ_W	0.4497	0.4867	0.4702	0.6191	0.5168	0.5696
	(0.0312)	(0.0604)	(0.0443)	(0.0278)	(0.0402)	(0.0121)
p	0.1208	0.2398	0.7242	0.1074	0.9998	0.0003
	(0.0875)	(0.2045)	(0.3361)	(0.1480)	(0.0189)	(0.0121)
k	1.5765	1.5765	0.2731	0.2731	0.0718	0.0718
	(6.9760)	(6.9760)	(0.0803)	(0.0803)	(0.0626)	(0.0626)
w_M^*	11.8227	12.5000	8.9373	10.2427	10.8382	10.8800
w_W^*	9.2520	10.0750	6.6678	7.4010	8.9373	10.0713
lnL	−5309		− 17222		−23545	
N	1365		4532		7086	

Note: Asymptotic standard errors in parentheses. Joint estimation on all years by education level.

gender-specific productivity distribution; λ refers to the exogenous arrival rate of job offers and η to the exogenous termination rate; p is the proportion of prejudiced employers in the economy; while k is the ration between the disutility from hiring women suffered by prejudiced employers (d) and the expected value of productivity for male. We estimate k instead of d to better scale the comparison across years and samples.

As mentioned in the main text, our results are potentially sensitive to the distributional assumptions. In order to analyze how sensitive the estimation results are to assuming a log-normal, we have estimated the model using two additional distributions. In the first exercise, we have assumed that productivity follows a gamma distribution, that is $x\sim\Gamma(k, \theta)$ where α and θ are the shape and scale parameters and the average productivity and its variance are defined as $\alpha\theta$ and $\alpha\theta^2$ respectively. In the second exercise, we have assumed that productivity follows a normal distribution, that is $x\sim N(\mu_x, \sigma_x^2)$, where μ_x and σ_x^2 are directly the average productivity and its variance. It is important to mention that these three distributions satisfy the recoverability condition, which is crucial under the identification strategy of Flinn and

Table 2A.4. Maximum likelihood estimation results (married with children) – structural parameters

	Master and PhD		College		High School	
	1995	2005	1995	2005	1995	2005
λ_M	0.0540	0.2297	0.2661	0.1651	0.3350	0.3187
	(0.0382)	(0.0812)	(0.0711)	(0.0352)	(0.0515)	(0.0438)
λ_W	0.2191	0.2499	0.3439	0.2055	0.4628	0.2689
	(0.1550)	(0.2501)	(0.0829)	(0.0373)	(0.1098)	(0.0497)
η_M	0.0005	0.0075	0.0059	0.0047	0.0141	0.0176
	(0.0005)	(0.0038)	(0.0022)	(0.0014)	(0.0031)	(0.0035)
η_W	0.0030	0.0011	0.0167	0.0084	0.0187	0.0159
	(0.0030)	(0.0015)	(0.0043)	(0.0021)	(0.0035)	(0.0029)
μ_M	3.7216	3.8587	3.6094	3.6555	3.2409	3.2540
	(0.0437)	(0.0433)	(0.0248)	(0.0246)	(0.0180)	(0.0195)
σ_M	0.5837	0.6190	0.5986	0.6259	0.5320	0.5486
	(0.0343)	(0.0340)	(0.0189)	(0.0193)	(0.0139)	(0.0153)
μ_W	3.6790	3.8450	3.4401	3.4105	2.9184	2.9246
	(0.1417)	(0.3251)	(0.1286)	(0.0536)	(0.0487)	(0.0500)
σ_W	0.4411	0.4653	0.5333	0.6217	0.4883	0.5849
	(0.0695)	(0.1078)	(0.0548)	(0.0344)	(0.0244)	(0.0329)
p	0.3201	0.9040	0.4054	0.0716	0.3533	0.1330
	(0.6467)	(0.9055)	(0.6454)	(0.1752)	(0.0704)	(0.1312)
k	0.2014	0.2014	0.2981	0.2981	0.8393	0.8393
	(0.1636)	(0.1636)	(0.5072)	(0.5072)	(0.8497)	(0.8497)
w_M^*	12.7675	13.2727	8.9373	10.6917	7.9797	8.5000
w_W^*	7.8903	9.2250	6.6221	7.2904	5.4262	6.0000
lnL	−3282		−10934		−13397	
N	841		2865		4064	

Note: Asymptotic standard errors in parentheses. Joint estimation on all years by education level.

Heckman (1982). The starting values used in the likelihood maximization procedure were the same for all the estimation exercises. The equivalence between the distributional parameters was found using the definitions for the average productivity and its variance.

The results of this sensitivity analysis indicate that some estimated parameters are indeed sensitive to the distributional assumptions. Comparing the estimates under the gamma distribution assumption with the benchmark estimates obtained using a log-normal distribution, we do not find large difference in the mobility parameters (e.g. the largest difference in job arrival rates is just 0.04) but we find large differences in the prejudice parameters (the largest differences for p and k are, respectively, 0.7 and 1.4). Comparing the estimates under the normal distribution assumption with the benchmark we find larger differences in the prejudiced parameters, and we experience converge problems on some samples.

3

Gender Gaps in Spain: The Role of Children in Career Development

Sara de La Rica and Ainara González de San Román

3.1 Introduction

The shrinking of the working-age population and the high educational level achieved by women over recent decades[1] make it essential to consider women as a fundamental part of the workforce. Governments and institutions may play an important role in creating the legal framework for improving women's choices and their participation in the economy, as well as helping societies to break away from the traditional gender role that affects women's behavior in many countries. It is also crucial that firms positively believe in the need to create a suitable working environment where men and women can combine work and family.

Needless to say, women have made huge progress in the workplace, especially in the more industrialized countries. In particular, Goldin (2004a) refers to the mass arrival of women in the workforce during the 1970s as the "quiet revolution." Describing the evolution of women in the labor market during the 20th century in the US, she states that until the 1920s working women were basically young and single and worked in factories or as domestic servants. From the 1930s onwards many more went to school and got jobs in offices. In the 1950s many married women entered the labor market and got jobs as secretaries, teachers, or nurses. By the 1970s, their daughters saw their mothers working and took it for granted that they would also work. And since the end of the 1980s, women are overtaking men in graduating from college. This process, to a greater or lesser degree, has been observed in most industrialized economies.

---

[1] See Goldin, Katz, and Kuziemko (2006) for an exploratory analysis of the catch-up and reversal in the gender gap in university graduation of American college women.

However, in spite of this revolutionary process, gender differences still persist. This chapter provides a complementary analysis to Chapter 2. While in that chapter Flabbi and Tejada isolated employer discrimination as a possible source of gender differences, here we look at the impact of family issues on labor market outcomes of men and women. Family issues play a crucial role in understanding the observed gender differences in the labor market. Women combine employment with home responsibilities to a much larger extent than their male partners. This affects their decisions with respect to labor supply, human capital accumulation, and hence their labor market performance. Several studies explore the trade-offs between family and career among similarly educated men and women. Wood, Corcoran, and Courant (1993) find that 40% of the gender gap among American lawyers is explained by the presence of children in the family. More recently Goldin and Katz (2008) and Bertrand, Goldin, and Katz (2010) point to the differences in hours worked as the main determinant of the gender gap in male and female careers. Finally, Molina and Montuenga (2009) confirm the existence of a wage penalty for Spanish working women with children.

This chapter adds to the literature by focusing on highly educated men and women and by exploring the trade-offs between family and working career in Spain, where changes in female behavior with respect to the labor market have been recent and substantial. We compare male and female behavior with respect to labor supply and labor market performance along the life cycle for different birth cohorts. Furthermore, we compare the impact of children on labor supply decisions and on women's labor market performance in two years – 1994 and 2008 – separated by a period of substantial change with respect to the role of women in the labor market. Our results indicate that family plays a crucial role as a source of gender differences in the labor market in Spain. By 2008, children are the main determinant of the observed gap in labor supply between college men and women. With respect to hours worked, children are also an important determinant for the decision of mothers to work part time. However, children do not seem to contribute to an explanation of the observed gender wage gap (5%) between college-educated men and women.

3.2 Descriptive Evidence: Gender Gaps in the Labor Market during the Life Cycle

In this section we describe the extent to which family issues are related to the gender gap in the labor market (labor supply and performance) for highly educated workers. In particular we show gender gaps in labor supply (employment rates and part-time rates) and labor performance (incidence in top jobs) during the life cycle for different birth cohorts. This allows us

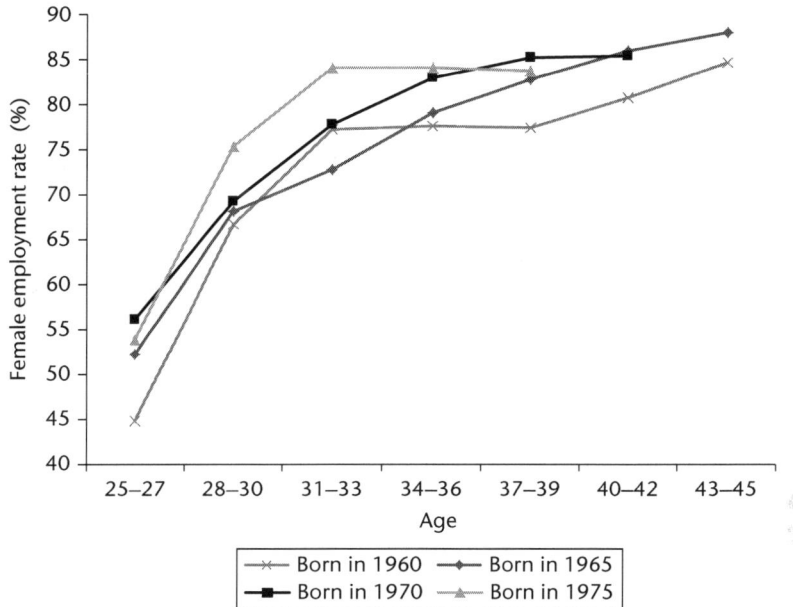

Figure 3.1. Life-cycle employment rates (%) – college-educated women.

Source: Encuesta de población Activa (INE) (1986–2011).

to compare gender gaps at pre-maternal and post-maternal ages. The fact that gender gaps increase during childbearing ages (25 to 40) provides a first indication of the importance of family for the professional careers of college-educated women versus those of their male counterparts. Second, by comparing gender gaps during the life cycle for different birth cohorts it is possible to assess the change of this profile over time.

3.2.1 *Employment Rates during the Life Cycle*

We use the Spanish Labor Force Surveys beginning in 1986 to construct the employment rates as the ratio of individuals who were working at the time of the survey divided by the total population between 25 and 60 years of age. Moreover, in order to assess how these rates evolve for different groups in our sample, we construct this indicator by gender, education group – college/non-college, and for different age intervals. Figure 3.1 shows life-cycle employment rates for college females (y-axis) across seven age groups (x-axis). Each line corresponds to a different birth cohort,[2] and therefore for each of them it is

[2] Given the data availability we can construct four different cohorts, five years apart from each other, and thus cover those born between 1960 and 1975. Moreover, since we have constructed seven age categories that group three years each, the cohort born in 1960 refers to those individuals

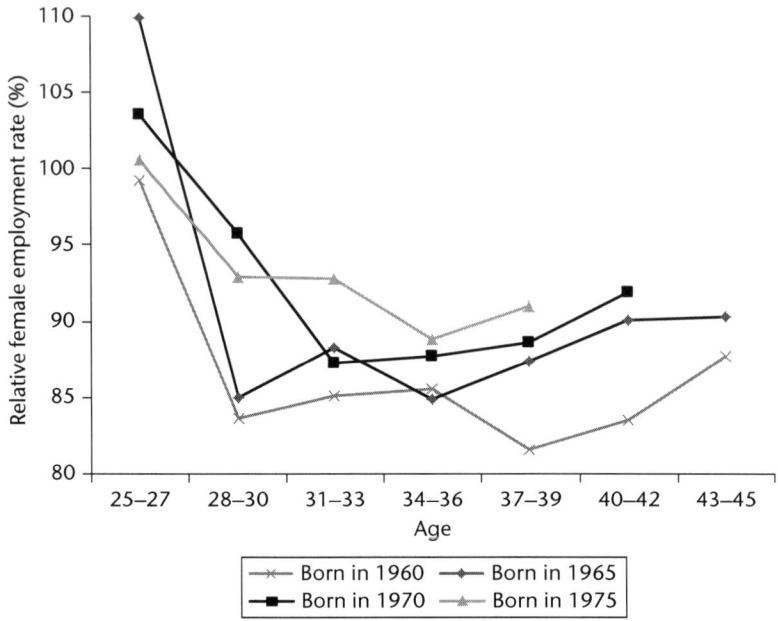

Figure 3.2. Life-cycle relative female employment rates (%) – college-educated women/men.

Source: Encuesta de población Activa (INE) (1986–2011).

possible to look at average changes in labor market indicators throughout the life cycle.

It is apparent that for the two earlier cohorts – the one born in 1960 and the one born in 1965 – the life-cycle profile is different from the corresponding one for later cohorts. In particular, the two youngest cohorts have a more apparent concave profile than the oldest ones, with an employment rate continuously increasing even at child-bearing ages. When comparing employment rates of college men and women, significant differences emerge at different stages of the life cycle. Figure 3.2 presents the relative employment rate of college educated women with respect to college educated men.

At very young ages, employment rates for college-educated women are higher than those of men. However, by the age of 30 there is an employment gender gap of 15% for the oldest cohorts and 7% for the youngest one. The gender gap along the life cycle has a U shape, and by the 40s, the employment gap seems to shrink again, although parity in employment rates is never reached at older ages. This figure, and the timing of lower female participation, suggests that family and childbearing may be the reasons

born between 1959 and 1961 who are between 25 to 27 years of age in 1986. The same applies for the rest of the cohorts.

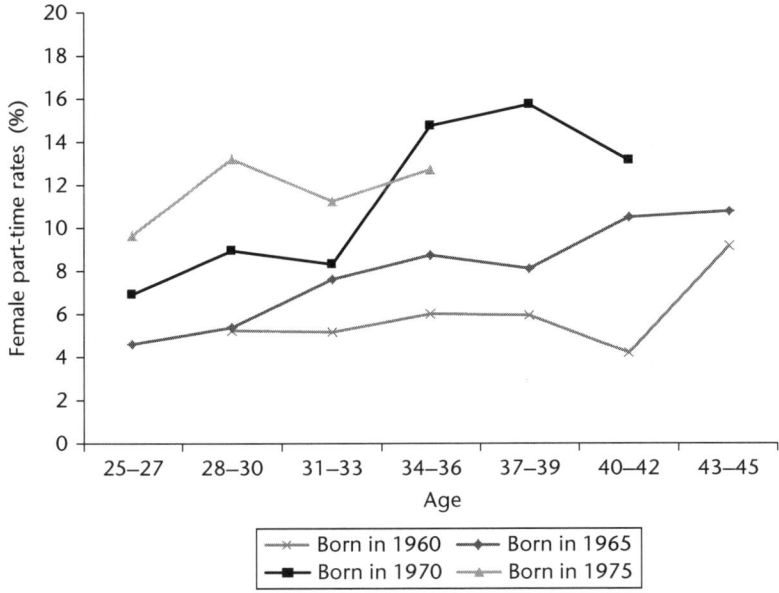

Figure 3.3. Life-cycle part-time rates (as % of employment) – college-educated women.

Source: Encuesta de Población Activa (INE) (1989–2011).

for the different time profile of participation. The evolution across cohorts suggests on the other hand that more recent generations have been affected less by family constraints in their labor participation.

3.2.2 Part-Time versus Full-Time Jobs during the Life Cycle

Family issues are also very likely to affect the hours worked. Childcare is very time intensive and competes with work outside the home during childrearing years. In absence of precise measures of actual hours worked we use indicators of part-time work to capture this phenomenon. Figure 3.3 describes life cycle part-time rates (as a percentage of employment for college-educated women)[3].

Two issues deserve notice. First, part-time work has been increasingly used by recent cohorts at all ages. Second, among college-educated workers, we observe an increasing pattern with age. This confirms the fact that the youngest generations of women use part-time employment to a greater extent especially at childbearing ages, presumably to reconcile work and family. Indeed, this is confirmed by the percentage of women indicating

---

[3] We do not provide either evidence of part-time rates for college males or relative male/female part-time rates because they are negligible at all ages and for all birth cohorts for the male population. They are available upon request.

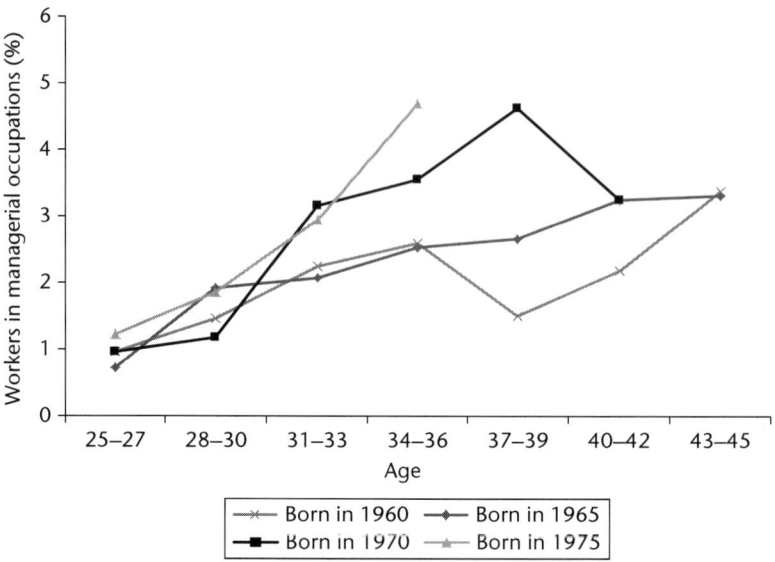

Figure 3.4. Life-cycle incidence of workers in managerial occupations – college-educated females.

Source: Encuesta de Población Activa (INE) (1986-2011).

"family reasons" as the reason for part-time work in the Labor Force Survey. In 1996, only 15% of college-educated females aged 35–39 gave such a reason for working part time. However, by 2011, 45% of part-timer work was owing to family reasons. This increase was also encouraged after 1998 by the law on part-time work, which improved the working conditions for part-timers and encouraged more females to make use of such a work pattern.

3.2.3 *Gender Gaps in the access to Managerial Jobs during the Life Cycle*

Gender gaps in the access to top jobs may also reveal differences in the labor market performance of college men and women during their life cycles and for different birth cohorts. Figure 3.4 shows the percentage of workers employed in managerial jobs. Lacking information on wages, this is a useful measure of labor market outcomes. The figure shows that on average the incidence of these jobs is very low. However, when looking at different age groups, we can see a clear increase in the prevalence of managerial jobs with age. Moreover, this increase is more pronounced in the later cohorts.

Finally, when comparing men and women during the life cycle, we can see from Figure 3.5 that there is a clear decrease in the relative presence of women in managerial jobs with age, and the pattern is similar across cohorts. Given the age at which this decline begins, this profile might suggest that raising a family becomes harder to reconcile with a high-profile career over time.

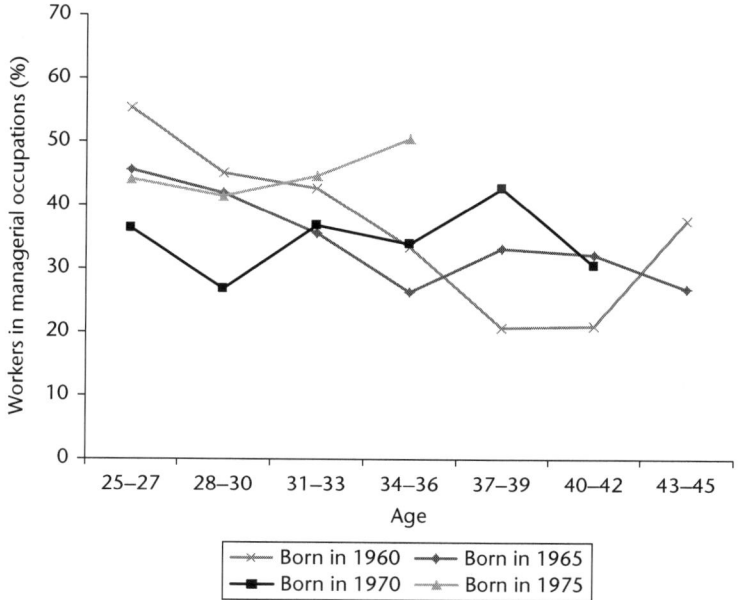

Figure 3.5. Life-cycle relative incidence of females working as managers – college-educated women/men.

Source: Encuesta de Población Activa (INE) (1986-2011).

3.3 The Impact of Children on Gender Gaps in Labor Supply and in Labor Market Performance

In this section we quantify the impact of having children on the gender gap in the labor market indicators mentioned above – employment rate, incidence of part-time work, wages, and presence in managerial jobs. We make use of two micro-data sets. The first is the first wave (1994) of Spanish data from the European Household Panel, and the second corresponds to the 2008 wave of Spanish data from the European Survey of Living Conditions. The college-educated individuals included in the 1994 sample, whose age is between 25 and 45 years, belong to the two oldest birth cohorts described in Section 3.2.1 – (aged between 60 and 65 in 2008), whereas those included in the 2008 sample are individuals who belong to the two latest cohorts, born in 1970 and 1975. Changes in the condition of women with respect to their role in the family and in the labor market have been remarkable during this 15-year period.

3.3.1 *Average Gender Gaps: 1994 vs. 2008*

Before estimating the impact of children on the observed gender gaps, it is interesting to look at the raw average gaps for the relevant groups of men

Table 3.1. Labor market statistics of college-educated men and women age 25–45 in Spain 1994–2008

	Employment Rates		Part-Time Rates		Managers Incidence	
	1994	2008	1994	2008	1994	2008
1. All Men	93.12	91.82	2.31	1.84	6.85	3.14
	(25.34)	(27.41)	(15.03)	(13.47)	(25.30)	(17.45)
2. All Women	68.52	85.20	12.33	14.45	0.98	0.80
	(46.49)	(35.52)	(32.93)	(35.18)	(9.91)	(8.93)
3. Men without children	87.19	88.93	3.04	2.58	4.71	1.39
	(33.54)	(31.38)	(17.24)	(15.86)	(21.27)	(11.74)
4. Men with children	95.73	96.72	2.01	0.71	7.76	5.84
	(20.24)	(17.88)	(14.06)	(8.38)	(26.80)	(23.48)
5. Women without children	76.07	87.65	15.03	11.06	1.61	1.18
	(42.81)	(32.91)	(35.89)	(31.38)	(0.66)	(10.84)
6. Women with children	65.01	82.29	10.86	18.73	0.66	0.50
	(47.76)	(38.19)	(31.19)	(39.04)	(8.12)	(7.05)
Gender Gap All (2–1)	−24.60	−6.62	10.02	12.61	−5.87	−2.34
Gender Gap no child (5–3)	−11.12	−1.28	11.99	8.48	−3.10	−0.21
Gender Gap children (6–4)	−30.72	−14.43	8.85	18.02	−7.10	−5.34
Family Gap Women (6–5)	−11.06	−5.36	−4.17	7.67	−0.95	−0.68
No. observations	1033	3452	842	3027	842	3027

Notes: Standard deviations in parenthesis. Rates are computed using individuals' weights.
Source: Household Panels Phogue (1994) and EU-Silk (2008).

and women for the two periods under consideration. We have restricted individuals to be between 25 and 45 years of age, when family concerns should matter most, and we focus on those individuals with the highest level of education (ISCED 5–7).[4]

Table 3.1 presents the average employment rates, part-time employment rates and percentage in managerial positions (following the corresponding ISCO classification of occupations for each period) for different groups of college-educated individuals, namely all men, all women, men and women without children and men and women with children.[5] Average gender gaps are reported for all individuals and separately depending on the family situation. We will call "family gap" the differences in average values between childless women and mothers.

Table 3.1 reveals interesting features for each of the indicators that we summarize next.

---

[4] This is the most standard age interval of other studies which have analyzed the impact of children on gender issues; see Harkness and Waldfogel (2003) and Molina and Moluenga (2009), among others.

[5] With children refers to having at least one, regardless of the total number of children or their age.

Table 3.2. Log mean hourly wages of college-educated men and women age 25–45 in Spain 1994–2008

	1994			2008		
	All	Without Children	With Children	All	Without Children	With Children
1. Men	1.987	1.819	2.056	2.445	2.353	2.591
	(0.678)	(0.746)	(0.636)	(0.448)	(0.418)	(0.457)
2. Women	1.923	1.926	1.921	2.334	2.237	2.459
	(0.696)	(0.719)	(0.685)	(0.452)	(0.444)	(0.432)
Gender Gap (2−1)	−0.064	0.107	−0.135	−0.111	−0.116	−0.132

Note: Standard deviations in parenthesis.
Source: Household Panels Phogue (1994) and EU-Silk (2008).

Employment Rates: There was a substantial increase in employment rate of all college women between 1994 and 2008. This increase was equal to 17 percentage points (pp) for women with children, whereas for childless women the increase was equal to 11 pp. The employment rate of men, on the contrary, remained very stable. Notice that the gender gap in the employment rate among men and women with no children disappears by 2008. The family gap was substantial in 1994 (11%), but it decreases by a large extent (to just 5%) by 2008.

Part-Time Employment Rates: Both in 1994 and 2008, part-time employment was basically a female choice. For women with children the increase in the use of part-time work between the earlier and the later year was substantial (from 11% to 19%), whereas for childless women we observe a decrease from 15% to 11%.

Access to Managerial Jobs: The presence of college-educated men and women aged 25–45 Years working in managerial jobs is very low. For women with children the presence among managers is virtually zero, while 1–2% of women without children are managers. For comparison 7% of men aged 25–45 were managers in 1994 but by 2008 only 3% were.

Table 3.2 shows descriptive evidence for wages, namely **(Log) Hourly Wages.** Notice that fathers earn more than childless men in the two periods, whereas the contrary happens for women. With respect to the gender wage gap, it is slightly higher in 2008 than in 1994 – it rises from 3.2% to 4.5%. In addition women without children earn more than their male counterparts in 1994 (6% more), but by 2008 the gender gap is reversed, favoring men by around 5%. When comparing men and women with children, men earn 5–6% more in the two periods under consideration. Finally, note that these gender gaps are much lower than those observed for the whole population of men and women. In this case education seems to reduce the hourly wage gap.

3.3.2 The Impact of Children on Each of the Labor Market Indicators

We now proceed to isolate the impact of children on the gender gap in labor market performances, distinguishing it from other potential determinants. Tables 3.3 and 3.4 present discrete choice (probit) estimations of (i) probability of working versus non-working and (ii) probability of part-time versus full-time employment.[6] Table 3.5 presents standard hourly wage regressions. In all estimations, we consider the sample of college-educated men and women aged 25–45 years.[7]

Depending on the specification, controls for age, presence of a working spouse, other family income, and regional fixed effects are also included. Our variable of interest is "Any child", a dummy equal to one if the family has any number of children of any age.[8] Estimations are done separately for 1994 and for 2008 to compare the impact of having children on the outcomes in the two periods. Given the potential simultaneity of the decision to have children and the decision relative to the labor market, we use as an instrument the children variable in order to obtain its causal effect on the estimated presence of children on labor market outcomes. Specifically we use the following two instruments:

- **IV1:** Following Harkness and Waldfogel (2003) we use as an instrument the fraction of women who have any child in the same region, age, and marital status (married or single). The identification assumption is that the local (regional) culture about having children affects the individual decisions of having children but not the local labor market conditions. Clearly if regional fertility averages are affected also by economic (labor market) conditions the instrument would not be valid.

- **IV2:** Second, we construct an instrument based on the Spanish Time Use survey of 2002–2003. To be consistent, we restrict to individuals aged 25–45 and compute average daily time devoted to housework by region (18 regions), gender, age range (25–34 and 35–45), and type of household (presence or not of children). This allows the creation of 144 different cells with different values with respect to time devoted to housework.

---

[6] We have decided not to report the impact of children on the incidence in managerial jobs because the almost complete lack of women in these jobs prevents the identification of any significant effect. Nevertheless, results can be obtained from the authors upon request.

[7] Tables 3.3 and 3.4 display the marginal effects of the variables related to having children, as well as the marginal effect of children for different groups: women with children versus women without children – marginal contribution to the family gap, and women versus men – marginal contribution to the gender gap. Table 3.5 displays the OLS and IV coefficients of the wage regressions.

[8] We also estimated other specifications, allowing the impact of the family to depend on the age of the child. We found that, conditional on the age of the mother, the impact of very young children on employment is marginally higher than that of older children. Given that the additional contribution is small, we finally decided to present only the average impact of any child on employment. Results for the other specification can be obtained from the authors upon request.

Table 3.3. Probability of employment – probit estimation college-educated men/women

	1994			2008			
	[1]	[2]	[IV1]	[1]	[2]	[IV1]	[IV2]
1. Female	-0.101**	-0.088*	0.032	-0.012	-0.015	0.020	0.017
	(0.047)	(0.047)	(0.065)	(0.017)	(0.017)	(0.019)	(0.022)
2. Any child	0.138***	0.098*	0.111	0.117***	0.073**	0.080*	0.120
	(0.046)	(0.050)	(0.084)	(0.027)	(0.028)	(0.046)	(0.078)
3. Female*Any child	-0.214***	-0.192***	-0.212***	-0.161***	-0.162***	-0.258***	-0.256***
	(0.058)	(0.059)	(0.091)	(0.032)	(0.032)	(0.043)	(0.049)
Adjusted Family Gap							
For Women (2+3)			-0.101*			-0.177***	-0.136*
			(0.065)			(0.034)	(0.072)
For Men (2)			0.111			0.080*	0.120
			(0.084)			(0.046)	(0.069)
Adjusted Gender Gaps							
Women any child vs. Men any child (1+3)			-0.180***			-0.237***	-0.239***
			(0.039)			(0.033)	(0.035)
Childless Women vs. Childless Men (1)			0.032			0.020	0.017
			(0.065)			(0.019)	(0.022)
Control variables	No	Yes	Yes	No	Yes	Yes	Yes
Observations	1033	1033	1033	3452	3452	3452	3452
Pseudo R^2	0.1262	0.1484	0.1509	0.0339	0.0671	0.0765	0.0649
Family contribution to the gender gap (%)		10.08 [-0.025]	10.82 [-0.027]		30.19 [-0.019]	56.73 [-0.035]	46.60 [-0.029]

Notes: Standard errors in parenthesis; *** $p < 0.01$, ** $p < 0.05$, * $p < 0.1$. The set of control variables include age, presence of a working spouse/partner, other family income in the household, and regional fixed effects. Individual sampling weights are used in the estimations. The presented coefficients are marginal effects from probit models. The computation of the family contribution to the overall gender gap follows the methodology of probit decomposition into coefficient effects developed by Yun (2004). Absolute contributions in brackets.

Table 3.4. Probability of working part-time versus full-time – college-educated men/women

	1994			2008			
	[1]	[2]	[IV1]	[1]	[2]	[IV1]	[IV2]
1. Female	0.097***	0.106***	0.171**	0.096***	0.089***	0.088***	0.099***
	(0.035)	(0.036)	(0.058)	(0.018)	(0.017)	(0.020)	(0.025)
2. Any child	−0.020	−0.008	0.090	−0.067**	−0.045	−0.085**	−0.064
	(0.034)	(0.043)	(0.081)	(0.032)	(0.029)	(0.043)	(0.070)
3. Female*Any child	−0.003	−0.012	−0.075	0.112***	0.111***	0.128***	0.097**
	(0.042)	(0.045)	(0.075)	(0.035)	(0.034)	(0.046)	(0.054)
Adjusted Family Gap							
For Women (2+3)			0.015			0.044	0.033
			(0.057)			(0.028)	(0.061)
For Men (2)			0.074			−0.085**	−0.064
			(0.096)			(0.043)	(0.070)
Adjusted Gender Gaps							
Women any child vs. Men any child (1+3)			0.096**			0.216***	0.196***
			(0.031)			(0.036)	(0.038)
Childless Women vs. Childless Men (1)			0.171**			0.088***	0.097***
			(0.060)			(0.020)	(0.025)
Control variables	No	Yes	Yes	No	Yes	Yes	Yes
Observations	841	750	750	3027	3027	3027	3027
Pseudo R^2	0.0898	0.1079	0.1112	0.1220	0.1502	0.1392	0.1337
Family contribution to the gender gap (%)		−5.43 [−0.005]	4.44 [0.004]		10.79 [0.014]	8.55 [0.011]	6.53 [0.008]

Notes: Standard errors in parenthesis; *** $p < 0.01$, ** $p < 0.05$, * $p < 0.1$. The set of control variables include age, presence of a working spouse/partner, other family income in the household, and regional fixed effects. The presented coefficients are marginal effects from probit models. Absolute contributions in the last raw in brackets.

In this case the identifying assumption is that the time spent on housework identifies local attitudes towards women and family and can be correlated with fertility decisions. Then we merge these values with the two household panels for 1994 and 2008. The correlation of this variable with the variable Any Child measured in 2008 is 0.227, significantly lower than the corresponding correlation with the other instrument, but still significant considering that the variable is extracted from a different data source and a different time period. The first stage estimation of Any child on this instrument (once the controls are added) turns out to be statistically significant, with a value of 0.242 and a standard error of 0.031. However, we encounter some data limitations for 1994, given that in the Household Panel for that period the regional information available covers only 7 regions instead of 18 autonomous communities. This reduces the number of cells to 56, which introduces very limited variability when merging these values with the 1994 Household Panel. Indeed, the correlation between this potential instrument and Any Child for 1994 is 0.067, and insignificant in the selection estimation. Therefore we will present IV1 and IV2 results for 2008, but only IV1 results for 1994.

Given that the model we face here is non-linear, we cannot use 2SLS to calculate the IV1 and IV2 estimates since there is not a guarantee that first-stage residuals are uncorrelated with fitted values and covariates.[9] Hence, the computational method that we use is a three-stage estimator. In the first-stage, Any Child is regressed on all of the exogenous control variables by using a probit model. The instrument is included among the regressors in this first stage estimator. In the second stage, Any Child is regressed on the fitted values of the first stage plus the exogenous variables by OLS – which guarantees that residuals are orthogonal to fitted values and covariates. And finally in the third stage the regression of interest is estimated as usual, except that the endogenous variable is replaced with the predicted values from the second stage. From the results of the first stage estimation, we can assure that the instrument is a good predictor of the endogenous variable[10] – Any Child. Unfortunately, the additional requirement for the instrument to be valid (it should be uncorrelated with the error term in each equation of interest) is not testable in exactly identified models as we have here.

We report the results of the estimations in Tables 3.3 and 3.4. With regard to the impact of children, the first column for each of the two

---

[9] This is one of the forbidden regressions in *Mostly Harmless Econometrics* by Angrist and Pischke (2009).

[10] To verify that the chosen instrumental variable is not weak, we compute the F-statistic against the null that the instrument is irrelevant in the first-stage regression which turns out to be much larger than 10, which ensures that the instrument is a good predictor of the endogenous children variable.

periods – Column 1 – shows the marginal effect of children when no additional controls are included. Columns 2, 3, and 4 report adjusted marginal effects of having children when including the additional set of controls in the estimation. The set of control variables, although not reported, include age, presence of a working spouse/partner, other family income in the household, and regional fixed effects. All of them have the expected signs and we omit them to restrict table size.

In Column 2 we assume exogeneity of the children variable, whereas in 3 and 4 we use 2SLS to account for the possible endogeneity in the decision of having children. Column 4 corresponds to the estimation using the second instrumental variable and it is only reported for 2008.

3.3.2.1 THE IMPACT OF CHILDREN ON THE EMPLOYMENT DECISION

Results from Table 3.3 indicate that in 1994, having any child decreased the probability of working for women with respect to men by around 21%. By 2008, this differential was 26% – the estimated impact is very similar regardless of the instruments used, which adds robustness to the result. However, the total gender gap, which is composed of the specific gender effect plus the children differential effect for women, decreases from 28% in 1994 to 24% by 2008. This is because the specific gender effect, coefficient of Female, decreases significantly from 1994 to 2008. In addition, having children decreases the probability of working by 10% in 1994 and by 17% in 2008 (family gap).

Our interpretation of these results is as follows. In 1994 college women who entered the labor market were a more selected sample than in 2008 and average wages of childless women were higher than those of childless men (the opposite in 2008). As a result, the impact of children was comparatively smaller in 1994 than in 2008, although in both periods children clearly decreased the probability of working for women. By 2008, given that there was no gender gap at the entrance to the labor market among the college educated, the presence of children was basically responsible for the whole gap. As a result, the impact of children was higher and the family gap was also higher.

3.3.2.2 THE IMPACT OF CHILDREN ON THE DECISION TO WORK PART TIME

Table 3.4 presents the estimations of the impact of children on the part-time versus full-time choice for people in the labor force. The most interesting result is that the impact of children in the use of part-time employment for women with respect to men (coefficient of Female*Any child) is not significant in 1994, but increases to 13% by 2008. In addition, and consistently with this (given the small incidence of part-time work among men), having children did not increase the use of part-time employment for women in 1994 but it did by 2008. If we consider the whole adjusted gender gap in part-time rates, in other words the specific gender plus the family effect, this amounts to 9% in 1994 and rises to 22% by 2008, where the specific female effect is added to the significant family effect. Very similar results are found regardless of the instrument used in the IV estimation for 2008.

Overall, by 2008, a large share of women with children used part-time work to reconcile family and career. They did not do so in 1994 probably because the number of part-time jobs was much more limited.[11] Hence many more women decided to quit the labor force. In fact the frequency of those college women who report that they work part time because of "housework, looking after children or other persons" increases by 50% in this 15 year period – it goes from 23% in 1994 to 73% in 2008.

3.3.2.3 THE IMPACT OF CHILDREN ON GENDER WAGE GAPS
Table 3.5 shows the estimate of the presence of children on the observed gender wage gap. Estimations for 1994 and 2008 are presented separately. In Column 1 we include only indicators of family to obtain the impact of children in the raw wage gap. Column 2 adds the standard controls (age and its square, tenure, part-time employment, industry dummies, and regional dummies) but without conditioning on occupation. Column 3 adds controls for occupation. The aim for presenting these two specifications separately is to measure the extent to which the gender gap in wages is due to the fact that women segregate into low-paid occupations. Finally, Column 4 reports the IV estimation corresponding to this last specification. We just present the IV1 results for both periods.

The most interesting result is that the impact of the family differs to a great extent when comparing 1994 with 2008. In 1994, there is no significant gender wage gap between childless women and men (coefficient of female of Columns 3 and 4). However, the presence of children decreased female wages by around 13% when compared to their male counterparts. In 2008, results are the opposite: the adjusted gender wage gap between childless women and men is significant (9% without conditioning for occupation and 7% conditioning for it) but the impact of children is negligible. This result is consistent with what we saw in the estimations of employment probability: as we argued before, in 1994 there is high positive selection in labor market entrance of college women, which results in average higher wages for them and hence in no gender wage gap. Hence the whole wage gap is down to the impact of

---

[11] We have not taken into account the possible selection of women into the labor market in this estimation because our aim is not to infer the part-time decision for all college women, but rather the determinants of this decision for women who have already decided not to quit the labor market. Our aim is to measure to what extent women with children who have decided not to quit the labor market decide to go on to part-time work to facilitate family and work life. The same applies to the estimation of the incidence in managerial jobs, as well as the wage estimations.

Table 3.5. Log wage regressions college-educated men/women – dependent variable: log hourly wages

	1994				2008			
	[1]	[2]	[3]	[IV1]	[1]	[2]	[3]	[IV1]
Female	0.085	0.066	0.039	0.119*	-0.115***	-0.092***	-0.066***	-0.063***
	(0.063)	(0.061)	(0.052)	(0.073)	(0.022)	(0.021)	(0.019)	(0.022)
Any Child	0.189***	0.010	0.055	0.085	0.116***	0.099***	0.056**	0.229***
	(0.050)	(0.052)	(0.044)	(0.084)	(0.029)	(0.026)	(0.025)	(0.033)
Female*Any Child	-0.209***	-0.138**	-0.136***	-0.236***	-0.016	-0.004	-0.005	-0.045
	(0.076)	(0.069)	(0.062)	(0.096)	(0.034)	(0.031)	(0.028)	(0.038)
Age		0.089**	0.049	0.058		0.054**	0.056***	0.044***
		(0.043)	(0.040)	(0.043)		(0.020)	(0.017)	(0.017)
Age squared		-0.001	-0.001	-0.001		-0.001	-0.001	-0.001
		(0.001)	(0.001)	(0.001)		(0.001)	(0.001)	(0.001)
Tenure		0.009**	0.013***	0.013***		0.002	0.006***	0.006***
		(0.004)	(0.003)	(0.004)		(0.002)	(0.002)	(0.002)
Part–Time		0.145***	0.045*	0.036		-0.151***	-0.117***	-0.126***
		(0.068)	(0.063)	(0.063)		(0.030)	(0.026)	(0.026)
Industry dummies	No	Yes	Yes	Yes	No	Yes	Yes	Yes
Regional dummies	No	Yes	Yes	Yes	No	Yes	Yes	Yes
Occupations	No	No	Yes	Yes	No	No	Yes	Yes
Observations	828	802	796	793	2602	2537	2533	2533
R^2	0.021	0.1955	0.3917	0.3963	0.0795	0.3132	0.4533	0.4539
Family contribution to the gender gap			85.50 [-0.055]	100 [-0.101]			-16.51 [0.018]	0 [0.065]

Notes: Standard errors in parentheses; *** $p < 0.01$, ** $p < 0.05$, * $p < 0.1$. The set of control variables include age, age squared, years of tenure in the actual job, industry dummies, occupations, four digits of the ISCO classification of occupations, and regional fixed effects. Individual sampling weights are used in the estimations. Absolute contributions in brackets.

children. By 2008, given that there was no selection at entrance for college women, the wage gap was basically at entrance (childless men and women), with no negative impact of children on female wages.

This interpretation is consistent with the estimates by Christofides et al. (2010), who show that the European countries with the lowest observed unconditional wage gap are also those with the lowest employment rates for women. Hence when labor market participation of women is highly selected, their high quality may reduce the observed wage gap.

It is also interesting to see the different correlation between part-time and hourly wages in 1994 and 2008. In 1994, part-time employment's impact is either positive or null, depending on whether we condition for occupation or not. However, by 2008, its impact is clearly negative, which is a more usual result. Given the low incidence of part-time work in 1994, it is likely that workers who made use of it were a selected sample of workers. Finally, when comparing the impact of children on wages with and without controlling for occupation (two-digit disaggregation of the corresponding ISCO classification for each year), Columns 3 and 4, we find very small differences. This means that gender gaps in wages of college individuals are not driven by segregation of women with children in low-paid occupations in order to reconcile family and work.

3.3.3 *Contribution of the Family to Average Gender Gaps*

To conclude this section we quantify the absolute and relative contribution of children to each of the average outcome gaps, based on the estimations presented above. In the case of wages the contributions are computed by simply multiplying the estimated coefficients of having children by the mean frequency of having children in the sample for men and women respectively. However, given that for employment rates, part-time employment rates and incidence of managerial jobs the estimated models are non-linear, the absolute contribution of children to the average gap is obtained following Yun (2004), who uses an extension of the Oaxaca Decomposition Method to account for non-linear estimations.[12] The relative contribution is the ratio between the absolute contribution and the raw corresponding average gap. The computed contributions are presented in the last raw of Table 3.5, both for the most general specification that includes controls and for the IV estimates.

---

[12] There are alternative ways of decomposing probit functions, see Even and Macpherson (1990), Nielsen (1998), but the one proposed by Yun (2004) is the most suitable in our setting since the emphasis of our approach relies on decomposing the differences into coefficient effects. To compute the absolute contributions we just need to multiply the estimated coefficient of interest by a proper weight, which in this context is the standard normal probability density function evaluated at the mean predicted characteristics.

We observe that the relative contribution of the family to the employment gender gap was very small in 1994 but increases to 57% by 2008. However, note that average gender gaps in employment are much higher in 1994 than in 2008. Second, having children contributes to explaining 4% of the gender gap in part-time work use in 1994, but this increases to 8% by 2008. Although the contribution of the family is not very remarkable in the two years studied, it is interesting to observe that in 15 years it has doubled, whereas the gap has remained quite stable. This means that college women with children are increasingly using part-time jobs to remain in the labor market instead of quitting because of childcare issues. Finally, whereas average gender wage gaps have doubled in these 15 years, the contribution of the family to it has decreased substantially: having children contributed to explaining 85% of the average gender gap in wages in 1994, whereas by 2008 the family does not explain it at all.

3.4 Policy Implications

The results reveal that by 2008 college women perform very similarly to men when entering the labor market in their labor supply decisions. However, childless women still use part-time jobs more extensively than their male counterparts (11% versus 2%). In addition, men on entrance earn approximately 5% more than their female counterparts. One important question is to identify the underlying reasons for these differences. Is working part time a supply-driven or a demand-driven decision? The proportion of childless women who report working part time because they cannot find a full-time job was 42%, which clearly indicates that at least for many childless women, there are demand restrictions which prevent them working on a full-time basis. Therefore, there seems to be room for policy actions to improve the intensive margin of female labor supply.[13]

The first important result from which to draw some policy implications is that by 2008 the observed gap in employment rates – whereas negligible between childless men and women – was still equal to 14% between fathers and mothers, and that the presence of children accounted for 56% of this gap. This indicates clearly that the presence of children leads many women to quit the labor market. The situation can be improved upon if firms and institutions develop possible mechanisms to combine family and work and hence allow mothers to participate in the labor market as much as fathers if they wish to do so. This can be achieved by developing flexible work schedules and home-work practices (tele-trabajo) not only for mothers, but also for fathers. Even

[13] One possibility that has been proposed is differential marginal tax rates for women who are working.

though some big firms are slowly starting to implement these measures, there is still a long way to go in Spain. Only if these mechanisms are widely available for mothers and fathers will women with children be able to access working careers similar to their male counterparts.

The second important result of this study is that by 2008 the use of part-time work by mothers has increased substantially (from 11% in 1994 to 19% by 2008). This may partly be a result of the 1998 Part-Time Law, which introduced the following changes with regards to part-time jobs: (i) part-time job decisions had to be the result of a voluntary acceptance by workers; (ii) employers had to provide information to the workers committee with regards to additional hours worked by part-time workers; (iii) Social Security contributions for additional hours were included in the calculation of contribution periods for entitlement to Social Security benefits; (iv) discrimination against part-time workers in terms of social welfare protection was reduced, and (v) job stability in part-time contracts was reinforced with incentives for indefinite contracts and the changeover from short-term part-time contracts to indefinite ones.

These reforms have probably made it easier for mothers to combine family and work. In 2007, the Gender Equality Law introduced some provisions concerning paternity leave and childcare leave which have allowed and encouraged work reductions for mothers and fathers with small children. The challenge for the future, particularly for the highly educated population, is not so much about allowing leave from work. It is rather about developing flexibility measures which enhance the possibility for women to remain in the labor market and make it possible to develop career paths similar to those of men if they wish to do so.

3.5 Conclusions

In this chapter we have explored the trade-offs between family needs and work career development for highly educated men and women in Spain, and we have described how these trade-offs have changed over time. Although women reach higher educational attainments in terms of graduation rates from college, their careers often diverge substantially from those of men. Part of this may be due to a different choice in the fields of study, as Chapters 4 and 5 of this book will analyse. Part of it may be due to discrimination, as Chapter 2 suggested. In addition, however, family issues have undoubtedly been shown to be an important determinant of this divergence. Women must combine employment with home responsibilities to a much larger extent than their male partners, and this conditions their decisions with respect to their labor supply and hence to their labor performance in the future.

We presented evidence of gender gaps in labor supply (employment rates, use of part-time), wages, and incidence in managerial jobs during the life cycle and for different cohorts – those born in 1960, 1965, 1970, and 1975. By comparing gender gaps during the life cycle for different birth cohorts we can assess changes over time in the way Spanish women combine family and work. In addition to this descriptive evidence we use two micro-datasets to account for the impact of having children on the observed gender gaps. Our findings suggest the following insights. First, we observe a very different pattern of employment when comparing the mid-1990s (1994) with the 2000s (2008): in the former year, gender gaps in employment rates are quite substantial even among childless men and women. However, by 2008, the pattern of gender gaps in employment rates has changed substantially: there is basically no gap between childless men and women.

Second, we find that the use of part-time employment is basically a female choice only. At this stage, we see interesting differences in the behavior of women with respect to the use of part time work in the mid-1990s as compared with the late 2000s: the use of part-time employment was higher among childless women as compared to mothers (15% versus 11%) in 1994. This has changed completely by 2008, when the use of part-time employment by childless females is only 10% but rises to 18% for mothers. Additionally, the fact that children account only for a small fraction of the gap in part-time employment suggests that there may be other determinants, among others demand restrictions, which lead some women to work on a part-time basis.

Third, with respect to performance in the labor market, we show that in the mid-1990s childless women earned on average 6% more than men, which suggests that working women at that time were not a random sample among college females but, rather, a highly skilled one. However, when we compare fathers with mothers, the gap was 7% in favor of men. By 2008, the pattern was different: the gender gap between childless men and women was of the same magnitude to that between fathers and mothers (5% in favor of men). The reason for this could be discrimination or different skills or differences in occupation/career choice of women.

4

Gender Gap in Italy: The Role of College Majors

Massimo Anelli and Giovanni Peri

4.1 Introduction

In this chapter we present a database that quantifies the impact of the choice of major for college-educated men and women on long-run labor market outcomes such as their employment rate, occupational choice, and income 5 to 15 years after finishing their studies. To our knowledge this database is the first to collect such a substantial amount of information about potential determinants of wage gaps, following individual choices and performance from high school to college and into the labor market, including family backgrounds. We are interested in exploring two new dimensions of the gender gap in wages and the choice of major. In this chapter we analyze how the difference in choice of major affects the male–female earnings gap as measured during the early years of their working career while controlling in much more detail than previously for individual characteristics, family background, academic quality, and environmental variables.

In Chapter 5 we examine potential explanations for male–female differences in the choice of college major, including differences in abilities, preferences, skills, and the differential effect of peers and teachers on men and women.

There is abundant evidence from the literature that women are significantly under represented in math- and science-intensive college majors such as engineering, mathematics, computer science, and economics, while they are over represented in humanities, classics, and education. This is a feature prevalent in many industrialized countries (as we documented in Chapter 1). In the US, Turner and Bowen (1999) show that women are significantly less likely to choose math and physical science subjects as their college major, relative to men. For the UK, Chevalier (2011) also shows the very different propensity of women to choose some college majors, such as engineering and economics. He also documents how relevant this is for some labor market outcomes. This difference in the choice of college major is responsible, we argue, for a significant portion of female underperformance in terms of wages. College majors are a very important determinant of the access to highly paid occupations.

We focus on Italy because we have personally collected a novel and unique database on the high school career, university career, and labor market performance of young Italians who graduated from high school between 1985 and 2005 and are currently between 28 and 48 years old. A large part of the previous analysis of college major and performance in the labor market has used data from the US and the UK. A country such as Italy, with its early and strong differentiation in college majors, provides an environment which should be extremely interesting. The choice of college major in Italy is potentially more relevant in determining a future job, than in the US or the UK. In the Italian educational system, in fact, college majors correspond closely to the choice of a career/occupation and are chosen right out of high school with high costs attached to changing the choice later. Each student satisfies general education requirements during high school, and then he/she applies and is admitted to a specific major in a specific university. In the US it is more common to apply to a university and to declare the major afterwards. Once the person is admitted to a major he/she focuses, from the beginning of the college career, on courses pertaining to that major. Also, law, medicine and veterinary medicine in Italy are college majors rather than postgraduate degrees; hence becoming a doctor or a lawyer is a choice made out of high school. As postgraduate education is still very rare in Italy (less than 0.5% of the population achieves a post graduate degree), the choice of college narrows the choice of occupation to a specific set. Hence, its effect on the income of a person will be very prominent and long-lasting.

The sample that we analyze is a group of highly educated Italians who graduated from a college-preparatory high school between 1985 and 2005 and hence are currently between 28 and 48 years of age. We collected a database that includes the majority (around 90%) of individuals who graduated from public college-preparatory high schools in the city of Milan (Italy) in the period mentioned. The sample includes around 30,000 individuals. The database includes information about their family background, school career, university career, and labor market outcomes. For a representative 10% subsample we also have information on occupation, education and job of the mother and the father and current labor, location, and family conditions, obtained during interviews in the summer 2011. We also put together data on the average value of houses in Milan at a very fine disaggregation so that we can associate the location where a student used to live at the time of high school with the average house value and use this as a proxy for family wealth.

The next section and Appendix 4.1 at the end of the chapter describe in detail the database, the original data, the method of collection, the variables included in the database, and our merging and cleaning procedures.

We first present descriptive statistics and then a regression approach to quantify the gender gap in the income of these college-educated individuals. We quantify how much gender-specific differences in the choice of college major contributed to the overall measured gender gap in income and employment for the individuals in our sample. Our findings indicate that the choice of college major is the most relevant aspect of the school career of individuals in predicting their future income and in explaining the gender gap in income. We also explore for the first time how the gender gap interacts with the academic ability of men and women, as measured by their high-school exit test scores and by other measures of performance in college, such as their exit grade and the time taken to graduate. We find that the gender gap in choosing highly paid majors becomes particularly strong among highly performing students. This is a sign that academic quality, even in math and science subjects, is not likely to be the determinant of the gender differences in choice of major. Strong differences in preferences for specific topics or preferences for post-college outcomes (such as flexibility or complementarity with rearing children) must therefore determine the differences.

Another interesting finding of our analysis is that the gender gap within our sample (of college-educated people in a city with relatively high income) is mainly specific to income. We find that there is not much gender gap in employment, as most of the women in the sample work, at least part-time.[1] We do not have data on hours worked and hence we cannot quantify the gender gap in that variable. We can, however, restrict our sample to women and men with no children, for which several studies show that the difference in hours worked is not significant, to isolate the differences in wages. We also gathered from the Italian Labor Force survey the average difference in hours worked by college-educated men and women (in northern Italy) to get an idea of how large that is and what fraction of the earnings gap found in our data can be explained by differences in worked hours.

4.2 The Data and some Descriptive Statistics: High School and College

In this section we describe our new data, the method of collection, and their main characteristics.

---

[1] The Italian Labor Force survey confirms that the difference in employment rate between men and women with a college education is smaller than 7%.

4.2.1 *Description of the Database*

For the analysis we use a new database collected and organized by Giovanni Peri and Massimo Anelli between September 2010 and March 2012. This database merges information from several sources and includes a sample of the large majority of individuals who graduated between the years 1985 and 2005[2] from 13 college-preparatory public high schools (Liceo Classico and Liceo Scientifico) in the city of Milan.[3] We collected this information manually by visiting all the college preparatory high schools in Milan and accessing hard-copies of the records directly from the schools. While there were some missing and destroyed records, we were able to cover more than 90% of all records for students who graduated between 1985 and 2005. This includes about 30,000 individuals. Milan is a large service-oriented metropolitan area in the richest part of Italy. The college-educated individuals from this city are an interesting group, which allows us to analyze the gender gap at the top of the income and educational distribution in Italy. For these individuals we have information on the year of graduation from high school, the grade in the high school exit exam, the school attended, the street address where they lived during high school, and the identity of their parents. We were able to link these data with the student records from all universities in Milan (there are five of them: two private universities, Universitá Cattolica and Universitá Bocconi, and three public universities, Politecnico, State University of Milano, and State University of Milano-Bicocca). We could, therefore, reconstruct the university career of the individual who graduated from a college-preparatory high school in Milan, including the following information: whether they graduated, in what year, in what field and subfield of study, at what university, and their final exit grade.

We linked these records to the data on the personal income of these individuals, as revealed to the internal revenue service. We could access, through the internal revenue service of Italy, the income reporting for 2005. These data include total income reported for tax reasons by each individual in the country and whether the individual was an employee or self-employed. There are advantages and disadvantages in using these income data. The primary advantage is that the administrative file of reported income includes all individuals in the national territory and reporting is mandatory. Hence if a person does not appear it is because he/she has no income or because he/she has left the country. The self-employed are included in the sample, and we will check whether the income gap between men and women for that group is different from that of the rest of the population. The main disadvantage

---

[2] There are few private high schools in Italy and they tend to select those students who, for some particular reason, do not make it in public high schools. We did not include them in our sample.

[3] We were not able to gather data for just two college-preparatory high schools, the Vittorio Veneto and the Carducci, as the principals of those schools denied us access to their data.

is that vis-à-vis the precise measure of income we do not have a measure of hours worked. We will, however, identify some measures of hourly wages, and we obtain some measures of gender differential in hours worked for a similar sample from the Italian Labor Force survey, and we will discuss in the results what part of the gender gap in income may be due to differences in hours worked.

Data on income or wages are very rare in Italian datasets, and hence this data provides a very important step in the analysis of income differential and gender gap. These data are the only source (to the best of our knowledge) to link school performance and income for such a large sample of individuals. We use these income data only for people who graduated from high school before 1995. Considering, in fact, an average college attendance of five years, people in our sample would have been on the labor market between 5 and 15 years in 2005. Hence this provides a good assessment of the long-run consequences of the abilities, school quality, and school choice on labor market outcomes during the early career. The total number of individuals for which we have data on high school and university career is around 30,000. For 21,430 of them we were able to match schooling data with income in 2005, and we selected 14,000 of these, those who graduated between 1985 and 1995, for our analysis.

For a stratified[4] 10% random subsample of the initial universe (equal to 3,069 individuals) we collected much more detailed information from telephone interviews conducted in June 2011 by the professional company Carlo Erminero & Co.[5] The additional information covers several variables regarding the family background, parental income, activities at the time of high school, current job and education, and current family situation of the individual. Finally, using online information from Agenzia del Territorio, we collected the information on the average value of housing in 55 districts of Milan that we associated with the street address of the individuals in the data, in order to gain an approximate value for their house and hence an indication of the wealth of their family.

Therefore this new database is the first to collect administrative data tracking individual information from cradle to the labor market. The possibility of controlling for family background characteristics, the detailed data on academic performance, and income information 5 to 15 years into the labor market make this dataset an exceptional contribution to the study of determinants of the gender gap and labor market outcomes in general, with major improvements with respect to published literature.

---

[4] The stratification has been done along the following four dimensions: type of high school, year of graduation in four-year bins, final test score in high school, in five-point bins, gender. We obtain a total of 80 cells.

[5] We are very thankful to Carlo Erminero and Fausta Faini for their very kind and professional collaboration.

4.2.2 *Description of College-preparatory High Schools and College Major for Men and Women*

The Italian system of education encourages students who are planning to go to college to select a specific track in high school. The very large majority of people who enroll in college, about 80% of the total, attended a type of college-preparatory high school called a Liceo. This can be a Liceo Classico, with an emphasis on arts subjects such as literature, philosophy, Latin and Greek, or a Liceo Scientifico, with an emphasis on mathematics and sciences.[6] Either of these preparatory high schools allows access to any type of college major. Students finish their general education in high school and, beginning with the first year of college, focus only on the topics of their major. Among the students who attended the high schools included in our sample almost 80% enrolled into college. Of those enrolled, about 70% graduated. This is a very high graduation rate by Italian standards. This is because college-preparatory schools in Milan are, generally, of very high quality; they select highly achieving individuals usually from families with high education and medium to high income.

The population of students who attend college-preparatory high school is an interesting one in which to study gender differences between young Italian individuals in the scholastic careers and then in the labor market. First, these are the upper part of the distribution (in terms of ability and possibly income of the family). Second, their family background is relatively similar, especially in our case, as they come from middle-class families, living in the same city, valuing college education, and certainly with income levels around or above the average for the city. Finally, the high school experience represents a substantial educational experience for Italian teenagers. It lasts for five years and it usually generates a very close-knit group of classmates and teachers, who play an important role as educators and models.

As for university education, the Italian system essentially pushes the choice of a career to the end of high school. The college major (field of study), in fact, is highly focused on courses that are related to the specialty of the major. So students essentially choose to become engineers, doctors, accountants, lawyers, economists by choosing at the end of high school the corresponding field of study (engineering, business, accounting, law, economics). The correlation between college major choice and the type of occupation is much stronger in the Italian system than in Anglo-Saxon systems.

We first present some key features of the gender differences, beginning with the choice of major and high school performance. As shown in Figure 4.1, the first difference between men and women apparent in our data (the

---

[6] There is also a very small number of Liceo Artistico, with an emphasis on art.

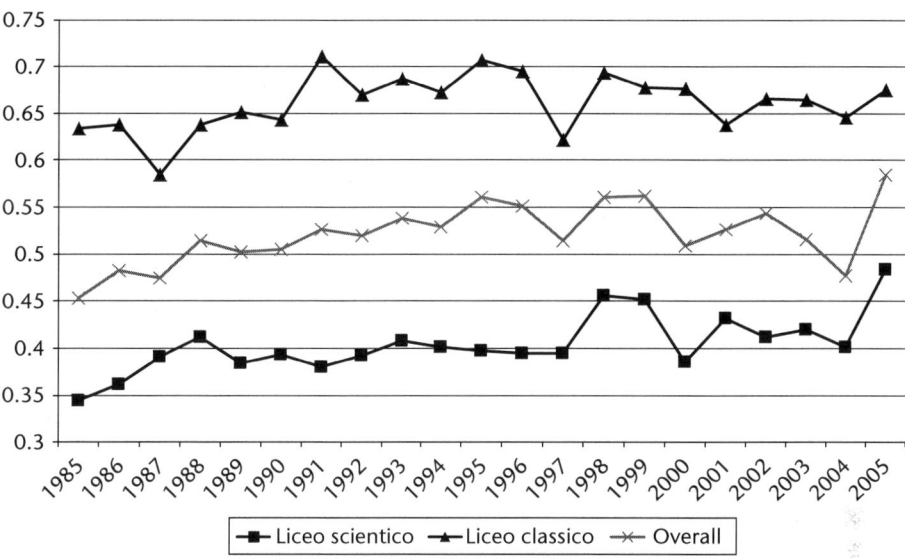

Figure 4.1. Share of women among high school graduates by high school type.

Note: Liceo Classico is the college-preparatory school with a stronger concentration on humanities and languages. Liceo Scientifico is the college-preparatory school with a stronger concentration mathematics and sciences. The universe is represented by the students graduating each year from those schools in the city of Milan, Italy.

gender gap) is that women are much more heavily represented in the Liceo Classico, the high school more focused on humanities and classics. While overall in our universe of graduates from college-preparatory schools women are about 50% of the total, in Liceo Classico they are 66% of the population while in Liceo Scientifico they are only 40% of the population. As that choice of high school is made when students are 13 years old, this gender imbalance has two important consequences. First, the majority of men and women will be tracked early on into classes with different exposure to science and math. Second, this implies that a broad choice of career (whether associated with language and classics or with math and science) is made at age 13 with very little information for the students and, possibly, a heavy influence from the family (and their generation's choice).

Figure 4.1 shows the evolution over time of the percentage of women overall and in each of the two types of school. While overall the percentage of women among high school graduates is close to 50%, with some fluctuations over time, the percentage of women in Liceo Classico fluctuates around 65% (with not much of a trend) while for the Liceo Scientifico the percentage fluctuates around 40%, with an initial upward sloping trend that flattens in the 1990s and 2000s.

85

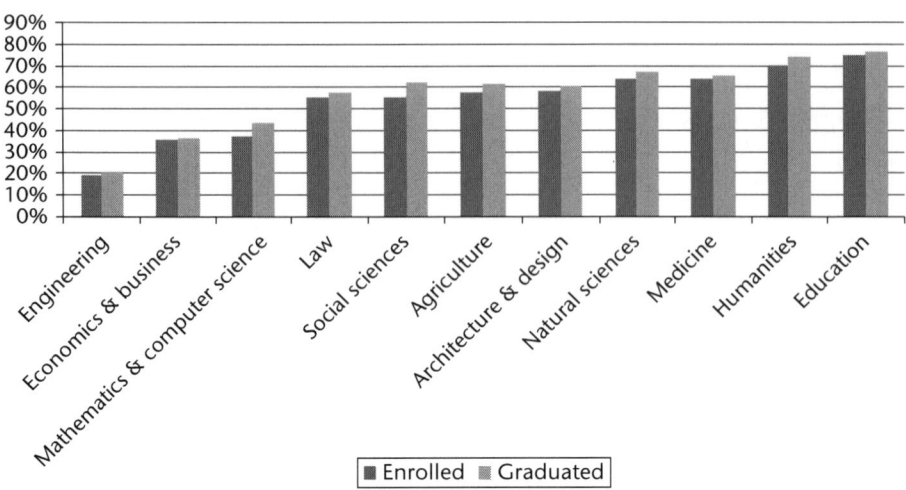

Figure 4.2. Percentage of women by college major.

Note: The universe is represented by all college-preparatory students graduated between 1985 and 2005 in Milan, Italy.

This revealed preference of women for languages, humanities, and arts and of men for science and mathematics subjects becomes even clearer when we analyze the choice of college major for students graduating from the high schools in our sample (over the whole period 1985–2005). Figure 4.2 shows the percentage of women among those who enrolled and graduated in 11 different college major groups that span all the possible choices available to the Italian students.[7]

Three things emerge very clearly. First the three majors of engineering, business and economics and math/computer-science have a very low percentage of women (lower than 50%). They are also large majors and, as we will see, they are associated with relatively high income. Hence this compositional difference will contribute significantly to the gender gap. Second, because of the significant attrition rate in college we report both the gender ratio among the enrolled (dark bar) and graduated (light bar). It is clear that, for each major, the graduation rate of women is larger than the graduation rate of men as the percentage of women among graduates is always larger than the percentage among the enrolled. Third, humanities and education, but also medicine and natural sciences have a very large share (higher than 60%) of women among the total of enrolled and graduated individuals. Some of those are large majors and they are usually not associated with high income.

---

[7] Each of the 11 groups merges several specific majors; the exact definition of majors in each of our groups is reported in Appendix 4.1.

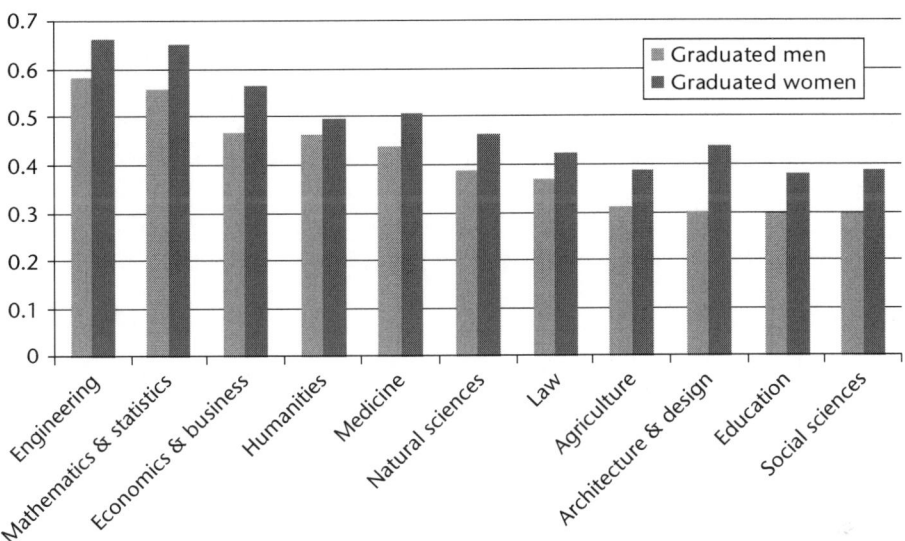

Figure 4.3. High school grade by college major (graduated).

Note: The universe is represented by all college-preparatory students graduated between 1985 and 2005 in Milan, Italy.

Do some major select better students? In our sample and during the considered years some of the degrees in engineering and business economics, as well as medicine, had entry tests while others (typically the majors in the humanities and political science, biology, and classics) did not. It is likely, therefore, that some of those majors were more selective than others. Figure 4.3 shows the average grade in the final high school exam, rescaled to be between 0 (barely passing) and 1 (top grade), for each of the considered college major-groups. The average grade of men in the major is represented by the light grey bar, while the average grade of women by the dark grey one.

The figure reveals significant differences in "average quality" of the students admitted in different majors and, interestingly, several of the most selective majors, in particular engineering, economics/business and mathematics/statistics are those that Figure 4.2 revealed as "male dominated". The female-dominated majors, instead, are spread through the distribution (humanities has a rather high average quality of admitted students while education has a low average quality). Two further interesting things emerge from Figure 4.3. First, women admitted to each major exhibit higher quality than men, as measured by their average high school exit-test score.[8] Second,

---

[8] The high school graduation test in Italy is identical for all schools in the nations and is graded on the same scale. However as it is not multiple choice, but involves essays and problems as well as an oral exam there may be differences in the grading. We will account for these potential differences in using the high school test as measure of academic quality, in regressions.

in some majors, such as social sciences and architecture design, the gender gap in high school grade is larger than 0.1 (10% of the total range), which is an extremely large value. This may be the sign that several academically gifted women direct themselves toward these two majors (rather than towards more demanding ones) while those majors attract relatively less talented men.

The previous graphs reveal a striking gender difference in major choice. But is the choice of college major driven mostly by the previous choice of high school type? Namely, is it the case that graduates from Liceo Scientifico choose engineering and business-economics (independently of their gender) while graduates of the Liceo Classico mainly chose humanities and law (also independently of their gender)? Or are women graduating from Liceo Scientifico still less likely to choose engineering and economics/business than men from the same type of school? Figure 4.4 (part a and b) shows that the second scenario is the relevant one. Even among the Liceo Scientifico graduates, women are much less likely to choose engineering and economics/business. In fact more than 55% of male graduates from that Liceo choose one of these two majors, while only about 20% of women do. Interestingly natural sciences and architecture design (besides humanities) are among the very top choices for women in the Liceo Scientifico. The more math and science-oriented women (i.e. those attending the Liceo Scientifico) seem to prefer natural science and architecture/design to engineering and business/economics, relative to comparable men.[9] The distribution of choices in the Liceo Classico is more similar between men and women. However there is still a large difference in engineering and business-economics (chosen by 25% of men and by less than 10% of women). Law and humanities, together, absorb more than 50% of both men and women graduates (with a bias in favor of law for men and in favor of humanities for women).

Do these choices contribute to determine the labor market performance of men and women, especially with respect to their future income? While we will devote the later sections to a more formal analysis of this issue, the answer is a resounding yes and Figure 4.5 already shows the main reason why. The figure shows the average gross (pre-tax) yearly income in Euros as of 2005, reported to the internal revenue service by the individuals in our sample, divided by college major. Among the four top-paying college majors two are strongly male dominated. Conversely the two bottom-paying majors are those strongly female dominated. Notice that the three college majors at the bottom of the distribution, which graduate about 35% of the women, are associated to average yearly income, in our sample, of less than €13,000 (about $17,000). Only 10% of the men graduate in those majors. On the contrary, a very large

---

[9] Dolado, Felgueroso, and Almunia (2010) show a comparable finding among women within the field of economics: a larger share of them choose fields such as labor and development (with more human content) and fewer choose finance and theory (with more abstract content).

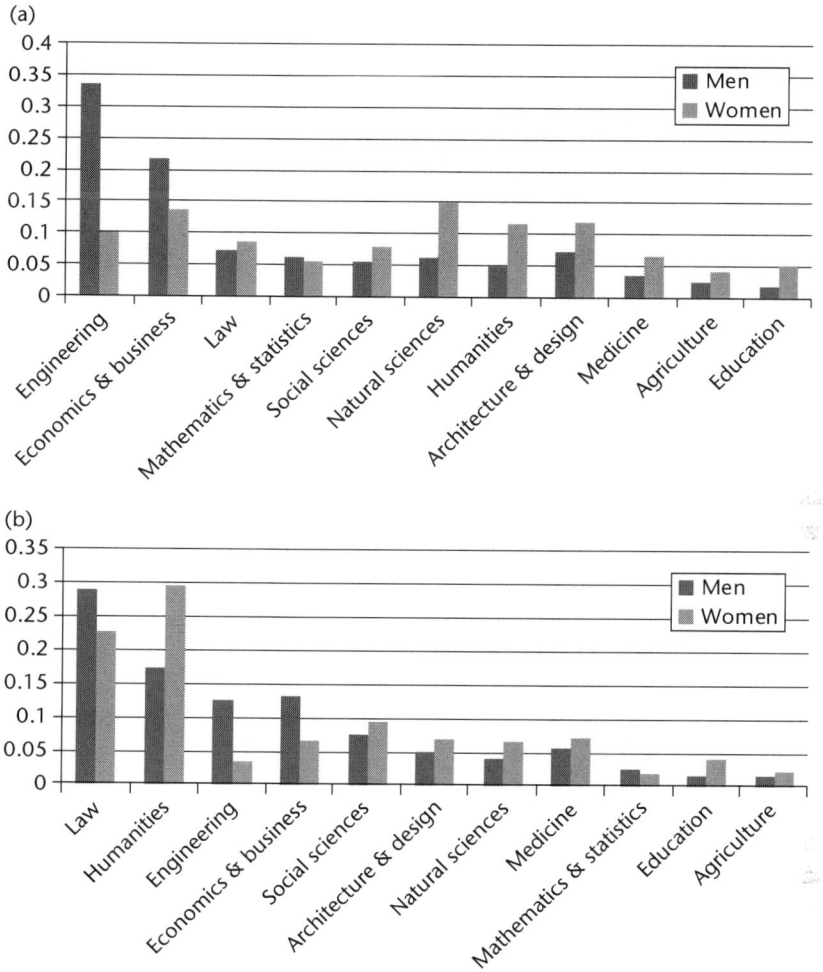

Figure 4.4. a) Liceo Scientifico – distribution over majors; b) Liceo Classico – distribution over majors.

Note: Each graph represents the percentage of total graduates, by gender, during the period 1985–2005 enrolling in each of the listed college majors.

portion (65%) of college-educated men graduated from one of the four top-earning majors, whose average income in our sample is above €30,000 per year.

Not only is the gender difference in the choice of highly paid major large and correlated with earnings, it has also not changed much over time. Considering the four top-paid majors (engineering, medicine, economics and business and law) and the four least-paid majors (humanities, art/design, agriculture, and education), Figure 4.6 shows the evolution of the share of women

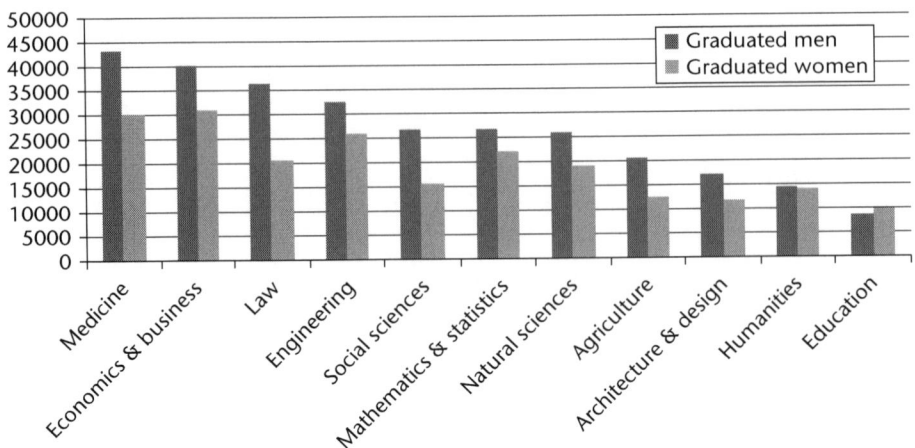

Figure 4.5. Average income by major (graduated).

Note: We measure the average yearly income for the sample of individuals who graduated from college–preparatory high school in Milano in the period 1985–2005. The income data are those reported to the internal revenue service in 2005 in euros.

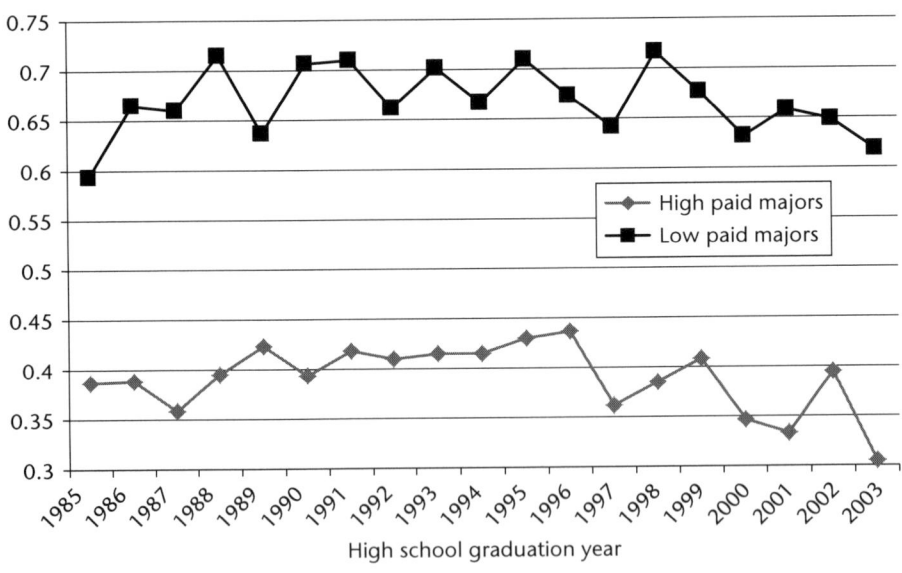

Figure 4.6. Percentage of women by high–paid vs. low–paid majors.

Note: High–paid majors are engineering, medicine, economics business and law and the low-paid majors are humanities, art design, agriculture, and education.

in each group between 1985 and 2005. In high-paid majors the share of students who are women has been below 40% for most of the period, and possibly it has declined in the last seven years of the sample. In low-paying majors the share of students who are women has been above 65% and stable.

4.3 Gender Gap in Academic Quality in High School

A possibility to explain the stylized facts presented in section 4.2 is that women have an absolute advantage academically, both in math and science subjects and humanities and the arts, but a comparative advantage in humanities and the arts. They outperform males, that is, in those subjects by more than they do in science and math. However, at least as revealed by the test score in high school, there seems to be only a small relative advantage of women in humanities, versus math and science, certainly not comparable with the very large difference in choice of major.[10] Moreover as math and science majors are associated to much higher wages than humanities majors, if the motivation to choose humanities is higher productivity (skills) on the labor market in order to obtain higher wages, such a differential should further attenuate the incentive to choose those majors. Something besides wages must motivate women.

To inquire further into how academic quality interacts with gender and choice of major we begin by analyzing in greater detail the academic quality of women and men as revealed by their high school final test grades. In particular we first check, by exploiting the difference in the scores in the exit test at the Liceo Classico and Liceo Scientifico, whether women have a disadvantage in math scientific fields, as revealed by those scores.

Figure 4.7 below shows the distribution of exit test grades, smoothed with a kernel, for men and women in the Liceo Scientifico (panel a) and in the Liceo Classico (panel b). The similarity of the two is apparent, and in both cases the women's distribution is significantly shifted to the right relative to men's distribution. Hence even in the Liceo Scientifico, whose exit test is much more intensive in math and science, women outperform men. The distribution of test scores is not centered and reflects the tradition of Italian schools to give very few high grades and concentrate most of the grades in the lower part of the distribution.

A formal test of the difference in average test scores between men and women reveals that for both Liceo Classico and Liceo Scientifico the standardized average exit test score for women is around 0.43 while for men it is 0.39

---

[10] We see below that women outperform men in their exit test score in both Liceo Classico and Scientifico. While their test score gap is a bit larger in the Classico (revealing comparative advantages in Humanities) the difference is quite small, certainly too small to justify the very large difference in college major choice.

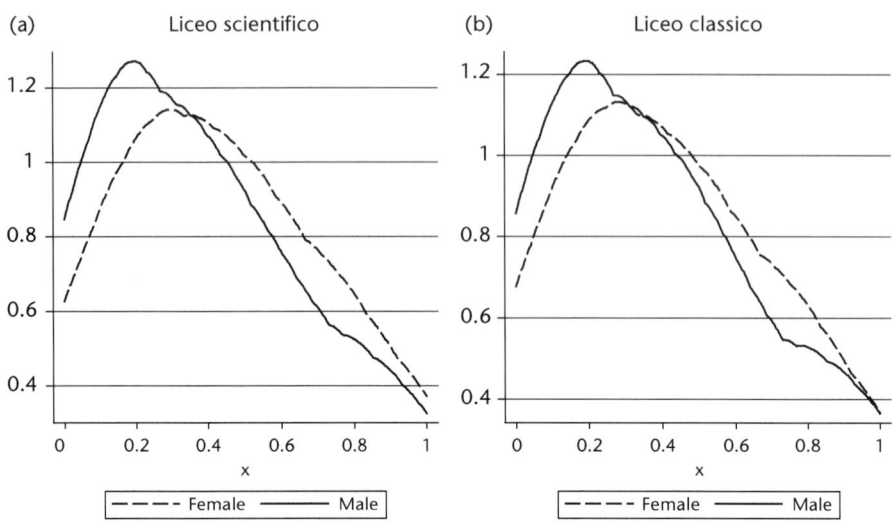

Figure 4.7. Distribution of high school graduation grade by gender.

Note: The high school exit test scores were standardized to be between 0 and 1, where 0 is the lowest passing grade and 1 is the highest score one could get. We only consider people who graduated, hence 0 is the lowest available score.

with a difference around 0.04 points, significant at any level of confidence. Also interestingly, we do not observe a larger dispersion in the performance of males, so that even if we use the percentage of students above a certain grade threshold as a measure of quality, women tend to dominate.

To control for differences in high school quality and family location we also perform a simple regression of the high school graduation test score on year school dummies, on the house value in the area where the student lived, and on a gender dummy equal to one for females. The coefficient on this dummy is 0.045 with a standard error of 0.004. This confirms the raw data. Empirical evidence from other countries shows that female students tend to get better grades in high school because of their better behavior, rather than higher innate abilities. This may certainly be true, but the measured academic quality of women in the high school considered seems higher.[11]

In spite of this better performance a large number of women did not choose the most demanding math-intensive and highly selective college majors that would also be associated with higher pay later on. Understanding why this is

---

[11] A rapid comparison with the available PISA test scores relative to the region of Italy where Milan is (Lombardy), for year 2000 (within our sample) reveals that men outperformed women in math (530 vs. 513), but did worse in both reading and sciences (496 vs. 537 in reading and 541 vs. 545 in sciences). If we look at an equally weighted average of the scores in these tree skill categories we see that girls outperform boys overall (532 vs. 522).

Table 4.1. Measures of performance in college and gender–ability

Dependent Variable	Graduated = 1	Time to Graduation	Final Grade in College	Final Grade in College	Final Grade in College
Specification	(1)	(2)	(3)	(4)	(5)
VARIABLES					
Female	0.063***	−2.972***	0.065***	0.038***	0.046***
	(0.01)	(0.769)	(0.005)	(0.004)	(0.008)
(Female)X(grade)	−0.062***	−0.711	−0.020**	−0.054***	−0.003
	(0.022)	(1.281)	(0.008)	(0.007)	(0.012)
HS exit test grade	0.424***	−17.031***	0.207***	0.263***	0.247***
	(0.015)	(1.072)	(0.006)	(0.006)	(0.007)
School X Year Dummies	X	X	X	X	X
Major Dummies				X	
Constant		62.768***	0.712***	0.748***	0.650***
		(0.174)	(0.003)	(0.007)	(0.003)
Sample	enrolled	graduated	graduated	graduated	graduated in high paid majors
Observations	22,873	16,035	16,561	16,561	8,406
R-squared		0.165	0.221	0.392	0.265

Note: Method of estimation is probit for specification 1 and OLS for all other specifications. Standard errors are clustered at school/year level, *** $p < 0.01$, ** $p < 0.05$, * $p < 0.1$.

the case, or at least where and how this gender bias arises and what effect it has on the labor market outcomes of women, is the goal of the rest of this chapter.

4.4 College Majors and Income Gender Gap: A Regression Approach

4.4.1 *From High School to College: The Gender Gap in University Performance*

We have considered so far high school exit exam scores as a measure of academic quality of the students. But are these test scores good predictors of their performance in college? Is it possible that men, who were underperforming relative to women in high school then outperform them in college? Table 4.1 analyzes these issues. Conditional on their choice of college, we consider three measures of academic performance in college. The first is the graduation rate. The second is, conditional on graduation, the time to graduation. The third is the final grade at college graduation. Specification 1 in Table 4.1 shows the marginal effects of a probit regression in which the probability of graduating from college is regressed on the high school exit test grade, a female dummy, and the interaction between female and high school grade. The other specifications perform OLS regressions of the outcome variables on the high school exit score, on school-year dummies, on a female dummy, and the interaction between female and high school grade.

Three results emerge from specification 1. First, the high school exit score is a very significant and strong predictor of the probability of graduation. Going from the lowest to the highest grade in high school is associated with an average increase in the probability of graduating by 42 percentage points. Second, even controlling for the high school exit score (which was higher for women), being a woman carries a significant additional advantage in graduating probability (six extra percentage points at the average probability). Third, such gender advantage is particularly strong for students who performed at the bottom of the high school test score distribution, while at the top it is close to zero. This can be seen by using the coefficient on the interaction between gender and grade for lowest score (0) and highest score (1) and adding it to the main gender effect. Each regression controls for dummies absorbing the "year by high school" effects, hence eliminating the effect of cohort and school quality. Specifications 2 and 3 consider Least Square regressions, using as dependent variables two alternative measures of college performance. One is the time to graduation expressed in months and the other is the final score at graduation. That score is also rescaled to be between 0 (barely passing) and 1 (top). Those regressions are restricted to those who graduated from college only and confirm the first two findings described above. The high school exit test score is a very strong predictor of time to graduation. The magnitude of that coefficient implies that a student graduating with top grades will, on average, take almost one and a half years less (17 months) to graduate relative to one graduating at the bottom of the high school grade distribution. Similarly each increase in the standardized high school grade by 0.01 corresponds to a 0.02 increase in the standardized college exit grade. Second, women take on average three months less to graduate than men and earn a final score higher by 0.065 standardized points even after controlling for their high school test scores. Is this because a larger percentage of women choose "easier" college majors? Columns 4 and 5 dispel that thought. First, by including major dummies women still outperform men, by a very significant average of 0.038 points. Second even focusing only on the highly paid majors, three of which (engineering, economics business, and law) are dominated by men in the enrollment, the advantage of women is still large and extremely significant (estimates in column 5).

Hence women outperform men academically in high school, both in the Liceo Scientifico and Classico. Controlling for the quality in high school, they outperform men in terms of probability to graduate, time to graduation, and exit score in college. This is true overall and also in the math-intensive, male-dominated highly paid majors. Hence, this evidence points to the higher academic quality of women, emerging in high school and deepening in college. If academic quality is associated with productivity and if skills developed in highly paid majors are in high demand, our analysis reveals the presence of two opposite effects affecting the gender gap. On one hand, based on pure academic performance (even in math-intensive majors) women should have an advantage in productivity relative to men. On the other hand they choose majors associated with lower wages at a much higher rate than men, and this would generate a disadvantage.

4.4.2 *Choice of Majors and Gender Income Gap*

After having analyzed the academic performance of this group of college-preparatory graduates it is interesting to see how this relates to their labor market performance. We have three types of outcome measures for these individuals and each of them has some limits. One is their personal gross income earned in 2005, as recorded by the internal revenue service. As we consider only the group that graduated from high school between 1985 and 1995, as of 2005, most of those individuals graduated from college between five and fifteen years earlier. The other two outcomes that we consider are employment status (whether a person is working or not) and the occupation/sector of activity. These last two outcomes are available only for the subsample on which we conducted telephone interviews (10% of the total, around 3,000 individuals).

We illustrate with a regression approach how large the wage gap between men and women in the sample is, and then we analyze what percentage of the income gap is explained away by the inclusion of controls measuring academic quality, school performance, and college career of the individuals. Specification 1 of Table 4.2 shows a regression of the logarithm of income in 2005 on year of graduation dummies, age of the individual, and a female dummy. The regression includes all the high school graduates over the period 1985 and 1995. These individuals were mostly between 28 and 38 years of age in 2005, and hence well into their working career. The coefficient on the female dummy is an estimate of the average gap in logarithmic points of gross income between women and men (controlling only for age and type of high school attended). Remarkably, this difference equals 0.45 logarithmic points (about 37%), which is by all standards a very large average difference. This is yearly income, and it combines the difference in average wage, including bonuses, overtime, and other incentives to production, and in average hours worked, which can compound the effect. To have an idea of what fraction of this gap can be due to difference in hours worked we selected from the European Union Statistics on Income and Living Conditions (EU SILC 2005) a sample which was as comparable as possible to our data (within the constraints of EU SILC 2005). In particular we compute the average hours worked by employed individuals aged 18–38 who attended at least a college-preparatory high school in densely populated areas of north-western Italy. The values are equal to 43.1 hours per week for the men and 37.1 hours per

Table 4.2. Gender gap in log income and the importance of college majors

Dependent variable: Log of Income in 2005

SPECIFICATIONS VARIABLES	(1)	(2)	(3)	(4)	(5)	(6)	(7)	(8)
Female	-0.451***	-0.422***	-0.437***	-0.434***	-0.432***	-0.329***	-0.292***	-0.267***
	(0.023)	(0.023)	(0.026)	(0.030)	(0.031)	(0.028)	(0.029)	(0.031)
HS exit test grade				0.375***	0.395***	0.125**	0.033	0.032
				(0.047)	(0.047)	(0.051)	(0.054)	(0.054)
Value of real estate				0.011	0.025	0.021	0.032	0.032
				(0.038)	(0.042)	(0.042)	(0.041)	(0.041)
College exit grade				-0.025	-0.038	0.720***	0.817***	0.820***
				(0.092)	(0.090)	(0.096)	(0.110)	(0.111)
Self-employed = 1								-0.112**
								(0.057)
(Self-Employed = 1) X Fem								0.029
								(0.053)
Constant	10.369***	10.373***	10.475***	10.272***	10.159***	9.481***	9.155***	9.141***
	(0.050)	(0.055)	(0.043)	(0.315)	(0.344)	(0.352)	(0.362)	(0.363)
Observations	13,472	11,036	8,323	6,872	6,872	6,872	6,872	6,872
R-squared	0.091	0.089	0.100	0.109	0.124	0.186	0.200	0.201
Sample	All	Enrolled	Graduated	Graduated	Graduated	Graduated	Graduated	Graduated
Year Dummies	X	X	X	X	X			
School/Year Dummies						X	X	X
High-paid majors Dummy						X		
Low-paid majors Dummy						X		
Majors Dummies							X	X

Note: Method of estimation is OLS. The dependent variable is the natural logarithm of the income in 2005. Standard errors are clustered at school/year level in parenthesis, *** $p < 0.01$, ** $p < 0.05$, * $p < 0.1$.

week for women. This implies a difference of around 13% in hours worked.[12] Hence we should keep in mind that of the total gap of 37% possibly one third of it (13%) is explained by worked hours.[13]

If we keep in mind that our sample includes only college graduates, all from a rich city in northern Italy, with relatively homogeneous family background, a gender gap in income of 37% is remarkable. Recent estimates of the gender earning gap in Italy in recent years reveal values that are comparable with those estimated in column 1 of Table 4.2. For instance the Global Gender Gap report of 2011, by the Global Economic Forum, reports that the earnings of women were 46% below those of men in Italy overall. The gender gap in yearly wages estimated from the EU-SILC data and limited to college-educated workers over 25 was 34% in 2005, while for all workers it was 40%. Notice also that while schooling seems to have an effect in reducing the gender gap, it is very far from eliminating it. This is also consistent with what was found by Burda, Hamermesh, and Weil (2008). They show that college education does not seem to reduce the time worked at home by women, so that even with a college degree they are at a disadvantage relative to men as they need to perform most of the home-making work.

Consistent with the previous finding that more education per se does not solve the issue of a gender gap in income, when restricting the sample to individuals who actually enrolled in college (specification 2) and to those who graduated from college (specification 3) the gender income gap does not change much, and in specification (3) it is still equal to 0.45 logarithmic points. Hence selection into college and then into the group that graduated from college does not affect the gender gap. In specification (4) we include controls for the academic quality of the individual, namely the score in the high school exit exam, the score in the college exit exam, and a control for the value of the real estate in the part of town where the student lived at the time of high school as a proxy of the wealth of his family of origin.[14] This specification reveals that the high school score is highly significant in affecting the logarithmic wage of an individual. A student graduating at the top of the class (score of 1) would on average earn 0.37 logarithmic points

---

[12] An alternative "back of the envelope" calculation of how much difference in hours worked affects the gap can be based on differences in hours worked by college graduates in typically male and typically female majors. For the US, Hamermesh and Donald (2008) find that differences in major can account for about 10% difference in hours worked between men and women. Hence the contribution of hours worked to the gap would be similar to what we obtain with our calculations.

[13] It is still important to explain why college educated women work fewer hours than men. However, as we saw in Chapter 3, the uneven distribution of family duties could be an important reason especially for women between 30 and 40 years of age.

[14] The value of the house in the area was calculated based on the exact address where the student was living at the time of high school, merged with a map of the real estate values of homes in Milan in 2008, by block. The location in the city of Milan is the most important determinant of value of the house and highly correlated with average income.

(44%) more than a student graduating at the bottom (score of 0). Academic merits, as measured by the high school test scores, have a strong correlation with income. However the inclusion of these controls does not affect the gender gap much. Column 5 also includes more detailed controls for the quality of high schools attended by students in the form of high school by year effects. This does not change the estimated gender gap either.

In column 6 we simply add two dummies to the previous controls. These are a dummy for graduating from a highly paid major (engineering, business/economics, law, or medicine) and one for graduating from a low-paying major (humanities, art and design, education, or agriculture). This, by itself, reduces the gender gap by 0.11 log points (11%), one-fourth of the whole difference. If we include all the 11 major dummies (Column 7) the female gap is reduced by 0.14 logarithmic points to 0.29. This corresponds to a wage gap of 25% vis-à-vis the 37% estimated in specification 3. Hence the choice of college major is responsible for one-third of the gender gap between college-educated young Italians in this sample. Notice also, interestingly, that when we control for the college major dummies the grades in high school have no predictive power on logarithmic income, while the grades in college, now within major, are very relevant. This is consistent with the interpretation that the high school exit score affects the working career mainly by affecting the choice of major in college, and then the specific academic performance within the major further affects income.

Finally, in specification (8) we use the information about self-employment. It is possible that the self-employed tend to earn less than employees and as women have a higher rate of self-employment than men (to have more flexibility) this may result in a wage gap. Hence we include a dummy for being self-employed and its interaction with the female dummy. While the regression reveals that self-employment is associated with a significantly lower income, this inclusion only reduces the gender gap by a further 0.025 logarithmic points. Hence the overrepresentation of women among the self-employed affects the gap slightly but does not explain a large part of it. We also learn from the regression that the gender gap is not very different among employed or self-employed workers (the coefficient on the interaction term is not significant). This suggests that if part of the gap is due to discrimination, it is not due solely to employer discrimination but could be due to customer discrimination.

Overall the results in Table 4.2 reveal that up to one–third of the gender gap (12 percentage points out of the overall 37) in observed income can be explained by the choice of major. The data on hours worked reveal that another third of the gap (13 percentage points) can be due to hours worked. The remaining third does not seem to be explained by the remaining family background, academic quality, and self-employment characteristics. While discrimination and family choices could be important to explain the

Table 4.3. Gender bias in the choice of highly paid majors and interaction with academic quality

Dependent Variable: High-Paid Majors = 1	Full Sample of High School Graduates			10% Random Sample of Graduates Interviewed		
	(1)	(2)	(3)	(4)	(5)	(6)
VARIABLES	Probit	OLS	OLS	Probit	OLS	OLS
Female	−0.191***	−0.204***	−0.218***	−0.139***	−0.139***	−0.145***
	(0.014)	(0.015)	(0.014)	(0.040)	(0.041)	(0.040)
Female X grade	−0.105***	−0.096***		−0.091	−0.100	
	(0.027)	(0.027)		(0.075)	(0.076)	
Fem X (grade low range)			−0.028*			−0.036
			(0.015)			(0.042)
Fem X (grade intermediate range)			−0.029*			−0.059
			(0.017)			(0.048)
Female X (grade high range)			−0.070***			−0.067
			(0.022)			(0.061)
HS exit test grade	0.262***	0.258***	0.246***	0.169***	0.177***	0.166***
	(0.021)	(0.021)	(0.020)	(0.055)	(0.058)	(0.055)
Constant		0.523***	0.526***		0.371***	0.372***
		(0.010)	(0.010)		(0.114)	(0.115)
Observations	16,560	16,561	16,561	1,965	1,965	1,965
R-squared		0.110	0.110		0.070	0.070
School Dummies				X	X	X
Year Dummies				X	X	X
School X Year Dummies	X	X	X			

Note: The dependent variable is a dummy equal to 1 if the individual has attended a major among the following four groups: medicine, economics/business, engineering, and law. The first three columns use all the individuals who graduated from college in the sample. Columns 4 to 6 only use the 10% subsample which we also interviewed in the Summer of 2011. The reported standard errors in parenthesis are clustered at school/year level. *** p < 0.01, ** p < 0.05, * p < 0.1.

remaining 13 percentage points of the gap we will focus here on the choice of college major, its determinants, and how it is related to abilities, preferences, and the experience of men and women.

In Table 4.3 we analyze the gender bias in choosing high-paid college majors[15] and the interaction of gender and academic quality in such a choice. Column 1 reports the marginal effects in a probit regression in which we include the high school grade of the individual female dummy (that exhibits a very strong negative effect) and the interaction between female and grade. Column 2 reports the estimates of the same coefficients with a linear probability model, and shows very similar values. The meaning of those estimates is that, for given quality (grade in high school), a woman has a 20% lower probability of choosing a high-paid major relative to men. As on average 65% of men choose a high–paid major, then the difference is very

---

[15] They are, as above, the four majors associated to the highest paid jobs: medicine, economics/business, law and engineering.

large. Even more surprising is the interaction effect. This means that among high–performing students (say those at the very top of the distribution with a score of 1) there is a further 10% probability gap between women and men in choosing a high-paid major. Hence women at the top of their class are fully 30% less likely than men to choose a high-paid major.

In column 3 we add an interaction of the female dummy with dummies for the range of high school grade, rather than linearly with the grade. The dummy for the lowest interval (scores between 0 and 0.25) of the distribution is omitted, then the female dummy is interacted with the second lowest interval (low, between 0.25 and 0.5), the third lowest (intermediate, between 0.5 and 0.75), and the top. The estimates confirm that the bias against high-paid majors is particularly strong among women of high academic quality. Column 4 to 6 repeat the same specifications, limited to the sub sample of individuals for which we have more detailed information on family background and on labor market outcomes (which we will use in the next section). The estimates are similar, although with higher standard errors.

The results shown in Table 4.3 are robust to changing the definition of high-paid majors, including only three majors in each group. Those results

Table 4.4. Gender bias in major-imputed income

Dependent Variable: Ln(Major-Imputed Income) in 2005

Specification Period:	(1) 1985–2005 Full Sample	(2) 1985–1995 Full Sample	(3) 1985–2005 10% interviewed
VARIABLES			
Female	−0.157*** (0.011)	−0.135*** (0.013)	−0.091*** (0.024)
Female X grade	0.003 (0.019)	−0.004 (0.023)	−0.064 (0.045)
HS exit test grade	0.119*** (0.012)	0.099*** (0.015)	0.093*** (0.033)
School Dummies			X
Year Dummies			X
School X Year Dummies	X	X	
Constant	10.366*** (0.006)	10.426*** (0.011)	10.229*** (0.069)
Sample	graduated	graduated	graduated
Observations	16,561	8,615	1,965
R-squared	0.109	0.089	0.098

Note: Method of estimation is OLS. The dependent variable is the logarithm of the Major-imputed income in 2005. The first column includes all the individuals who graduated from high school in the whole sample (1985–2005). Column 2 includes only those individuals who graduated from high school and were also matched to income in 2005. Column 3 includes those individuals who graduated from high school in the period 1985–2005 and were also interviewed in the summer of 2011. The reported standard errors in parenthesis are clustered at school/year level. *** $p < 0.01$, ** $p < 0.05$, * $p < 0.1$.

are useful but they do not provide a clear measure of how much of the wage differential across genders is explained by this choice. To do this we produce, in Table 4.4, a synthetic measure of how much of the income gender gap is determined by the different choices in major, combining all majors. We construct as dependent variable the "major-imputed" income. This variable is constructed by associating to each individual the average income of male individuals with the same college degree from the 2005 income sample. This translates majors into wages, at the value of the average male wage earned by an individual with that college major as of 2005. Then we regress this "major-imputed" wage on the female dummy, the high school grade, and the interaction. The estimated coefficient on the female dummy (and its interactions) expresses how large the wage gap is on average because of the choice of major of men and women.

Column 1 of Table 4.4 shows the results when we include the sample of all high school graduates (between 1985 and 2005). As the wage is imputed on the major we can use all observations as long as we have a college major for them, and this is what we do in the first column. Column 2 of Table 4.4 shows those estimates, including in the sample only the individuals who graduated between 1985 and 1995, who are those for whom we also have actual reported income, which we used in Table 4.2. Column 3, finally, shows the results obtained on the 10% sample on which we have conducted a telephone interview. In all three cases the major-imputed wage is associated with a gender gap of between 0.13 and 0.15 log points, which is almost exactly the difference in the point estimate of the effect of the gender gap in Table 4.2 with (Column 7) and without (Column 5) the inclusion of the major dummies. Hence the difference in the choice of major is a crucial channel through which gender affects wages, producing an income differential between 12 and 15 percentage points, around one third of the income gender gap among Milanese college graduates and (likely) about half of the part not explained by differences in hours worked. A measure of the significance of the wage effect of gender gap through the choice of major is obtained by comparing the coefficients on the female dummy and the effect of high school grade estimated in Table 4.4. The difference between men and women in major-imputed wage is somewhat larger than the difference between the bottom and the top high school performer (e.g. taking the estimates in specification 1, the top–bottom score gap determines a difference of 12 percentage points while the men–women gap is 15 percentage points). Hence the income effect purely channeled through the choice of major implies that the women graduating at the top of their class will be at a disadvantage relative to a man graduating at the bottom of his. Whatever the reason for this difference in the choice of major, women are giving up substantial income opportunities and the Italian economy is

Massimo Anelli and Giovanni Peri

Table 4.5. Gender gap in income and employment rate

Dependent Variable:	Log Income in 2005	Log Income in 2005	Employment Status in 2011	Employment status in 2011
Specification VARIABLES	(1)	(2)	(3)	(4)
Female	−0.399***	−0.313***	−0.007	0.002
	(0.117)	(0.115)	(0.024)	(0.024)
Female X grade	0.139	0.191	−0.003	0.012
	(0.220)	(0.210)	(0.044)	(0.045)
HS exit test score	0.202	0.131	0.027	0.017
	(0.157)	(0.148)	(0.027)	(0.030)
School Dummies	X	X	X	X
Major Dummies		X		X
Year Dummies	X	X	X	X
Constant	10.128***	9.850***	0.939***	0.943***
	(0.203)	(0.257)	(0.048)	(0.053)
Sample	graduated & interviewed	graduated & interviewed	graduated & interviewed	graduated & interviewed
Observations	1,297	1,297	1,965	1,965
R-squared	0.274	0.335	0.176	0.192

Note: Method of estimation is OLS. The dependent variable in column 1 and 2 is the logarithm of the income measured in 2005 by the internal revenue service. The dependent variable in Columns 3 and 4 is a dummy equal to 1 when the individual is employed in year 2011. The sample is equal to the 10% interviewed individuals. The reported standard errors in parenthesis are clustered at school/year level. *** $p < 0.01$, ** $p < 0.05$, * $p < 0.1$.

giving up a large share of their productivity (captured by wages) through this channel.

In table 4.5 we analyze the gender gap in the probability of being employed. We only know the employment status of individuals in the 10% interviewed subsample; hence in Table 4.5 we reproduce the regressions that estimate the income gap for this subsample without and with controls for college major, respectively in Columns 1 and 2. These two regressions confirm the fact that one-fourth of the total gender gap in income (difference between column 1 and 2) is explained by the college major choice and that the overall size of the gap is around 40 log-points even in the sub-sample. Table 4.5 also shows regressions in which the dependent variable is a dummy for being employed in 2011, the time of the interview. The estimates show no difference in employment rate (Column 3 and 4), at least in the restricted sample, between men and women. This is reasonable as most of these college–educated women work (at least part time) and, as we will see below, the fertility rate of these women is very low. They may work a different number of hours, as we have argued above, but the differences in employment rate are small.

We performed several robustness checks (not reported, but available upon request) to verify that the inclusion of several family background controls

Table 4.6. College major choice of siblings

Dependent Variable:	Probability Highly Paid Major = 1		
Specification	(1)	(2)	(3)
Method	Probit	OLS	OLS
Female	−0.363***	−0.232***	−0.470***
	(0.080)	(0.059)	(0.130)
Fem X HS Grade	−0.175	−0.055	−0.113
	(0.159)	(0.103)	(0.234)
HS Grade	0.463***	0.292***	0.439***
	(0.114)	(0.083)	(0.166)
Year Dummies	X	X	X
School Dummies	X	X	X
Family Dummies	X	X	X
Constant		−0.361	1.728***
		(0.281)	(0.440)
Sample	Mixed gender siblings choosing different major	Mixed gender siblings	Mixed gender siblings choosing different major
Observations	751	1,525	751
R-squared		0.585	0.337

Note: The dependent variable is a dummy equal to 1 if the individual has attended a major among the following four groups: medicine, economics/business, engineering, and law. The first and third column include only families with at least two siblings in the sample, with differences in the choice of major between children. Column 2 includes families with at least two children in the sample, including those with children graduating from the same major. The reported standard errors in parenthesis are clustered at school/year level. *** $p < 0.01$, ** $p < 0.05$, * $p < 0.1$.

does not affect the gender gap in choice of major and the impact of major on labor market outcomes. We control for the imputed wage of the father at the time the child was in high school, his education (coded as years of schooling), the mother's education, and the average value of houses in the area where the family lived at the time of high school. None of these controls modifies the estimates, and the strong bias of women away from high-paid majors is very robust, as is its effect on the income gender gap.

4.4.3 *College Major Choice of Siblings*

We only show the most demanding and perhaps cleanest test to see that the disproportionate choice of highly paid major by men does not depend on family-specific factors such as income, location of the home, education, and parental job. While the career choice of parents certainly affects the choice of children, we demonstrate that the overwhelming tendency to prefer different college majors is as strong within a family as in the whole sample. We begin by selecting families that have more than one sibling in our sample. Then we perform probit and OLS estimates of the gender bias in choosing highly paid major on this subsample, including family dummies in it. Table 4.6 reports the coefficients. The total sample includes 1,525 siblings. Out of those there are 751 siblings making different choices of major within a family (between highly paid and non-highly paid majors). The gender gap identified only on the families with siblings making different choices in specification 3 (and using the OLS estimates) implies that men from the same family are 47% more likely to choose a high-paid major than their sisters. If we include all siblings, as in specification 1 (also those making the same choice of major in a family), then brothers are 23% more likely to choose a high-paid major than their sisters. The gap in the overall sample (estimated with OLS and same controls) from Table 4.3 implies that women are 20% less likely to choose highly paid majors than their brothers. Hence the differences across families do not explain any of the significant negative bias of women towards highly paid college majors. That bias is as strong within the average family as it is in the overall sample.

4.5 Gender Gap in Occupational Choice

The last outcome that we can analyze with our data is the occupation of people revealed by the interviews in 2011. We have grouped occupations into 12 groups and the sectors of activity into 8. Then we constructed a grid by occupation and sector of activity and we assigned to each individual the average hourly wage in Italy for that group, in 2011. This is a way of summarizing with one variable the occupation sector choice of an individual, and to capture the wage differential that is associated with differences in occupation sectors. As we are measuring hourly wages, this variable will not include any difference in hours and weeks worked. Hence we expect the variation of this variable and, possibly, of the estimated gender gap, to be smaller than for the actual income. Table 4.7 shows the gender gap in (the log of) wage imputed by sector and occupation. We notice some interesting features, all consistent with the previous findings. First, the occupational wage gender gap is around 6.3% when we do not control for major dummies, and decreases by about a fifth to 5.4% when we do. Hence it is much smaller than the gender gap in logarithmic income. Variation of specific jobs within an occupational category, differences in hours worked across jobs, differences in non-wage income across people: all will contribute to generating the larger variance for income. Second, quite significant and also affecting the gender gap, is the inclusion of the wage of the father (also imputed through the occupation and sector of activity). The occupation of the father is significantly correlated with the occupational choice of the children, and including this variable explains a fifth of the gender gap in occupational wage. A reasonable explanation for this would be that in several professions (lawyer, doctor, accountant, notary), where the intergenerational transmission within the family is common in Italy (see Pellizzari and Orsini, 2012), this takes place more through the

Table 4.7. Gender gap in occupation sector-imputed wage

Dependent Variable:	Imputed Log Wage by Sector & Occupation			
VARIABLES	(1)	(2)	(3)	(4)
Female	−0.063***	−0.054***	−0.052***	−0.045**
	(0.019)	(0.019)	(0.020)	(0.020)
Female X grade	0.018	0.028	0.001	0.013
	(0.037)	(0.036)	(0.040)	(0.040)
HS exit test score	0.042	0.020	0.047	0.028
	(0.030)	(0.030)	(0.033)	(0.033)
Imputed wage of father			0.064***	0.059***
			(0.020)	(0.020)
Father education			−0.005	−0.009
			(0.009)	(0.009)
Mother education			0.007	0.007
			(0.009)	(0.009)
House value in top decile			0.046*	0.034
			(0.028)	(0.027)
House value in bottom decile			0.022	0.022
			(0.021)	(0.020)
School Dummies	X	X	X	X
Year Dummies	X	X	X	X
Major Dummies		X	X	X
Constant	7.448***	7.447***	6.942***	7.006***
	(0.048)	(0.055)	(0.147)	(0.151)
Sample	graduated & interviewed	graduated & interviewed	graduated & interviewed	graduated & interviewed
Observations	1,727	1,727	1,515	1,515
R-squared	0.102	0.145	0.121	0.162

Note: Method of estimation is OLS. The dependent variable is described in the header of the column. Specifications 1 and 2 do not include the family background controls. The reported standard errors in parenthesis are clustered are at school/year level. *** p<0.01, ** p<0.05, * p<0.1.

transmission to the son than to the daughter. In fact, if we also include an interaction of the occupational wage of the father with a female dummy (not reported), the effect is negative (−0.03) and the gender gap loses significance.

The other variable that is significant in determining the occupational income in the sample is the value of real estate in the area where the person lived. We only include a dummy for living in the part of town with the 10% highest value houses, which has a positive effect on occupational wage. We also performed some other regressions (not reported) including a few further controls, such as a dummy for having both working parents, and an interaction of that dummy with the female dummy. These controls do not change the gender gap, nor are they very significant in themselves.

4.6 Conclusions

Using this unique set of micro-data we have documented three very inter-esting and still unexplored features in the gender gap for college-educated Italians, currently in their 30s and 40s. The first is that there is a very significant gender gap in favor of women in all measures of academic performance, beginning in high school and continuing with college. Women show significantly higher exit test scores, higher percentage of graduation from college, lower time to graduation, and higher college grades. Even more interestingly, and in contrast with some of the previous findings but in line with other existing measures of academic performance of Italian men and women, we see that their better performance is not limited to the humanities or classic-oriented topics. Women outperform men also within the Liceo Scientifico and, once in college, they outperform men in each major, including the maths- and science-intensive ones.

The second fact is that the male and female choice of college major is very different. In particular women, somewhat in contrast with their higher academic performance, tend to shun the highly selective and highly paid majors of engineering and business/economics, and this tendency is particularly strong relative to men when their academic quality is very high. Women reveal a preference for the less selective, low-paying majors of humanities.

The third interesting fact is that this remarkable difference in the choice of major more than offsets the advantage that higher academic quality would afford to women in terms of income. It explains one-quarter to one-third of the gender gap in income and, once we correct for hours worked, half of the remaining gap. There are other factors that contribute to the significant gender gap, which may include the continuity of career, discrimination on the job (however, we have seen that there is no evidence of employer discrimination as self-employed women experience almost the same income gap as employees), and differential non-academic skills. The choice of major is still an extremely important component of the gender gap and by far the largest factor among those related to school performance, at least for college graduates.

These findings are novel, and certainly shed light on very important and not yet explored determinants of the gender gap, already arising in choices made in high school and college. In the next chapter we also analyze other yet unexplored determinants of the gender gap in college major choice and labor market income.

Appendix to Chapter 4

Massimo Anelli and Giovanni Peri

4A Description of the Data on Milanese High School Graduates

In this work we present for the first time a unique database collecting information on the high school career, university career, and labor market performance of young Italians who graduated from high school between 1985 and 2005. This dataset involves different sources that have been carefully matched in a complicated merging process. The collection of the database has involved the collaboration of many parties. The help from the following persons and institutions made the collection possible: the directors of the high schools in Milan, the company Ambroscuole, the Provincia di Milano, especially in the person of Dr. Sinnone-Corno, Professor Daniele Checchi (for Universitáy' Stat ale), Professor Carlo Lucifora (for Università Cattolic), Professor Francesco Peri (for Università di Milano, Bicocca), Professors Augusto Sarti and Mauro SantoMauro (for Politechnico di Milano). Divide Malacrino and Francesca Barbiero provided excellent assistance in collecting and organizing the data.

We summarize the sources of the single datasets merged, the information contained in each dataset, and the merging process in figure 4A.1. The diagram representing the merging process must be read from left to right.

The core dataset includes the universe of all high school graduates attending 13 out of 15 college-preparatory schools in the city of Milan between 1985 and 2005 (around 30,550 individuals). Data have been collected manually by inputting the information contained in hard copies of the school records.

The list of the 13 college-preparatory high schools in the city of Milan involved in the data collection process by type of school (classical studies vs. scientific studies) is included in Table 4A.1.

Among the five major universities of Milan involved in the collection of our data three are public universities (Università' degli Studi di Milano, Università' degli Studi di Milano – Bicocca, Politecnico di Milano) and two are private (Università' Bocconi, Università' Cattolica di Milano). The first two public universities mentioned (Università' degli Studi di Milano,

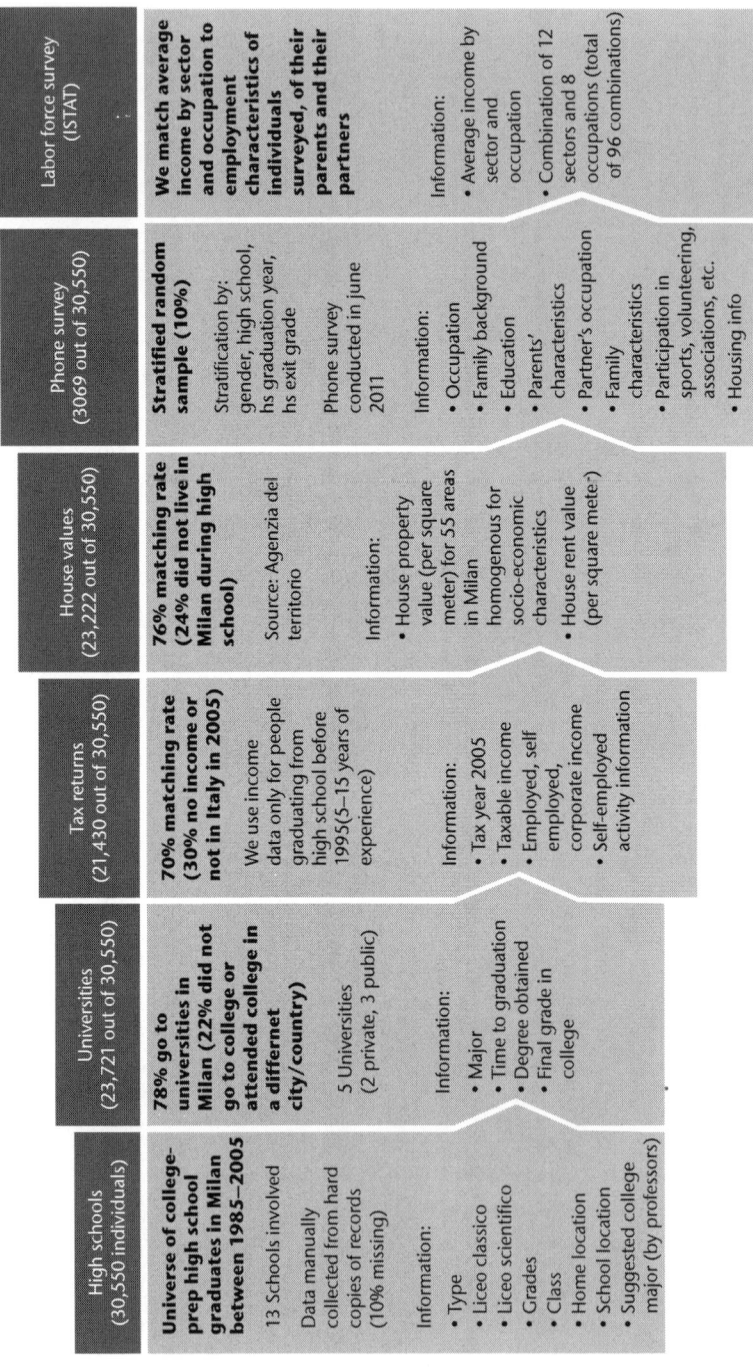

Figure 4A.1 Scheme illustrating the original data and merging process to obtain the final data.

Table 4A.1. List of high school institutions under analysis by type of high school curriculum offered

Liceo Classico (focus on classical studies and humanities)	Liceo Scientifico (focus on math and sciences)
• ISTITUTO LSLR PITAGORA	• DA VINCI
• BECCARIA	• DONATELLI-PASCAL
• BERCHET	• EINSTEIN
• MANZONI	• GALILEI
• OMERO E TITO LIVIO	• MARCONI
• PARINI	• SEVERI
	• VOLTA

Table 4A.2. List of college majors B by field of study as aggregated for this work

Fields of Study	College Majors Aggregated into the Field
Agriculture	Agriculture, Nutrition, Veterinary
Architecture and Design	Architecture, Design
Economics and Business	Economics, Business
Education	Communication Studies, Education, Nursing, Physical Education
Engineering	Engineering
Humanities	Literature, Languages, Philosophy, Cultural Heritage, Art History, Music, History, Archeology
Law	Law Studies
Mathematics and Statistics	Mathematics, Statistics, Physics, Computer Science
Medicine	Medicine
Natural Sciences	Biology, Bio-Technological Sciences, Pharmacy, Environmental Studies, Geology, Natural Science, Chemistry
Social Sciences	Political Sciences, Social Sciences, Sociology, Psychology

Università' degli Studi di Milano – Bicocca) have a very broad offer of majors while Politecnico di Milano offers degrees in engineering, architecture, and design only. Among the private universities Università' Cattolica di Milano has a broad offer of majors comparable with Università' degli Studi di Milano while Università' Bocconi is a school of business, economics and law.

The list of majors offered by universities located in Milan is very large. For our analysis we thus aggregated all these majors in 11 broader "Fields of Study", as described in Table 4A.2.

5

More Unexplored Dimensions of Gender Gap and College Choice: Attitudes, Choice of Partner, and Peer/Teacher Effects in School

Massimo Anelli and Giovanni Peri

5.1 Introduction

In the previous chapter we established that the choice of college major is a crucial determinant of the gender gap in earnings. In this chapter we explore new socioeconomic dimensions determining the choice of major and labor market outcomes and contributing to explain male–female differences. We take advantage of the unique and highly detailed information we collected on student careers through the interview of a 10% random sample to shed light on some previously unexplored motivations for the observed different choice of major. In particular we explore four channels that have been indicated by the recent literature as possible important components of women's decisions and of the gender gap.

First, there is a large recent literature that emphasizes the importance of attitudes (psychological factors) that are not easily measured in standard academic testing on labor market performance. These skills differ between men and women and may contribute significantly to their different choice/preference of major. Bertrand (2010) emphasizes two interesting and important "psychological attributes" that may differ systematically between men and women. The first is the attitude towards competition and the second is the attitude towards others, or altruism. While we do not have direct information on these, we have information on some of the choices made in high school that may indirectly inform us about these attitudes.

Second, we explore the idea that the choice of major not only affects job and career in the labor market, but may also affect the probability of marrying a partner with certain characteristics and income potential. Some majors may signal that an individual (especially a woman) is committed to a more flexible job and hence has a stronger family orientation. This, in a society in which family duties mainly fall to women, can be considered as a desirable feature of a future partner. We evaluate whether men or women choose majors associated systematically with higher expected income of their partner.

Finally we preliminarily investigate the role of high school peers and teachers in affecting the choice of major by women and men. Our database allows us to identify for each individual those in the same class school year (whom we call peers). Moreover, we have information about the college major that was suggested by professors at the end of high school. This information allows us to identify the impact of the gender of peers and of the recommendation by professors regarding the choice of college major by men and women. Several papers have studied the effect of academic quality of peers on the performance and choices of students (e.g. Sacerdote, 2001; Carrell et al., 2011; De Giorgi et al., 2010; Christofides et al., 2012). We focus here on the effect of the gender of peers in the choice of college majors for men and women.

5.2 Sport and Volunteering and Choice of College Major

While the literature on the gender gap has traditionally focused on measures of human capital and of academic quality related to activity in the classroom (as in the previous chapter), recent literature has also emphasized some complementary abilities and attitudes that may explain part of the gender gap in terms of choice of major and labor market performance. One is the attitude of an individual towards competition. As we cannot measure this directly, we posit that people engaged in sport on a regular basis are likely to be more competitive than people not involved in sport or at least they are likely to handle competitive pressure better than those not involved in sporting activity. Activity such as tournaments and official league games exposes young individuals to a competitive environment; hence choosing to practice sport on a regular/competitive basis may reveal that those individuals can better handle competition.[1] Gneezy et al. (2003) and Niederle and Vesterlund (2007, 2010) show in experiments that women tend to underperform when they are in a competitive setting and tend to shy away from competition, while men tend to perform better in competition and to seek competitive arrangements. Some studies (Gneezy et al., 2003) find that women exhibit a performance gap especially when competing against men, while others

---

[1] A recent paper (Stevenson, 2010) estimates the causal effect of sport activity in high school on some measures of performance in college and participation in the labor market, focusing particularly on women. Lacking a clear identification strategy to isolate the effect of sport on subsequent outcomes, however, we take the choice of sport activity in high school as more likely to reveal characteristics of the individual relative to her/his ability to compete.

(Gneezy and Rustichini, 2004) find that the gender gap in performance is highest when children compete with same gender players. Sport is a situation in which individuals compete with others of the same gender.

We would like to explore whether participation in competitive sports in high school is associated with the choice of specific college majors. We interpret practicing sport in high school as a sign of being more competitive, and we check its effect on the choice of highly paid majors (which are usually more competitive). We also explore whether this effect is different for men and women.

Similarly, there is a (mainly experimental) literature that regards the different social preferences of men and women, namely the fact that women are more "socially minded" and more altruistic than men, as another possible source of different choices and different performance in the labor market. In particular college majors such as education, humanities, and social sciences may be associated with higher concern with social goods, while majors such as economics/business and engineering may be associated with a more competitive and selfish view of the world. Several papers (e.g. Andreoni and Versterlund 2001; Eckel and Grossman, 1998) find that in experimental settings women are more willing to give than men. Our data include information about the participation of the student during high school in volunteer activities in charities or similar groups (social and religious). We consider participation in these activities as revealing the altruistic attitudes of individuals, and we analyze whether this is correlated with the choice of major in college, and whether the correlation is different for men and women.

Table 5.1 shows the results of including sport and volunteer dummies in our regressions on the probability of choosing a highly paid major in college. In particular the first two columns report the average marginal effects in a probit regression for the probability of choosing a highly paid major (as defined in the previous chapter and hence including medicine, engineering, economics/business, and law). Columns 3 and 4 show the effects of the same correlates on the choice of a low-paid major (education, humanities, art and design, the three lowest paying majors). Columns 5 and 6 summarize the effects of the correlates on major-imputed wage. For each dependent variable we include one regression that omits the sport and volunteering variables (specifications 1, 3, and 5) but includes the other individual characteristics, including the female dummy, and one specification that includes the sport and volunteer dummies (2, 4, and 6). Column 7 controls for the choice of major and analyzes any additional effect (not through the choice of major) of sport and volunteering on income in 2005. Finally Column 8 considers the correlation between the explanatory variables, including the sport and volunteering dummies, and the probability of employment.

Table 5.1. Sport and volunteering and choice of college major

Specification Method	(1) Probit	(2) Probit	(3) Probit	(4) Probit	(5) OLS	(6) OLS	(7) OLS	(8) OLS
Dependent Variable	High Paid Major = 1		Low Paid Major = 1		Log of wage imputed by major		Log of actual wage	Employed = 1
Female	-0.146*** (0.033)	-0.158*** (0.036)	0.084** (0.033)	0.106*** (0.037)	-0.111*** (0.020)	-0.128*** (0.023)	-0.172 (0.123)	-0.003 (0.023)
Fem X HS Grade	-0.111* (0.065)	-0.124* (0.065)	0.159** (0.069)	0.168** (0.070)	-0.054 (0.041)	-0.062 (0.041)	-0.214 (0.190)	-0.039 (0.040)
HS Grade	0.219*** (0.049)	0.232*** (0.049)	-0.174*** (0.055)	-0.184*** (0.056)	0.114*** (0.029)	0.122*** (0.030)	0.275** (0.131)	0.043* (0.024)
Sport		0.055* (0.031)		-0.017 (0.035)		0.024 (0.020)	0.274*** (0.087)	-0.008 (0.018)
Sport X Fem		-0.020 (0.052)		-0.029 (0.046)		0.010 (0.031)	-0.228 (0.153)	0.006 (0.033)
Volunteering		-0.066** (0.029)		0.062** (0.026)		-0.058*** (0.018)	-0.121 (0.084)	0.013 (0.017)
Volunt X Fem		0.076* (0.042)		-0.065* (0.034)		0.060** (0.027)	-0.060 (0.119)	-0.012 (0.022)
Family controls	X	X	X	X	X	X	X	X
Year Dummies	X	X	X	X	X	X	X	X
School Dummies	X	X	X	X	X	X	X	X
Major Dummies					X	X	X	
Constant					9.913*** (0.167)	9.936*** (0.166)	9.796*** (0.787)	0.790*** (0.152)
Sample	10% Random Sample of Graduates Interviewed							
Observations	2,261	2,261	2,261	2,261	2,261	2,261	1,234	2,261
R-squared					0.105	0.109	0.162	0.184

Note: Dependent variable in each regression is specified at the top of the column. The method of estimation is probit for specification 1–4 and OLS for the remaining specifications. Standard errors clustered at school/year level in parenthesis. The sample includes those individuals among the high school graduates who enrolled in college and have been interviewed in 2011. Family controls: father wage, father education, mother education. *** $p < 0.01$, ** $p < 0.05$, * $p < 0.1$.

The findings in Table 5.1 are very interesting and in large part consistent with the interpretation that highly paid majors are chosen with higher probability by individuals who are more competitive (practice sport regularly) and less altruistic (do not volunteer in charities). In all specifications we control for high school test score, a gender dummy, and the interaction of gender and test score, and we also include the controls for father's wage (imputed from his occupation and sector of activity), father's education, and mother's education. The coefficient on the sport dummy is positive on the probability of entering a high-paid major (Column 2). We also find a negative (and not significant) effect of the sport dummy on the probability of choosing a low-paid major. Conversely, being involved in volunteering activities has a positive and significant correlation with the choice of low-paid majors and a negative and significant correlation with the choice of high-paid majors. The combination of these two effects on major-imputed wage is shown in Column 6 and implies a positive but not significant effect of doing sport and a negative and significant effect of volunteering on that wage.

Interestingly, those effects on the choice of major are attenuated for women. Estimates regarding the interaction between the women dummy and the sport dummy reveal that the effect of participating in sport activities has less of an effect on choosing a high-paid major for women. Even stronger is the attenuation of the effect of volunteering for women. Women involved in volunteering in high school were not more likely to choose a low-paid major than women who did not. Adding the main effect and the interaction with women gives an effect of volunteering on the probability of choosing a high-paid or a low-paid major that is not significantly different from 0. Hence while sport and volunteering seem to be significantly associated with (respectively) higher and lower probability of choosing a highly-paid major and lower (and higher) probability of choosing a low-paid major, this correlation is significant only for men. Moreover, the estimate of the gender gap is statistically the same with and without these controls for all the outcomes analyzed in Columns 1–6.

It is also interesting to consider the correlation of sport and volunteering with the income of individuals, after we control for college major. Possibly the qualities revealed by participating in those activities have an impact on job performance, beyond the choice of major. Column 7 shows the effects of sport and volunteering in high school on income in 2005, once we control for college major. Hence these estimates capture the additional positive (or negative) effect on income associated with involvement in sport and volunteering, not channeled through the choice of college major. The only significant additional effect is a positive effect of sport on income, even controlling for college major. In fact the point estimate of this effect is quite large (equal to a difference of 27% between those who were and those who were not involved in sport). Moreover this effect only applies to men, as for women the effect (sum of the main effect and of the interaction) is not significantly different from 0. The competitive edge seems to help men (possibly with their choice of occupations) but not women in the labor market. Finally, in Column 8 we see whether sport and volunteering affect the employment probability of individuals in our sample. Given the very high participation rate of this sample there is no discernible effect of volunteering and sport on being employed.

5.3 Expected Partner Income and Marriage as Determinants of College Major

The choice of college major by women in our sample is hard to rationalize if we consider expected future income as their only motivation and academic ability as their constraint. In fact, women reveal a systematic strong preference against the choice of high-paid majors even while they exhibit higher academic quality.

An alternative explanation is that women value different outcomes from men when choosing a major. They possibly give lower weight to the monetary income that can be accessed after graduation and higher weight to other features of the college major. In Chapter 1 we emphasized that women value flexibility in their occupation, and the US data show that women are much more likely to choose majors that give access to an occupation where a large number of individuals are employed part time. This is likely because women, especially in their 30s and 40s, attribute high value to spending time with the family (see also the results in Chapter 3).

Here we consider a family-related motivation that would be perfectly in line with women maximizing income of their future household rather than their own. One possibility for the choice of major is that, while not paying high wages, enrolling and graduating from a low-paying major could increase the probability that a woman finds a partner; or choosing low-paid college majors may increase the expected income of the future partner. Given the preference of females for low-paid majors this story would be true only if there is an "assortative matching" in terms of majors on the marriage market. That is, if women in majors characterized as "typically female" (and low paid) have a higher probability of marrying high-earning men, from typically male majors. In such a case a rational choice for a woman could be to trade off her wage for the wage of the potential partner. This could happen if men consider the choice of a low-paid major by a woman, especially if she has high academic quality, as a signal of her commitment to the family. If men with higher potential income prefer to marry women with a stronger commitment to the family (guaranteeing a higher quality life for the children), then there could actually be assortative matching.

Table 5.2. Choice of college major, probability of marriage, and income of the partner

	Women		Men	
Specification	(1)	(2)	(3)	(4)
Method	Probit	OLS	Probit	OLS
Dependent Variable	Married = 1	Log wage of partner	Married = 1	Log wage of partner
HS Grade	−0.044	0.049*	0.031	−0.022
	(0.047)	(0.027)	(0.052)	(0.030)
Father wage	0.082*	0.111***	0.038	0.054
	(0.048)	(0.025)	(0.050)	(0.034)
Father education	−0.042*	0.023*	0.005	0.035*
	(0.023)	(0.013)	(0.023)	(0.018)
Mother education	0.032	0.130***	0.014	0.119***
	(0.020)	(0.014)	(0.021)	(0.016)
High-paid major=1	0.011	−0.008	0.046	0.027
	(0.037)	(0.020)	(0.032)	(0.020)
Low-paid major=1	0.001	−0.029	−0.003	0.016
	(0.037)	(0.019)	(0.041)	(0.023)
Year Dummies	X	X	X	X
School Dummies	X	X	X	X
Constant		6.008***		6.465***
		(0.190)		(0.234)
Sample	Enrolled & Interviewed	Enrolled & Interviewed	Enrolled & Interviewed	Enrolled & Interviewed
Observations	1,153	703	1,041	643
R-squared		0.365		0.263

Note: Dependent variable in each regression is specified at the top of the column. The method of estimation is probit for specification 1 and 3 and OLS for specifications 2 and 4. Standard errors clustered at school/year level in parenthesis. The sample includes those individuals among the high school graduates who enrolled in college and have been interviewed in 2011. Family controls: father wage, father education, mother education. *** $p < 0.01$, ** $p < 0.05$, * $p < 0.1$.

In order for this to be the case, we should observe three facts that would be consequences of this type of matching. First, women who have chosen low-paying majors should have a higher probability of being married (controlling for age, school, and individual characteristics). Second, conditional on being married, women who chose low-paying majors should marry men earning higher incomes. Third, there should be a positive female–male gap, controlling for other features, in the partner wage predicted by the major; namely, in order to offset the negative gender gap in major-imputed wages, women should have a positive gender gap in major-imputed partner wage.

Columns 1 and 3 of Table 5.2 show the average marginal effects on the probability of being married in 2011 (probit regression) of individual controls (including parents' education, father's wage, and high school grade) and of the high- and low-paid major dummies. Column 1 is limited to women and Column 3 to men. Then Columns 2 and 4 show the correlation, separately by

Table 5.3. Testing "assortative" matching in marriage

Specification	(1)	(2)	(3)	(4)
Dependent Variable		Log wage of partner imputed by major		
Female	−0.005***	−0.005**	−0.004	−0.006
	(0.001)	(0.002)	(0.003)	(0.007)
Fem X HS Grade		−0.001	−0.001	−0.002
		(0.004)	(0.005)	(0.005)
HS Grade		0.008***	0.007*	0.007*
		(0.003)	(0.003)	(0.003)
Father wage			−0.001	−0.001
			(0.002)	(0.002)
Father education			0.001	0.002
			(0.001)	(0.001)
Mother education			0.004***	0.003**
			(0.001)	(0.002)
Mother educ X Fem				0.001
				(0.002)
Father educ X Fem				−0.000
				(0.002)
Year Dummies	X	X	X	X
School Dummies	X	X	X	X
Constant	7.335***	7.331***	7.321***	7.321***
	(0.005)	(0.005)	(0.017)	(0.017)
Sample		10% Random Sample of Graduates Interviewed		
	1,514	1,514	1,346	1,346
	0.047	0.055	0.078	0.078

Note: Dependent variable in each regression is the logarithm of major-imputed wage of the partner. The method of estimation is OLS. Standard errors clustered at school/year level in parenthesis. The sample includes those individuals among the high school graduates who enrolled in college and have been interviewed in 2011. Family controls: father wage, father education, mother education. *** $p < 0.01$, ** $p < 0.05$, * $p < 0.1$.

gender, between the same explanatory variables and the expected income of the partner (imputed from his/her occupation/sector of activity).

The results do not support at all a theory of assortative matching in marriage, nor the idea that women increase their probability of marrying highly paid men by choosing low-paid majors. In fact the probability of marriage and the average income of the partner are not correlated to the choice of a low-paid major at all. Mother's education and father's education seem both to be correlated with higher income of the spouse, and interestingly, the academic quality of women (as measured by high school grade) has a positive effect on the expected income of the husband (suggesting homogeneous matching).

Table 5.3 is a further test that assortative matching in the marriage (in terms of income) is not a plausible explanation for the preference of women for low-paid majors. In that table we consider, for each major, the expected income of the partner. Then we regress it on the academic quality of the individual and on his/her background and family characteristics. If assortative matching is at work then a positive gender gap, namely women choosing majors that increase the probability of marrying a partner with higher income (relative to the choice of men). The four specifications of Table 5.3, which include progressively more background controls, do not support that idea. In fact women tend to choose majors with a lower predicted average income of the partner, relative to men, although the effect is small (0.5 logarithmic points). The effect is not significantly different from 0 when controlling for family background.

While concerns for the family can certainly enter the choice of major, improving the probability of getting married or increasing the expected income of the spouse does not seem to be what drives that choice.[2]

5.4 Peer Gender, Teacher's Recommendation, and Choice of College Major

Two other important and mostly unexplored determinants in the choice of college major are peer pressure and recommendations provided by high school teachers. Women may attach a larger weight to the opinion and choices of their peers and of their teachers. Or, driven by stereotypes, teachers may disproportionately suggest low-paid majors to women. In the analyzed Milanese high schools teachers were overwhelmingly women, potentially biased in suggesting low-paying majors to high-quality female students, and thereby contributing to a perpetuation of the bias. Several studies have shown relevant peer effects on several student outcomes. Sacerdote (2001) finds effects of randomly matched roommates (in Dartmouth) on the grade average and the probability of joining fraternities. He does not find any evidence of peer effect on choice of major, however. De Giorgi et al. (2010) find a significant effect of randomly assigned classmates in first-year college courses on the choice of major Bocconi University (one of the universities in our Milanese sample). Carrell et al. (2011) find a causal effect of peers on the level of physical fitness of US Air Force academy students and on their school performance. Christofides et al. (2012) exploit Canadian data and find that high school peers have a significant impact on both high school educational outcomes and on the probability of aspiring to and attending college. Neither of those studies focuses specifically on the gender dimension of peer effects.

Our data and our settings are ideal for identifying peer effects. First of all we can identify individuals belonging to the same class in high school. Second,

[2] Let us also notice that the fertility rate of women in our sample is very low. In general women in northern Italy have had among the lowest fertility rates in the world. The average number of children per woman in 2011, covering an age range between 29 and 45, was 0.71; the median number of children was one.

Table 5.4. Is class male ratio correlated with pre-determined characteristics?

Specification Variables	(1) Class Male ratio	(2) Class Male ratio
Class % in bottom 10% house value	−0.042 (0.052)	
Class % in top 10% house value	0.009 (0.055)	
Class mean house value		0.080 (0.053)
Class mean distance from school	−0.005 (0.004)	−0.004 (0.004)
Constant	0.424*** (0.012)	−0.229 (0.434)
Observations	1,160	1,160
R-squared	0.618	0.618
School/Year FE	X	X

Note: The dependent variable is the share of male in each class. The units of observations are classes within school year. The method of estimation is OLS. Standard errors are clustered at school/year level in parenthesis. *** p < 0.01, ** p < 0.05, * p < 0.1.

the gender composition of a class is plausibly exogenous as it is affected by many random events. Third, a class in an Italian high school is a set of students who share an identical choice of courses, with the same professors for five years. Hence students in the same class are exposed for a long period to mutual interactions at an age (14 to 18) in which peers are very important. We will analyze whether the gender composition of the class affected the choice of college major. While we cannot identify a peer effect in the choice of major, in the sense that we cannot identify if it was the choice of major itself or other features of the peers that affected choice, we can identify the final effect of the gender ratio in a class on the probability of choosing a highly paid major.

In our analysis we control for fixed effects at the school/year level and for fixed teacher effects (the most relevant types of common shocks), and, crucially, we can exploit the random distribution of gender composition across cohorts over time, in order to differentiate the effect of the male proportion in the class from common school/year shocks (and teacher effects) on the choice of major.

Table 5.4 reports the tests of randomness of the proportion of males across classes in our sample. In specification 1 we regress this ratio on the percentage of people living in rich districts of Milan (with houses in the top 10% of the value distribution) and on the percentage of people living in poor districts of Milan (with houses in the bottom 10% of the value distribution). Lacking information on family income for the students, the value of their house is a good proxy. We also include school by year fixed effects to test only within the school/year variation. The coefficients on the explanatory variables are not significant, showing no evidence that the gender ratio of a class is related to income or family status variables (predetermined characteristics). In specification 2 we enter directly the average student house value for the class and the average distance from school for the class. Again we do not find any evidence of a correlation between gender ratio and these variables. Hence we consider it plausible that the gender composition of a class is simply the result of sampling variation.

As the gender of a person affects dramatically his/her choice of major, we analyze here if the gender of peers, who spend five years together as students, may also affect his/her choice of major. Male peers are more likely to choose highly paid majors, but they also create a more competitive environment for women in the class and possibly encourage gender stereotypes in the iden-tification of male and female students. Would this encourage or discourage women from choosing highly paid majors? Would the effect of more male classmates be different for men and women? And ultimately, would these peer effects contribute to explain the very different choices made by men and women? Table 5.5 shows the results of regressions performed to shed light on these questions.

In Column 1 we simply add the share of male classmates as explanatory variable[3] to the standard specification (as in Table 4.3) in the choice of highly paid majors (dummy). We estimate the effect using OLS. The standard errors are, as usual, clustered at the school/year level. This specification does not reveal a significant effect of the proportion of males on the probability of choosing a highly paid major. However, Column 2, in which we split the effect of the proportion of males in the class between a main effect on males and an additional effect on women reveals a very interesting pattern. The percentage of males in a class increases significantly the probability of males choosing a highly paid major by 12 percentage points (as the main effect is positive and significant). For women the additional effect essentially offsets the main effect, so their probability of choosing a highly paid major is not affected, on average, by the presence of male classmates. This may reveal that women do not feel the pressure of their class mates, while men are pushed to imitate each other in a competitive class environment. Also interestingly, this behavior of males, reinforcing each other in the choice of highly paid major, while female are not affected by peer gender, explains more than a quarter of the Male–female gender gap in choice of highly paid major, as the estimate of the female dummy coefficient decreases from −0.22 to −0.16 in percentage points. Notice, finally, that higher grades in high school are associated with a higher probability of choosing a highly paid major and that coming from a rich home (measured by the value of the house) increases marginally the probability of

---

[3] The share of male classmates is calculated as the number of male classmates (except the individual) divided by the total number of people in the class (excluding the individual).

Table 5.5. Major choice and percentage of male peers in high school class

Dependent variable: Highly paid major = 1

Specification Variables	(1)	(2)	(3)	(4)	(5)	(6)	(7)
Female	-0.223***	-0.165***	-0.159***	-0.169***	-0.164***	-0.168***	-0.161***
	(0.009)	(0.028)	(0.029)	(0.028)	(0.029)	(0.028)	(0.029)
%male	0.057	0.121***	0.060	0.120***	0.060	0.086*	0.028
	(0.035)	(0.045)	(0.048)	(0.045)	(0.047)	(0.045)	(0.048)
%male X female		-0.125**	-0.136**	-0.116**	-0.128**	-0.116**	-0.130**
		(0.056)	(0.057)	(0.056)	(0.057)	(0.055)	(0.056)
%male X (grade90-100 = 1)			0.295***		0.292***		0.283***
			(0.076)		(0.076)		(0.077)
female X (grade90-100 = 1)			-0.015		-0.015		-0.022
			(0.055)		(0.056)		(0.057)
%male X fem X (grade90-100 = 1)			0.033		0.034		0.045
			(0.109)		(0.109)		(0.112)
grade70-80 = 1	0.072***	0.072***	0.073***	0.073***	0.074***	0.072***	0.072***
	(0.010)	(0.010)	(0.010)	(0.010)	(0.010)	(0.010)	(0.010)
grade80-90 = 1	0.143***	0.143***	0.143***	0.144***	0.145***	0.142***	0.143***
	(0.012)	(0.012)	(0.012)	(0.012)	(0.012)	(0.012)	(0.012)
grade90-100 = 1	0.196***	0.196***	0.058	0.197***	0.060	0.197***	0.065
	(0.014)	(0.014)	(0.042)	(0.014)	(0.042)	(0.014)	(0.043)
House value in top 10%	0.024*	0.025*	0.024*	0.025*	0.024*	0.025**	0.024*
	(0.013)	(0.013)	(0.013)	(0.013)	(0.013)	(0.013)	(0.013)

Table 5.5. *(Continued)*

Dependent variable: Highly paid major = 1

Specification Variables	(1)	(2)	(3)	(4)	(5)	(6)	(7)
House value in bot 10%	-0.006	-0.006	-0.005	-0.007	-0.006	-0.008	-0.007
	(0.012)	(0.012)	(0.012)	(0.012)	(0.012)	(0.012)	(0.012)
Constant	0.564***	0.532***	0.559***	0.039	0.048	0.039***	0.050**
	(0.043)	(0.045)	(0.045)	(0.070)	(0.069)	(0.019)	(0.020)
Observations	17,528	17,528	17,528	17,528	17,528	17,528	17,528
R-squared	0.094	0.095	0.096	0.098	0.100	0.105	0.106
Sample	Enrolled	Enrolled	Enrolled	Enrolled	Enrolled	Enrolled	Enrolled
School X Year FE	X	X	X	X	X	X	X
School X Section FE	X	X	X				
School X Section X 10 years FE				X	X		
School X Section X 5 years FE						X	X

Note: Dependent variable is a dummy equal to 1 for choosing a highly paid major. The method of estimation is OLS. Standard errors are clustered at school/year level in parenthesis, *** p < 0.01, ** p < 0.05, * p < 0.1.

choosing a highly paid major. Column 3 of Table 5.5 further decomposes the heterogeneity of the effect of male peers, by interacting the percentage of males with a dummy for having a grade in the exit test at the top of the distribution (between the score of 90 and 100) and with that dummy plus the female dummy. The results show that most of the positive effect of male peers in pushing the choice of highly paid majors is on high-quality students. A top student is 29% more likely to choose a high-paid college major in a class with all males than in one with all females, controlling for everything else. Women, on average, even exhibit a negative effect of the share of male classmates on their probability of choosing a highly paid major (adding the main effect and the interaction with women we get an effect equal to −7.6 percentage points when going from all male to all female classmates). However, for women at the top of the ability distribution, the presence of men increases their probability to choose highly paid majors (although not as much as for men). Columns 4 and 5 and Columns 6 and 7 reproduce the regressions in 2 and 3 with more demanding fixed effects that control for section by decade and section by five-year effects, so as to absorb the effect of a gradual turnover of teachers over time. All the specifications confirm the effects found in 2 and 3. Namely, the share of male peers increases significantly the probability of male students, especially those of high academic quality, choosing a highly paid major. Also, on average a higher percentage of male peers will leave unchanged or decrease the probability that a woman chooses a highly paid major.

Finally, in Table 5.6 we estimate specifications similar to those in Table 5.5 but including a dummy variable equal to 1 if the recommendation of the teachers at the end of high school was to enroll in a highly paid major. We obtain this variable from the high school records. Only if there is an explicit recommendation (which is present in about 46% of the cases) and such recommendation is for one or more of the four highly paid majors (medicine, engineering, economics/business, and law) do we code it as 1. Otherwise we code it as a 0.

First, let us note that the variable has a very large and extremely significant coefficient in all specifications (first row of Table 5.6). Teachers' suggestions contain information on the skills of the student and may be very influential when the student decides on a college major. Second, we may also see that the recommendations themselves have a huge gender bias, in the sense that after controlling for academic quality (test score) teachers are much more likely to recommend a highly paid major to men than to women. While 56% of men are recommended a highly paid major by teachers, only 36% of women are (this bias is not reported). Finally, while including the teacher recommendation does not much change the size of the male peer effects, which is still positive on high-quality males, negative on average women, and close to 0 for average men, this variable reduces further the gender gap

Table 5.6. Effects of teacher recommendation on the choice of highly paid major

Dependent variable: Highly paid major = 1

Specification Variables	(1)	(2)	(3)	(4)	(5)	(6)	(7)
Teacher suggested highly paid major = 1	0.412*** (0.013)	0.412*** (0.013)	0.411*** (0.013)	0.413*** (0.013)	0.412*** (0.013)	0.415*** (0.013)	0.414*** (0.013)
Female	−0.144*** (0.011)	−0.084*** (0.032)	−0.085*** (0.032)	−0.083*** (0.031)	−0.083*** (0.032)	−0.076** (0.030)	−0.076** (0.031)
%male	0.057 (0.038)	0.119*** (0.045)	0.059 (0.049)	0.117** (0.046)	0.057 (0.050)	0.103** (0.050)	0.044 (0.054)
%male X female		−0.125** (0.062)	−0.122* (0.063)	−0.126** (0.062)	−0.124* (0.063)	−0.135** (0.060)	−0.134** (0.061)
%male X (grade90−100 = 1)			0.277*** (0.077)		0.270*** (0.078)		0.263*** (0.079)
female X (grade90−100 = 1)			0.004 (0.057)		0.003 (0.058)		−0.002 (0.059)
%male X fem X (grade90−100 = 1)			−0.022 (0.116)		−0.016 (0.117)		−0.009 (0.119)
grade70−80 = 1	0.023** (0.011)	0.023** (0.011)	0.023** (0.011)	0.023** (0.011)	0.023** (0.011)	0.021** (0.011)	0.022** (0.011)
grade80−90 = 1	0.082*** (0.013)	0.082*** (0.013)	0.082*** (0.013)	0.082*** (0.013)	0.082*** (0.013)	0.080*** (0.013)	0.080*** (0.013)
grade90−100 = 1	0.162*** (0.014)	0.162*** (0.014)	0.032 (0.042)	0.162*** (0.014)	0.035 (0.042)	0.161*** (0.014)	0.038 (0.043)
House value in top 10%	0.027* (0.014)	0.028* (0.014)	0.026* (0.014)	0.030** (0.014)	0.028** (0.014)	0.030* (0.014)	0.028** (0.014)
House value in bottom 10%	−0.008 (0.013)	−0.008 (0.013)	−0.006 (0.013)	−0.010 (0.013)	−0.008 (0.013)	−0.011 (0.013)	−0.009 (0.013)

	(1)	(2)	(3)	(4)	(5)	(6)	(7)
Constant	0.394***	0.362***	0.391***	0.019	0.040	0.796***	0.804***
	(0.045)	(0.048)	(0.050)	(0.032)	(0.033)	(0.026)	(0.026)
Observations	12,740	12,740	12,740	12,740	12,740	12,740	12,740
R-squared	0.245	0.246	0.247	0.251	0.252	0.256	0.257
Sample	Enrolled	Enrolled	Enrolled	Enrolled	Enrolled	Enrolled	Enrolled
School X Year FE	X	X	X	X	X	X	X
School X Section FE	X	X	X	X		X	
School X Section X 10 years FE			X	X			
School X Section X 5 years FE					X		X

Note: Dependent variable is a dummy equal to 1 for choosing a highly paid major. The method of estimation is OLS. Standard errors are clustered at school/year level in parenthesis, *** $p < 0.01$, ** $p < 0.05$, * $p < 0.1$.

in the choice of highly paid major (to around 8%). Hence another quarter of the gender bias in the choice of major is "explained" by (or at least correlated with) gender bias in the teachers' recommendations. The gender (usually female) and degree (usually a low-paid major) of most high school teachers may explain why they suggest highly paid majors less frequently to women. This shows that high school teachers and their education may help to perpetuate the choice of low-paying majors for women, as teachers recommend majors such as education, humanities, and art rather than engineering or economics to high-quality women.

5.5 Policy Implications and Discussion

The chapters in the first part of the book have examined in great detail determinants of the labor market gender gap, some of which were previously largely unexplored. We learned about the role of discrimination, family, college major choice, and high school environment in a detailed and new way by using new methods and new data. These findings should be relevant in discussing and recommending policies that may address the issue of the gender gap in income and labor market outcomes. First, the gender gap in income and earnings still exists and it is particularly large in Spain and Italy, among the analyzed countries. Second, more schooling and education are not, per se, a solution to this problem: women are highly educated in all analyzed countries but the earning gender gap is as large among college educated as among other workers. In fact even among the highest educated (see Chapter 2) a large part of the gender gap may be due to discrimination. Third, the choice of college major (analyzed in Chapter 4) and early family and career choices (analyzed in Chapter 3) are responsible for a very large part of the gap. The fact that women shy away from math intensive highly paid college majors and then choose (or are forced) to put on hold their career to attend to family needs may be the largest causes of earning differentials. Fourth, focusing on the evidence presented in the last two chapters and based on the Italian case, women seem to have high academic quality, even in science and math-intensive curricula. They simply choose math-intensive/highly paid majors such as engineering and economics/business far less frequently. Fifth, it appears that, especially for women of high academic quality, lack of information and the perpetuation of social norms, also through teachers' recommendation of college majors, may be part of the reason for a suboptimal (from an economic point of view) choice of major. The very strong effect of teacher recommendations, which are biased in favor of majors such as education, classics, and art for women, can be another sign that social norms, pushing women into some occupations, are very persistent.

In the light of these results we briefly discuss three potential policies that could change women's choice of major. First, and least expensive, high school teachers (both male and female) should be educated on the importance of recommending highly paid majors to women, especially those with high academic achievements. At the very least they should provide more information and a more gender-neutral approach to recommending college majors to high-achieving men and women. Alternatively, high school teachers should be selected in larger part from those individuals with a math-intensive and science-intensive background. The college-preparatory high school curriculum should also be shifted towards more science and math.

Second, as peers may have an impact on the choice of major, especially on high-achieving students, it may be important to delay the tracking of students into specialized schools until later, when the students have a better idea of and more information about the job they would like to do. In the Anglo-Saxon system students remain in a single track until the end of high school, and then even at university they share most courses until they choose their major during the second year. This implies that when they choose their major they have benefited from observing diverse peers and may have learned valuable information about highly paid majors. In Italian schools, instead, a large proportion of high-achieving women are tracked in the Liceo Classico from the age of 12, and they mostly observe the major choice of other women.

Third, as women may value other things besides expected wages, providing more information on the math-intensive majors and giving incentives and rewards to choose them could push some of the high-achieving women towards them. For instance there could be fellowships for women with high exit test scores from high school who choose to undertake a highly paid math-intensive college major; or universities with math-intensive college majors could make an effort to reach out to high-quality women, by setting aside some places for them only (if there are an entry test and a fixed number of places). Both policies would be preferable to simple prizes based on high school exit test, because they combine an academic incentive (to do well in high school) with an incentive to choose highly paid (and highly productive) college majors. More simply, policies that create a larger flow of information between women studing highly paid majors (or who have graduated from them) and women in high school, or with teachers in high school, should also be encouraged. Tutoring of high-achieving female students in high school by women in highly paid college majors could also be successful.

5.6 Conclusions

In this chapter we have explored the potential determinants of college major choice that are in turn crucial determinants of the earning gap between men and women. We have identified and analyzed four factors that the previous literature has suggested are possibly relevant in determining the gender gap, but no empirical study has explored for lack of data. The first is the fact that women and men have different psychological attitudes towards competition and altruism. Being less competitive and more altruistic may generate a preference in women that drives them to more socially oriented majors (education, social sciences) and less towards profit-oriented ones (engineering, business). Regression analysis uses participation in sports and in volunteer activity during high school as revealing whether a person is more altruistic or more competitive. We find that involvement in sport and no involvement in volunteering are predictors of a higher probability of enrolling in a high-paid major. This relationship is much stronger for men than for women. Hence the psychological explanation goes part of the way to explain the different choice of majors.

Then we consider the possibility that women may choose a major because of its effect on the probability of marriage and on the average income of the spouse. Our results do not support this explanation, because we find that choosing a low-paid major neither increases the probability of marriage for women (given other characteristics) nor affects the expected income of the future spouse.

Finally we explore the possibility that women are affected by the gender of their peers in high school and by the recommendation of college major given by their teachers in high school. We find some evidence that male students are more likely to choose high-paid majors if they attended classes with a large male proportion. For women, however, there is a smaller effect; their choice of college major is less affected by class gender composition. We also find that the recommendation of college majors by teachers (which is very gender-based) has a very strong impact on student choice.

Overall, our attempts to explain the income gender gap for highly educated women in Italy, and even to study the gender gap in their choice of major, have explained only between one-third and one-half of the difference. While we think this is a very relevant portion, we also acknowledge that culture and possibly prejudice (which we saw in Chapter 2 is also important in determining the gender gap in the US) may still play important roles. In particular by directing women towards family roles early in their career and hence to a choice of major that leads to jobs where human capital does not depreciate and are possibly easier to combine with childrearing, the culture and tradition of countries such as Spain and Italy may still play a very important role in maintaining the gender gap. Only slowly and with time, and with the help of forward-looking parents and teachers, will the college and career choices of young Italian and Spanish highly educated women progressively increase their opportunities vis-à-vis their male colleagues.

Part I References

Albanesi, S. and Olivetti, C. (2006). "Gender and dynamic agency: Theory and evidence on the compensation of female top executives," Department of Economics, Boston University Working Paper No. 2006-061.

Albrecht, J., Björklund, A., and Vroman, S. (2003), "Is there a glass ceiling in Sweden?," *Journal of Labor Economics* 21/1: 145–177.

Altonji, J. G. and Blank, R. M. (1999). "Race and gender in the labor market." In: O. C. Ashenfelter and D. Card(Eds.), *Handbook of Labor Economics*, vol. 3. Amsterdam: Elsevier, pp. 3143–3259.

Andreoni, J. and Vesterlund, L. (2001). "Which is the fair sex? Gender differences in altruism," *Quarterly Journal of Economics* 116 (1): 293–312.

Angrist, J. and Pischke, J-S. (2009). *Mostly Harmless Econometrics: An Empiricist's Companion.* Princeton, NJ: Princeton University Press.

Arulampalam, W., Booth, A. L., and Bryan, M. L. (2007). "Is there a glass ceiling over Europe? Exploring the gender wage gap across the wage distribution," *Industrial Labor Relation Review* 60/2: 163–186.

Becker, G. (1971), *The Economics of Discrimination.* Chicago: The University of Chicago Press. (First ed. 1957).

Becker, G. S., Hubbard, W. H., and Murphy, K. (2010). "Explaining the worldwide boom in higher education of women," *Journal of Human Capita* 4/3: 203–241.

Beffy, M., Fougère, D., and Maurel, A. (2009). "Choosing the field of study in post-secondary education: Do expected earnings matter?," IZA Discussion Paper No. 4127.

Bertrand, M. (2010). "New perspectives on gender." In: O. C. Ashenfelter and D. Card (Eds.), *Handbook of Labor Economics*, vol. 4b. Amsterdam: Elsevier, pp. 1543–1590.

Bertrand, M. and Hallock, K. (2001). "The gender gap in the top corporate jobs," *Industrial and Labor Relations Review* 55/1: 3–21.

Blau, F. and Kahn, L. (2006). "The US gender pay gap in the 1990s: Slowing convergence," *Industrial and Labor Relations Review*, 60(1).

Blau, F. D. and Kahn, L. M. (2008). "Women's work and wages." In: S. N. Durlauf and L. E. Blume (Eds.), *The New Palgrave Dictionary of Economics*, second ed. Oxford: Palgrave Macmillan.

Bowlus, A. and Eckstein, Z. (2002). "Discrimination and skill differences in an equilibrium search model," *International Economic Review* 43/4: 1309–1345.

Brown, C. and Corcoran, M. (1997). "Sex based differences in school content and the male-female wage gap," *Quarterly Journal of Economics* 99: 31–44.

Burda, M., Daniel H., and Philippe W. (2008). "The distribution of total work in the EU and USA." In: T. Boeri, M. Burda, and F. Kramarz (Eds.), *Working Hours and Job*

Sharing in the EU and USA: Are Americans Crazy? Are Europeans Lazy?. New York: Oxford University Press, pp. 11–100.

Carrell, S. E., Hoekstra, M., and West, J. E. (2011). "Is poor fitness contagious? Evidence from randomly assigned friends," *Journal of Public Economics* 95/7–8: 657–663.

Charles, K, K. and Gurian, J. (2008). "Prejudice and wages: Anempirical assessment of Becker's 'The Economics of Discrimination'," *Journal of Political Economy* 116/5: 773–809.

Charles, K. K, Gurian, J., and Pan, J. (2010). "A woman's place: The role of sexism on labor market and non labor market outcomes," University of Chicago Working Paper.

Chevalier, A. (2011). "Subject choice and earnings of UK graduates," IZA Discussion Paper No. 5652.

Chiappori, P.-A., Iyigun, M., and Weiss, Y. (2009). "Investment in schooling and the marriage market," *American Economic Review* 99/5, 1689–1713.

Christofides, L. N., Hoy, M., Milla, J., and Stengos, T. (2012). "The implication of peer and parental influences on university attendance: A gender comparison," Department of Economics, University of Guelph Working Papers No. 1201.

Christofides, L. N., Polycarpou, A., and Vrachimis, K. (2010). "The gender wage gaps, 'sticky floors' and 'glass ceilings' of the European Union," IZA Discussion Paper No. 5044.

De Giorgi, G., Pellizzari, M., and Redaelli, S. (2010). "Identification of social interactions through partially overlapping peer groups," *American Economic Journal: Applied Economics* 2/2: 241–275.

Dolado J., Felgueroso, F., and Almunia, M. (2010). "Are men and women economists evenly distributed across fields? Some new empirical evidence," Universidad Carlos III de Madrid Discussion Paper.

Donohue, J. and Heckman, J. (1991). "Continuos versus episodic change: The impact of civil rights policy on the economic status of blacks," *Journal of Economic Literature* 29/4: 1603–1643.

Eckel, C. C. and Grossman, P. J. (1998). "Are women less selfish than men? Evidence from dictator experiments," *Economic Journal* 108/448: 726–735.

Eckstein, Z. and Nagypal, E. (2004). "The evolution of US earnings inequality: 1961–2002," *Federal Reserve Bank of Minneapolis Quarterly Review* 28/2: 10–29.

Eckstein, Z. and van den Berg, G. (2007). "Empirical labor search: Asurvey," *Journal of Econometrics* 136: 531–564.

Eckstein, Z. and K. Wolpin. (1995). "Duration to first job and the return to schooling: Estimates from a search-matching model," *The Review of Economic Studies* 62/2: 263–286.

Even, W. E. and Macpherson, D. A. (1990). "Plant size and the decline of unionism," *Economics Letter* 32: 393–398.

Flabbi, L. (2010a). "Gender discrimination estimation in a search model with matching and bargaining," *International Economic Review* 51/3: 745–783.

Flabbi, L. (2010b). "Prejudice and gender differentials in the US labor market in the last twenty years," *Journal of Econometrics* 156: 190–200.

Flabbi, L. (2011). "Gender differences in education, career choices and labor market outcomes on a sample of OECD Countries." Organization for Economic

Co-operation and Development Background Paper for the *WDR 2012*, World Bank, Washington, DC

Flabbi, L. and Mabli, J. (2012). "Household search or individual search: Does it matter? Evidence from lifetime inequality estimates," Georgetown University, Department of Economics Working Paper No. 12–02.

Flabbi, L. and Moro, A. (2012). "The effect of job flexibility on women labor market outcomes: Estimates from a search and bargaining model," *Journal of Econometrics* 168: 81–95.

Flinn, C. (2002). "Interpreting minimum wage effects on wage distributions: A cautionary tale," *Annalesd' Economieet de Statistique* 67/68: 309–355.

Flinn, C. and Heckman, J. (1982). "New methods in analyzing structural models of labor market dynamics," *Journal of Econometrics* 18: 115–168.

Gayle, G.-L., Golan, L., and Miller, R. A. (2011). "Are there glass ceilings for female executives?," *Journal of Labor Economics* 30/4: 829–871.

Ge, S. (2011). "Women's college decisions: How much does marriage matter?," *Journal of Labor Economics* 29/4: 773–818.

Gneezy, U., Niederle, M., and Rustichini, A. (2003). "Performance in competitive environments: Gender differences," *Quarterly Journal of Economics* 118: 1049–1074.

Gneezy, U. and Rustichini, A. (2004). "Gender and competition at a young age," *American Economic Review* 94/2: 377–381.

Goldin, C. (2004a). "From the valley to the summit: The quiet revolution that transformed women's work," NBER Working Paper No. 10335.

Goldin, C. (2004b). "The long road to the fast track: Career and family," *Annals of the American Academy of Political and Social Science*, 596: 20–35.

Goldin, C. and Katz, L. (2008). *The Race between Education and Technology*. Cambridge, MA: Harvard University Press.

Goldin, C., Katz, L. F., and Kuziemko, I. (2006). "The homecoming of American college women: The reversalof the college gender gap," *Journal of Economic Perspectives* 20/4: 133–156.

Goldin, C. and Rouse, C. (2000). "Orchestrating Impartiality: The impact of 'blind' auditions on female musicians," *American Economic Review* 90/4: 715–741.

Hamermesh, D. and Donald, S. (2008). "The effect of college curriculum on earnings: An affinity identifier for non-ignorable non-response bias," *Journal of Econometrics* 144: 479–491.

Harkness, S. and Waldfogel, J. (1999). *The Family Gap in Pay: Evidence from Seven Industrialized Countries*. Washington, DC: APPAM.

Harkness, S. and Waldfogel, J. (2003). "The family gap in pay: Evidence from seven industrialized countries," *Research in Labor Economics* 22: 369–414.

Heckman, J. J. (1998). "Detecting Discrimination", *Journal of Economic Perspective* 12/2: 101–116.

Holzer, H. and Neumark, D. (2000). "Assessing affirmative action," *Journal of Economic Literature* 38/3: 483–568.

Molina, J. A. and Montuenga, V. (2009). "The motherhood wage penalty in Spain," *Family Economic Issues* 30: 237–251.

Niederle, M. and Vesterlund, L. (2007). "Do women shy away from competition? Do men compete too much?," *Quarterly Journal of Economics* 122/3: 1067–1101.

Nielsen, H. S. (1998). "Discrimination and detailed decomposition in a logit model," *Economic Letters* 61: 115–120.

Orsini, J. and Pellizzari, M. (2012). *Dinastie d'Italia: gli ordini tutelano davvero i consumatori?* <http://www.egeaonline.it/editore/catalogo/dinastie-d-italia_.aspx> Università Bocconi Editore.

Paglin, M. and Rufolo, A. (1990). "Heterogeneous human capital, occupational choice, and male- female earnings differences," *Journal of Labor Economics* 8: 123–144.

Sacerdote, B. (2001). "Peer effects with random assignment: Results for Dartmouth roommates," *The Quarterly Journal of Economics* 116/2: 681–704.

Stevenson, B. (2010). "Beyond the classroom: Using title IX to measure the returns to high school sports," *The Review of Economics and Statistics* 92/2: 284–301.

Turner, S. E. and Bowen, W. G. (1999). The changing (unchanging) gender gap," *Industrial and Labor Relations Review* 52/2: 289–313.

Weber, A. and Zulehner, C. (2010). "Female hires and the success of start-up firms," *American Economic Review Papers and Proceedings* 100/2: 356 361.

Weber, A. and Zulehner, C. (2014). "Competition and gender prejudice: Are discriminatory employers doomed to fail?," *Journal of the European Economic Association* 12/2: 492–521.

Wood, R. G., Corcoran, M. E., and Courant, P. N. (1993). "Pay differences among the highly paid: The male-female earnings gap in lawyers' salaries," *Journal of Labor Economics* 11/3: 417–441.

Xie, Y. and Shauman, K. (2003), *Women in Science: Career Processes and Outcomes.* Cambridge, MA: Harvard University Press.

Yun M.-S. (2004). "Decomposing differences in the first moment," *Economic Letters* 82: 275–280.

Comments

Christopher J. Flinn

This part of the book contains a wealth of interesting empirical analysis on the gender gap in three labor markets: Italy, Spain, and the US. The authors confine their attention for the most part to the labor market performance of highly educated men and women, arguing persuasively that the gender gap here stubbornly remains (the "glass ceiling"), even while being reduced greatly among other segments of the labor market. This problem is of particular interest since gender differentials in compensation across fields that the highly educated enter can skew investment incentives by women in such a way that these gender differentials are reinforced.

Due to the size of Part I and the limited amount of time we have had to discuss it, Dan Hamermesh and I agreed to focus our attention on different aspects. My comments focus largely on the research of Flabbi and Tejada. This theoretical and empirical analysis of gender differentials follows on the extremely innovative work Flabbi performed in his dissertation. The results the authors obtain are interesting and credible given the structure of the model they uses, so there is not much to be criticized in that regard. As a result, I will address some more fundamental issues in thinking about discrimination in markets characterized by search frictions or informational asymmetries. I think these are important issues to consider when trying to interpret the empirical results obtained by Flabbi and Tejada and, to some degree, those found throughout the chapters in Part I.

Becker's Analysis of Discrimination

Recall that Becker (1957) considered three sources for discrimination: the employer (which is modeled here); buyers of the product; and co-workers. Using the data at their disposal (extracted from the Current Population Survey (CPS)), the authors have access to little information regarding the establishment at which the individual is employed, other than industry and occupation. In particular, there is no information regarding the exact nature of the products being produced or the demographic composition of the firm's employees. Even if firm identity was available to researchers, which it is not, the size of the CPS is such that the likelihood of sampling a significant number of employees from the same firm is minimal.

For these reasons, the most obvious route to take in addressing the extent of discrimination in a partial equilibrium framework is the one taken by the authors. Given the search and bargaining framework they use, they are able to separate the differences in the earnings distributions by gender into parts due to the rate of contacts between firms and job seekers, the rate of job separations, and most importantly, the underlying "ability" distributions. These models are largely identified through functional form assumptions regarding the underlying match productivity distribution, but the authors show that their results are fairly robust with respect to variations in these untestable assumptions.

I will first comment on some limitations of the approach taken by the authors even within the search and matching framework being used. These limitations may have some bearing on the nature of the estimates obtained and inferences drawn.

The fact that there are search frictions allows the authors to escape the Becker critique. The Becker analysis assumes competitive markets and argues that, as long as there exist some nondiscriminatory employers willing to pay a wage equal to the worker's marginal product irrespective of their gender, they will be able to "outcompete" discriminatory employers and drive them out of the market altogether. The competitive case assumes that in the long-run firms earn zero profits. In a model with search, or informational, frictions, individuals on both sides of the market will earn positive surpluses in any employment match due to the imperfect competition which results from the existence of search frictions. This will be the case even for women, and will be true whether or they accept employment at a discriminatory employer. Of course, for any given level of productivity, the size of the surplus the woman will obtain will be less at a discriminatory employer than at an unbiased one, but the point is that it will be positive in either case.

The view of the model is that discriminatory employers can take part of their "profits" from a match with a woman in the form of discrimination. Since models with search frictions insure that each side of the employment contract is better off than they would be if unmatched, this situation can survive in labor market equilibrium due to the imperfect competition characterizing the labor market. However, if we add other features to the model, this feature may not survive. For example, say that firms are financed by investors, and that investors care about the earnings performance of the firm, not the utility that the manager of the firm derives from discriminating against women or in favor of men. The firm profits for discriminators will be strictly less than those of nondiscriminators, meaning that all investment should go to the nondiscriminators. This investment route makes the model competitive essentially and is able to reassert the Becker claim that discriminators cannot exist in equilibrium.

In the search literature, there are (at least) two assumptions made regarding the nature of the search technology, which in any case largely remains a "black box." The first is that of random matching, which is the assumption made here. In this situation, firms and searchers behave as subatomic particles that come into contact in a more or less random manner, so that the likelihood that an individual of a certain type a and a firm of a type b meet and explore an employment possibility is the same for all a and b. The other prominent case is that of directed search, in which a firm of type b posts a vacancy and individuals apply to the firm. The likelihood that a given individual is given a job at the firm will depend on the number and types of other applicants for that position. The reason I bring this up is that the implications for discrimination from the directed search setting are analogous to those associated with Becker's argument concerning racial segregation at the firm level. His argument was that, given equal productivities of blacks and whites and a loss of utility from employing blacks on the part of some employers, an efficient outcome would be to have the discriminatory firms only employ whites with the nondiscriminatory employers employing both blacks and whites. One could make a similar argument here: an efficient outcome under directed search would have employers who are discriminators openly advertize their aversion to hiring women with those who are not explicitly stating so. In this way, women would not apply to jobs at discriminators. The resulting equilibrium would be efficient, even if we embed this story in the framework used here of random matching and bargaining. As long as men and women had the same match productivity distributions, the male and female wage distributions should be equal.

Of course, federal and state law prevents employers from stating their gender or racial biases when advertizing job vacancies. This is a case where the law, however well-intended, works against attaining efficient and equitable outcomes. Equal employment opportunity law also causes some problems for the basic setup of Flabbi and Tejada. The model assumes that employers are able to truthfully reveal their prejudices to job applicants when negotiating a wage. The first question that arises is, in this case, why can't the discriminated against female applicant/worker initiate a law suit against such an employer? The innovative empirical implication of the model is that discriminatory employers will be employing fewer women, on average, than will nondiscriminators. Checking the proportion of females working at a firm could provide a signal to the woman applicant whether the firm is in fact a discriminator. But this same objective evidence is available to government enforcers of equal employment opportunity laws, so why are these firms not prosecuted?

The second point is that if the only evidence available to the female job applicant is the employer's prejudice type as reported by him, it would seem to be in the interest of all firms to claim that they are prejudiced, since in this way they earn higher profits on their female employees, since she receives a lower share of the surplus. We know, however, that the critical productivity level for a match to result in an employment contract is greater at discriminators than at nondiscriminatory firms. Is the employer able to claim that it is a discriminator to some women and not to others? What is the mechanism that makes the employer's declaration of his discriminatory type credible to female applicants but not prosecutable in a court of law? These are a few open questions regarding how the equilibrium utilized in the chapter is actually attained.

The assumption of no on-the-job search is an important one, particularly in looking at the size of the set of discriminatory firms and the wage penalty women face. The authors' decision to neglect on-the-job search is completely defensible from an empirical point of view given the data used to estimate the model. However, from a policy point of view this is problematic. There now exist a number of models (e.g., Postel-Vinay and Robin 2002; Dey and Flinn 2005) in which firms compete directly over workers whenever a currently employed searcher contacts a new potential employer. In these models, the firms are assumed to compete for the worker by engaging in a Bertrand competition for their services. In the Dey and Flinn model, the firm at which the employee is most productive attains her services (efficient mobility). This would still be the case whenever a discriminator competed against another discriminator, or a nondiscriminator competed against another nondiscriminator. However, if a woman employed at a biased firm met a non-biased firm, she could leave for the non-biased firm even if her productivity was higher at the biased firm. These kind of competitions result in increases in a woman's wage, in general, but also reduce the proportion of employed women working at biased firms in the steady state. The size of this reduction will depend greatly on the number of biased firms in the population. If there are a large number of biased firms, then it is unlikely that a woman working for a discriminatory employer would encounter a non-biased one. On the other hand, if there are few nondiscriminatory employers, it is likely that they would lose female employees since the likelihood they contact a nondiscriminator is high. Estimating a model with on-the-job search could yield very different estimates of the proportion of discriminators and the size of their bias (k). Most importantly, it could yield vastly reduced welfare differentials between men and women in the steady state.

The analysis doesn't consider the vacancy creation process, which is an important element in equilibrium search models (even if the matching function on which it is based is largely a black box, it must be admitted). It is important in this application for the following reason. It is generally asserted that job vacancies are created by firms up until the point where the expected value of a created vacancy (in terms of profits to the firm) is equal to zero. The justification for this assumption is a free entry condition: there exist a large number of potential firms that could create vacancies and whose alternative value of not creating a vacancy is zero, so that firms will keep adding vacancies until they drive the expected value of a vacancy down to zero. But how is the condition modified when firms are differentiated in terms of how they feel about female employees? It would seem if biased firms actually dislike hiring women, then under the free entry condition only unbiased firms will create jobs. The argument is that unbiased firms will add jobs until the expected value of a vacancy for them is zero, which implies that the expected value of a vacancy for a biased firm will be negative (at least under random matching). On the other hand, if biased firms actually enjoy discriminating against women, then all the job vacancies should be created by them. To obtain a labor market in which both biased and unbiased firms create vacancies seems to require some modification of the model structure.

Statistical Discrimination

There is an alternative model of discrimination that does not require the existence of a set of biased employers. Instead, it requires some gender-bias in the expectations employers have about the job performance and attachment to the labor market of women. This model is one of "statistical discrimination." Very loosely speaking, the model requires that employers hold expectations about how women will behave as employees. Define all of the expectations held by employers regarding all of the (observable) types of workers in the labor market by E. The question is whether some E are consistent with a self-fulfilling prophecy or not. For example, say that employers feel that women are less productive workers than are men, and therefore offer a woman with some productive characteristics x a lower wage than a man with the same x. If a woman, given the lower wage, supplies less effort than a man, then these expectations on the part of an employer would be confirmed. This then could constitute an equilibrium in which women were paid less and as a result of this worked less hard. Replacing these biased expectations with unbiased ones, in which women and men with the same x were equally productive and as a result were paid the same wage should result in the same productivity level if women and men are truly equivalent as employees. The policy challenge is to shift biased expectations into unbiased ones.

There is some hope that biased expectations can evolve into unbiased ones. Instead of workers controlling their productivity through effort decisions (which are dependent on the wage), say that workers have an innate level of productivity, and that there is substantial heterogeneity in productivity in the populations of males and females. Furthermore, assume that one's productivity as a dependent worker is positively correlated with one's productivity in other activities (such as self-employment or raising children). Then when wages to women are low relative to those offered to men, only low productivity women will enter the labor market. As female wages increase relative to those of men, average productivity among female workers converges to that of male workers. The impetus for the wage convergence could be antidiscrimination law, positive signals regarding female productivity from the advantage women now have in educational credentials, and so on.

Some of the empirical results in the paper support this view. Gender wage differentials have substantially decreased in occupations where women now constitute a sizable proportion of employees. Change is slower at the top, the so-call "glass ceiling." One could hope that as women increasingly assume high profile executive positions, the expectations of boards of directors and share-holders will be substantially altered to equal ability and performance potential of men and women.

Household Considerations

While the proportion of single households in the population has increased, the proportion of married households is now slightly less than 50 percent in the US. Nevertheless, there are a significant number of cohabiting (heterosexual) households and the probability of ever marrying during one's lifetime remains high. It is natural to ask how discrimination affects household welfare when there is no (or positive) bias toward one gender and negative bias toward the other. In other words, are the biases offset in these households, so that gender-based discrimination is less of a serious issue from the viewpoint of the family than it would be when the analysis is restricted to individuals, as is the case in the Flabbi and Tejada analysis?

On the face of it, there is an obvious argument to make that the total income of the household is relatively less impacted by gender discrimination than when the analysis is conducted assuming one-person households. Men, who are favored in the labor market, are paired with women who are not. There is substantial assortative mating in the marriage market, so for the sake of argument assume that there is perfect sorting along the productivity dimension x. A husband with earnings $e_m(x)$ has a wife who has earnings

$e_f(x)$. In the absence of discrimination, household earnings would be higher. Since most expenditures in the household are public, that is, they are enjoyed by all members of the household, this reduces the husband's consumption and therefore his welfare. One would think that in such a case, men would be as vociferous in their opposition to gender-discrimination in employment opportunities as their wives. It is clear that employment discrimination against women also reduces the total income of the household, which one might think would reduce the welfare of the males they are married to or cohabiting with.

This may not be the case due to the positive impacts on the husband's welfare that may arise due to household bargaining. In this view of the world, husbands and wives bargain over the division of the surplus generated by the marriage, with their outside options being an important component of this division. It is often assumed that the outside option is equal to the value of either spouse living alone in the divorced or separated state. Since single women are substantially worse off than are single men due to the presence of discrimination, this results in a larger share of the surplus for husbands (even when husbands and wives are of the same productivity type x). For the husbands, a more equitable labor market means a larger household surplus but a smaller share of it for them. For their wives, the status quo of gender discrimination translates into a smaller household surplus and a smaller share of it for them. In this sense, marriage may mitigate the effects of market discrimination on female welfare, but by no means does it eliminate welfare differences between husbands and wives.

Bargaining Power

The last issue I want to discuss relates to the nature of male-female wage outcomes. In the bargaining problem, now between worker and firm instead of husband and wife, outside options play a key role in determining outcomes. In their model, due to the presence of discriminatory employers, women have a lower continuation value of search, which is what gives them wages that are inferior to those of men even when their productivity distribution is the same.

In addition to outside options, axiomatic Nash bargaining relies on a direct "bargaining power" parameter, which is denoted by α in the analysis of Flabbi and Tejada. In the empirical literature in which bargaining models are estimated, it is known to be notoriously difficult to obtain reasonable and precise estimates of α (for a discussion of this point, see Flinn (2006) for example). The authors impose the standard assumption that firms and workers have equal bargaining power independent of the gender of the worker or the bias of the firms, so that $\alpha = 0.5$ in all cases.

Given the difficulty of estimating α, particularly with the data the authors used, this assumption is understandable. But my concern is that there may be substantial differences in α across genders. There are many anecdotal accounts and scientific studies that point to the disutility suffered by women in bargaining situations, or competitive environments more generally (e.g., Babcock and Laschever 2003; Niederle and Vesterlund 2007). Reasonably small gender differences in α have the potential to produce marked differences in outcomes even when the underlying productivity distributions for men and women are the same and even in the absence of gender-biased employers. For this reason, I think that it should be a priority of the authors and other researchers to incorporate other data sources (as in Flinn 2006) in an attempt to identify gender-specific bargaining power parameters. The answer to ending gender discrimination may largely involve making women more comfortable in bargaining and competitive situations more generally.

References

Babcock, Linda and Laschever, Sara (2003). *Women Don't Ask: Negotiation and the Gender Divide*. Princeton, NJ: Princeton University Press.

Becker, Gary (1957). *The Economics of Discrimination*. Chicago: The University of Chicago Press.

Burda, Michael, Hamermesh, Daniel, and Weil, Philippe (2013). "Total work and gender: Facts and possible explanations," *Journal of Population Economics*, Springer, vol. 26(1), pp. 239–261, January.

Dey, Matthew and Flinn, Christopher (2005). "An equilibrium model of health insurance provision and wage determination," *Econometrica* 73: 571–627.

Flinn, Christopher (2006). "Minimum Wage effects on Labor market outcomes under search, matching, and endogenous contact rates," *Econometrica* 74: 1013–1062.

Niederle, Muriel and Vesterlund, Lise (2007). "Do women shy away from competition? Do men compete too much?" *Quarterly Journal of Economics* 122: 1067–1101.

Postel-Vinay, Fabian and Robin, Jean-Marc (2002). "Equilibrium wage dispersion with worker and employer heterogeneity," *Econometrica* 70: 2295–2350.

Comments

Daniel Hamermesh

The chapters in Part I focus on gender differences in outcomes among the highly educated. The focus is especially relevant for several reasons: (1) The highly educated are typically the leaders in any modern economy's industry, government and social activities; (2) Their behavior is very often the vanguard of behavior that will spread throughout society; and (3) They are us, and navel-gazing is fun! For these reasons these studies, which analyze data from the US, Spain, and Italy, are especially welcome.

What are the "take-aways"? Perhaps most important is the similar persistence of gender gaps in labor-market outcomes across these economies. The gaps are not the same in all three, and their sources and other impacts certainly differ; but in all three they seem remarkably resistant to change.

My only comments on the structural model for the US are, first, that it would be very valuable to use readily obtainable employer data (the EOPP or Four-City data) to get at these questions. After all, employers presumably are the ones who discriminate (or are the agents of others' discriminatory preferences). So why not base at least some of the analysis on data from employers? This seems especially important given worries about measurement errors in the CPS-based recall data, which seems an especially important concern in a model whose results are so crucially data dependent.

It would also be interesting to focus more closely on the disaggregation of gender differences among highly-educated workers. In terms of the gender mix of degree-holders, and perhaps in the distribution of earnings too, EdDs historically have looked a lot different from MDs. The Current Population Survey (the data set used in this chapter) aggregates EdDs and PhDs into one category, all other doctorates (medical, legal, veterinary, divinity, and a few others) into a second category.

Table 1 shows the fractions of younger employees (ages 25–39) with these degrees in 1992–94, the first years for which the data are available, and in 2009–11. The most striking thing to note in these data is the growth in the percentages of female advanced-degree holders. Women have surpassed men

Table 1. Advanced-degree holders ages 25–39, by gender, US, CPS 1992–94, 2009–11 (percent of all employees of the age and gender)*

	Male		Female	
	1992–94	2009–11	1992–94	2009–11
Masters	4.9	7.2	5.4	11.2
MD, JD, etc.	1.5	1.5	1.0	1.7
PhD, Ed.D., etc.	0.8	1.3	0.5	1.4

* Current Population Survey, MORG.

Table 2. Total fertility rate and average age at average birth, Spain, 1965–2004*

	1965	1985	2004
Total Fertility Rate	2.94	1.64	1.46 (2008)
Average Age at Average Birth	30.1	28.5	30.8

* European Commission, *Population Statistics* 2006; Eurostat, *Yearbook* 2011.

in both types of doctorates in the past twenty years. But the most rapid growth has been in PhDs and EdD.s, doctoral categories in which average earnings are low compared to JDs and MDs. So yes, women's educational attainment in the US has surpassed men's, even at the advanced-degree level; but it has grown especially rapidly in those degrees that are typically among the relatively lower-paid.

The Spanish case is most interesting, and Chapter 3 begins to expose some fascinating issues. To this non-European observer two crucial characteristics seem important and might be conditioning and be conditioned by women's labor-market outcomes. In the past quarter-century Spain has introduced and greatly expanded employers' access to fixed-term labor contracts. One would think that this would have raised female participation and lowered female–male relative earnings. Regardless, the effects of this fundamental change on female-male outcomes should be a major focus of interest here.

Another Spanish novelty that merits consideration here is the remarkable baby bust of the past several decades (mirroring that in much of Southern Europe). The average child is still born at the same age of his/her mother as earlier, as Table 2 shows; but today the kid is as likely as not to be an only child, whereas 40 years ago he or she was typically one of three.

Given these striking changes several research strategies might allow the authors to focus more on "why" the changes have occurred. Thus: (1) Why not take advantage of inter-area differences in changes in average fertility to model and examine the interactions of fertility decisions and labor-market behavior? Along these lines, working off changes in social programs (see, e.g., Nollenberger and Rodriguez-Planas 2011) might also be helpful; and (2) Since much of the revolution in fertility must stem from (perhaps exogenous)

Table 3. Time use by education, ages 22–40, Italy and US (minutes per representative day)*

	Italy		US	
	Laurea+	No Laurea	16+ years	<16 years
Paid Work:				
Women	252	173	240	203
Men	365	369	385	350
House Work:				
Women	232	324	317	315
Men	77	81	183	176
Of which child care*:				
Women	68	74	134	121
Men	22	23	68	62

* US also includes other family care. Calculated from *Indagine sull'uso del Tempo* 2002, ATUS 2003-06.

changes in attitudes, linking correlations between attitudinal changes and demographics in the repeated waves of the World Values Survey (available for Spain for 1981, 1990, 1995, 2000, and 2005 at least) would be a useful way to identify the causes of changes in gender outcomes.

One wonders how important attitudes might be in conditioning gender differences in behavior and how the impact of attitudinal differences varies as the educational attainment of men and especially women rises. The authors' construction of instruments based on Spanish time-use data makes the results more believable. That is not surprising, given that Spanish women on average do much more work in total (work for pay and household production) than Spanish men, a difference that also appears in other Mediterranean countries but is not present in wealthy non-Mediterranean countries (Burda et al. 2013).

Does this striking female–male difference persist among young women when they acquire more education? Table 3 presents data from young women's time diaries from Italy for 2002 and the US for 2003–06, with the focus on market work, household production and, within the latter category, time spent in child care. Less-educated young Italian women do about 45 minutes *more* work in total (for pay and in the home) than do less-educated young Italian men. One might think that education liberates Italian women; but the data show that, like their less-educated sisters, young Italian women with at least a *laurea* also do about 45 minutes more work in total than similarly highly educated young Italian men. In the US the analogous comparisons show that, regardless of educational attainment, young women do 10 minutes *less* work in total per day than young men. None of the conclusions here is altered qualitatively if we adjust for differences in age or for the ages and numbers of children.

These data are rather depressing. They suggest that education in Italy is very far from being a panacea that equalizes outcomes for men and women. They also suggest how different Italy is from the US (and other

Table 4. Weekly work hours in 2001 of University of Texas graduates, classes of 1980–2000*

	Average	Std. Error
"Female" majors		
Architecture, fine arts	41.8	1.4
Communications	41.0	1.1
Education	40.8	1.3
Humanities	42.4	1.2
Nursing, social work	33.9	2.6
AVERAGE	40.8	1.4
"Male" majors		
Accounting and finance	45.2	0.9
Other business	43.3	1.2
Engineering	44.8	0.8
Natural sciences	42.1	0.9
AVERAGE	43.9	0.9

* From Hamermesh and Donald (2008). Social sciences are excluded.

wealthy non-Mediterranean countries) and how little education does in Italy to allow women's outcomes to equal those of men. Persistent culture, which we study very rarely and about which we know so little, seems much more important for gender outcomes than relatively easily equalized gross educational outcomes.

The last half of the report deals with gender differences in outcomes in Italy, in particular among highly educated *Milanesi*. The authors are to be commended for having constructed an extremely interesting and useful set of data and for analyzing it in a very creative way. They demonstrate very convincingly that there is about a 40 log-point gender wage gap, which a large variety of beatings of the data only reduces by about 10 log points. The study is especially interesting, focusing as it does on choice of university major, because in Italy, as in most countries, but not the United States, university degrees are mapped nearly uniquely into occupational attainment.

The authors note that, while they have data on the respondents' employment status, they lack data on work hours. What difference does this absence make? Table 4 presents tabulations of weekly work hours from a sample of US university graduates, disaggregated by choice of major. These data complement and expand upon the authors' comparison of average hours by gender among educated young people in northwest Italy. Graduates in the "male" majors work about 7% longer per week than graduates in "female" majors. Since major and occupation are less highly correlated in the US than in Italy, it seems reasonable to conclude that perhaps an additional 10 log points of the Italian gender wage differential among the highly-educated might be explained by differences in work hours.

That still leaves half—20 points—of the gender wage differential unexplained. Part of this striking difference might arise from less female investment on the job in occupations held by educated Italian women. After all, why invest as much as guys if you know you will be spending a lot more of your time in home production? Another cause might be pure discrimination, although the authors' comparisons between self-employed and employed educated Italians suggests this may not be too important. (I use "may," because one might be concerned about the effects of gender differences in unobservables that alter selection into these two sectors.)

The authors perform a variety of interesting exercises to determine the causes of the large unexplained wage gap. They are all executed carefully and convincingly, and they all fail to alter the remaining wage gap in any important way. Women are less likely than men to engage in sports activities in school, and are more likely to volunteer; but the differences in participation in these activities are much too small to matter. The idea that women choose university majors as a husband-attracting strategy fails miserably, perhaps unsurprisingly given the segregation of students by faculty (so that women choosing a "female" major are most likely to encounter men in this low-paying field of study).

While the authors do demonstrate the existence of peer effects in choice of major, these seem far too small to account for much of the remaining 20 log-point gender wage gap. In the end, the estimated wage gap doesn't budge. Culture and attitudes about gender roles and behavior persist when women equal or even surpass men's educational achievements. The equalization of educational attainment has reduced gender inequality; but the evidence is clear that it has not and, without much more fundamental changes will not eliminate inequality of labor-market outcomes between men and women.

References

Burda, Michael, Hamermesh, Daniel, and Weil, Philippe (2013). "Total work and gender: Facts and possible explanations," *Journal of Population Economics*, Springer, 26(1): 239–261, January.

Hamermesh, Daniel and Donald, Stephen (2008). "The effect of college curriculum on earnings: An affinity identifier for non-ignorable non-response bias," *Journal of Econometrics* 144: 479–491.

Nollenberger, Natalia and Rodriguez-Planas, Nuria ((2011). "Child care, maternal employment and persistence: A natural experiment from Spain," IZA Discussion Paper 5888, July.

Part II
Unexplored Dimensions of Discrimination in Europe: Religion, Homosexuality, and Physical Appearance

6

Discrimination and Labor Market Outcomes: Theoretical Mechanisms and Existing Empirical Studies

Eleonora Patacchini, Giuseppe Ragusa, and Yves Zenou

6.1 Introduction

Discrimination in the labor market is perhaps one of the most studied topics in economics but certainly the least understood. Indeed, when explaining the adverse labor market outcomes of certain categories of workers (e.g. ethnic minorities or women), it is very difficult to disentangle discrimination from other (often) unobserved aspects such as low ability or social norms and peer effects. Recently, researchers in economics have been using new methods to tackle this issue: field studies (such as audit studies and correspondence tests) and natural experiments. The results convincingly show that there is discrimination against minority workers and women. Interestingly, several countries are currently analyzing the implementation of compulsory anonymous résumés that forbid candidates from including information such as a photograph and/or their name, age, marital status, gender, and nationality, which could trigger discriminatory hiring practices. As we will see below (Section 6.2), the economics literature has put forward two major sources of racial or gender discrimination: taste-based and statistical. The dislike of hiring ethnic minorities or women produces taste-based discrimination while statistical discrimination occurs in an environment of imperfect information, where agents form expectations based on limited signals that correlate with race or gender.

In the present and following three chapters of this book, we consider under-investigated categories of individuals that might be discriminated against in the labor market. Using the 2008 Eurobarometer data covering most of the European countries, Figure 6.1 shows some facts about the perception of discrimination in Europe. It reveals, for example, that discrimination on the

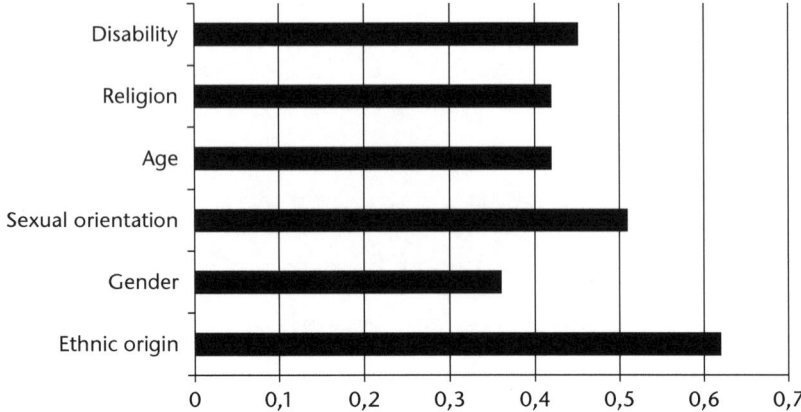

Figure 6.1. Perception of discrimination in the EU.

Notes: We show the percentage of people answering that discrimination on the basis of the listed source is "widespread." The percentages of people declaring that it is "Rare," "Do not know," and with missing values are not shown.

Source: Eurobarometer 2008, EU 27.

basis of sexual orientation is perceived as widespread by more than 50% of the people, whereas this percentage is only slightly higher than 35% for gender.

In the context of an evolving society, with different lifestyles and with a growing attention on cultural and social diversity, these issues are at the forefront of the political debate. The research on these topics, however, is still quite limited and the existing evidence for Europe is extremely scarce.

This chapter presents the theoretical mechanisms underlying discrimination in the labor market and surveys the existing related empirical literature.

6.2 Theoretical Mechanisms

The economics literature posits two major sources of discrimination: *taste-based* and *statistical*. The first one takes place because employers dislike some categories of the population, while statistical discrimination occurs in an environment of imperfect information where agents form expectations based on limited signals that correlate with some observable characteristics.[1]

To be more precise, *taste-based* models originate from Gary Becker's seminal work (1957). In Becker's model, discrimination in hiring or wages is caused by a "taste for discrimination" that leads the employer to hire or pay higher wages

[1] See the overviews by Altonji and Blank (1999), Lang and Lehmann (2012), Kofi Charles and Guryan (2011), and Boeri and van Ours (2012).

to members of his/her own group. In this approach, discrimination is costly and leads to segregated workplaces.

In Becker's model, prejudiced employers, workers, or consumers dislike employing, working with, or purchasing from people with observable traits (e.g. race, gender, beauty, obesity, homosexuality). Although the Becker model is well known, it is worth reviewing briefly. The profit π of a prejudiced employer is given by:[2]

$$\pi = f(L_{ND} + L_D) - w_{ND}L_{ND} - w_D L_D - d L_D$$

where L_D and L_{ND} are the number of discriminated and non-discriminated workers employed, $f(.)$ is the production function, which is assumed to be well-behaved, w_D and w_{ND} are the wages of discriminated and non-discriminated workers, and d is a taste for discrimination. In this framework, the parameter d corresponds to the psychological cost of hiring and working with a discriminated person, and enters in the profit function as a cost associated with the hiring of a discriminated worker. It measures the intensity of the employer's discriminating preferences. In this context, the subjective cost of hiring a discriminated worker takes into account both wage and psychological costs and is given by $w_D + d$. Observe also that, in this formulation, discriminated and non-discriminated workers are equally productive and perfect substitutes.

Each employer chooses L_{ND} and L_D that maximize her profit and wages:

$$w_{ND} = f'(L_{ND} + L_D)$$

$$w_D = f'(L_{ND} + L_D) - d$$

which implies that

$$w_{ND} - w_D = d.$$

Therefore, whenever the wage gap $w_{ND} - w_D$ exceeds d, the employer will strictly prefer to hire discriminated workers, and whenever it is less than d, she strictly prefers to hire non-discriminated workers. Assume that there is a distribution of d among employers so that some are more prejudiced than others. If, as seems reasonable, the distribution of d has no mass points, then, assuming the labor market is otherwise perfect, $w_{ND} - w_D = d$ implies that either there is no discriminatory wage differential or (almost) all firms are completely segregated. However, as noted by Becker and emphasized by Arrow (1973), employers with weaker prejudicial tastes will make more profit and will expand. Demand for discriminated workers will grow, and in the long run, if there are sufficient employers with no aversion to hiring discriminated workers, the wage differential will fall to zero. Those employers who are averse

---

[2] The subscripts D and ND stand for "Discriminated" and "Non-Discriminated" respectively.

to hiring discriminated workers and who survive in the labor market will hire only non-discriminated workers. In short, employment will be partially segregated, but there will be no wage discrimination.

If the Becker model is correct, the market should relentlessly eliminate discrimination except where it cannot provide sufficient segregation. This is most likely to occur for workers in specialized occupations requiring customer awareness of the characteristic of the worker, where firm entry is limited, where the proportion of discriminated workers in the labor force is large, and where prejudice is widespread.

There is also another theory of discrimination, related to the previous one, which is *coworker discrimination* or *customer discrimination*. This theory has different implications for wage and employment gaps than pure employer discrimination. Consider a model where coworkers prefer not to work with people from a specific group (this is referred to as coworker discrimination).[3] The utility of a prejudiced worker depends whether she works or not with a discriminated worker. Her utility in a firm that hires n workers is given by:

$$U = w \left(1 - d \sum_{i=1}^{n} I \right)$$

where w is the wage of the prejudiced worker, d is the taste for discrimination and I is an indicator function that takes 1 if the coworker is a discriminated worker and 0 otherwise. This means that this prejudiced worker prefers to work only with workers like her or, if not, to be compensated for the disutility of working with workers from a different group. This model has different predictions. First, in firms where the discriminated and non-discriminated groups cooperate, the non-discriminated worker has to earn more to overcome her disliking of discriminated coworkers. Therefore, firms will hire either non-discriminated or discriminated workers and the workforce will be segregated. Second, if employers are not prejudiced there will be no wage gap even if all non-discriminated workers are prejudiced.

Consider now a model where customers prefer to buy from individuals from the same group (this is referred to as customer discrimination). In this case, the customers' willingness to pay p_w for a particular product depends on the presence of other workers in the production process:

$$p_w = p \left(1 + d \sum_{i=1}^{n} I \right)$$

where p is actual price, d is the taste for customer discrimination and I is an indicator function that takes 1 if the worker involved in the production

---

[3] We follow here the presentation of Boeri and van Ours (2012, Chapter 4).

process is a discriminated worker and 0 otherwise. We obtain here similar conclusions to those obtained by the coworker discrimination model, since prejudiced consumers will only buy from firms with discriminated workers if the price of the product is sufficiently low.

The second main explanation for discrimination is defined as *statistical discrimination* and is based on incomplete information (Arrow, 1973; Phelps, 1972). According to models of statistical discrimination, employers have incomplete information about the employee's performance and consequently base their hiring/wage-setting decisions on (erroneous) stereotypes. In Arrow's (1973) model and in a similar model developed by Phelps (1972), employers have (erroneous) beliefs that individuals from some particular groups (homosexuals for instance) are less productive and act accordingly. Models of statistical discrimination differ in the fact that some authors consider that stereotypes are erroneous, while others argue that stereotypes may correspond to actual group averages in equilibrium. In the first case, imperfect information would arise because discriminated groups emit noisier signals. Consequently, employers who observe ability with greater error (rationally) discriminate against people belonging to discriminated groups (Phelps, 1972; Aigner and Cain, 1977; Cornell and Welch, 1996). In the second category of statistical discrimination models, negative prior beliefs about members of a particular group may become self-fulfilling in equilibrium (Lundberg and Startz, 1983; Coate and Loury, 1993). This may be the case for instance if individuals of a specific group under-invest in human capital because they anticipate a discriminatory treatment, and therefore they will receive a lower return to education.

There are also some theories that are specific to particular groups, such as homosexuals. Just as in the case of gender and ethnicity, there might be several possible means through which sexual orientation is independently related to a number of economic outcomes, such as earnings or the probability of finding a job. Two hypotheses have dominated in this literature. The first is the discrimination hypothesis, based on Becker's (1957) taste-based discrimination theory, or Arrow's (1973) and Phelps' (1972) statistical theory of discrimination. The second is the hypothesis of *specialization within families*. The predictions are the same: gay males are predicted to experience earnings disadvantages compared with heterosexual males, while lesbians are expected to experience earnings advantages compared with heterosexual females.

According to taste-based discrimination or statistical discrimination (see Section 6.6), employers may act on their bias against homosexuals, which may result in disadvantages on the labor market such as lower earnings or lower chance to find a job. This outcome is, however, more likely for gay males than for lesbians since attitudes towards gay males are much more hostile than are attitudes towards lesbians (Herek, 2000; Kite and Whitley, 1996). The statistical discrimination model is typically used to make predictions about lesbians. Stereotypes about lesbians, for example that they are more focused on their career, that they are less likely to have children, or that they are more masculine, are considered to be an important source of bias. In the statistical discrimination framework, lesbians therefore are predicted to do better than their heterosexual counterparts.

The idea of *specialization within families* was put forward by Becker (1981), who argued that heterosexual males specialize in market labor and hetero-sexual females in household labor because of comparative advantages caused by biological differences. Heterosexual females therefore acquire less market-related human capital and more home-related human capital. In contrast, heterosexual males will acquire more market-related human capital. This results in earnings differentials between males and females. On the contrary, homosexual households are unable to specialize to the same extent as heterosexual households, because the gains from gender differences between spouses in comparative advantages do not exist. Lesbians who expect to form households will therefore not acquire less market-related human capital, and will therefore earn more than heterosexual females. In contrast, gay males are predicted to earn less than heterosexual males, because they will invest less in market-related human capital than heterosexual males.

6.3 Overview of the Empirical Literature

From an empirical viewpoint, it is extremely difficult to distinguish between taste-based discrimination and statistical discrimination. This is because the result of both types of discrimination is the same: similar individuals who differ only by some traits (such as race, gender, physical appearance) experience different outcomes. A simple examination of differential treatments sheds little light on the source of discrimination and potentially explains why few studies are able to find conclusive evidence of statistical discrimination. In the next section, we review the studies (mostly field experiments) that have tried to disentangle these two aspects of discrimination. Then we will review the specific literature on the discrimination of homosexuals (Section 6.3.2), obese (Section 6.3.3.1), and unattractive individuals (Section 6.3.3.2).

6.3.1 *Field Studies on Discrimination*

Economists have accumulated a large body of evidence on the existence of both gender and ethnic/racial discrimination using various empirical approaches ranging from traditional empirical data analysis (Kahn, 1991;

Knowles et al., 2001; Altonji and Pierret, 2001) to field experiments (see Riach and Rich, 2002) for an exhaustive survey of field experiments discrimination). Two main procedures of field experiments have been used to carry out tests for the extent of discrimination. A first procedure consists in matching two testers who attend job interviews or buy products, one from the majority group and the other from the minority. These experiments have provided strong evidence of discrimination in different contexts, including the housing market (Galster, 1990), sports car market (List, 2004), car sales (Ayres and Siegelman, 1995), and television shows (Levitt, 2004). Another field approach to measure the extent of discrimination at the hiring stage consists of sending matched CVs that vary in only one variable (e.g. the name) to employers in response to job advertisements (see, for instance, Neumark, 1996; Bertrand and Mullainathan, 2004).

In this section, we will review the evidence on discrimination using field experiments since it is so difficult to be sure that discrimination is at work in standard empirical analyses. Experimental economists have developed tools to elicit beliefs and infer preferences from observed behavior in the laboratory,[4] but such measurement can be difficult if subjects are aware of being observed because of the illicit nature of discrimination. Researchers have developed clever designs (so-called correspondence tests and audit studies) to circumvent that problem using natural field experiments in which potential discriminators are not aware of being observed (e.g. Bertrand and Mullainathan, 2004).

As a result, *field studies* measuring discrimination can be split into two categories: *audit studies* and *correspondence tests*. The former method uses actual testers and personal contact of the testers with those transacting on the other side of the market. A good example of this type of study is Neumark (1996). The latter approach does not use personal contact, thereby avoiding potential bias from tester behavior differences across groups. A recent example of this approach is Bertrand and Mullainathan (2004).

Whereas experimental modification of an individual's race is impossible, *random manipulation of an observer's beliefs* or knowledge about the racial classification of an agent with whom that observer interacts is something that social scientists can do. One could, for example, imagine researchers randomly telling some subset of market actors that a person of superficially indeterminate race is in fact black and telling another subset that the person is white. A comparison across these groups in their treatment of the individual would provide some evidence about whether those actors discriminated against people they thought to be black.

---

[4] Several *laboratory experimental studies* have also been conducted to measure the extent of discrimination as well as its determinants (see Anderson et al., 2006, for a survey).

Bertrand and Mullainathan (2004) essentially conduct exactly this type of analysis in their study of firms' treatment of résumés sent in for entry-level job applications. Bertrand and Mullainathan find that résumés that had been randomly given "black-sounding" names as opposed to "white-sounding" ones, but that were otherwise the same, were significantly less likely to receive callbacks. A fair reading of these results is that firms engage in discrimination against applicants thought to be black. Fryer and Levitt (2004), however, find no impact of name on a wide range of life outcomes, while controlling for initial circumstances at birth. Arai and Skogman Thoursie (2009) examine data for immigrants who changed their surnames to Swedish-sounding or neutral names during the 1990s in Sweden. The underlying research question is whether the labor market offers equal opportunities to individuals regardless of their names and the associated ethnic background. The results imply that there is a substantial increase in annual earnings after a name change, no effects on earnings prior to a name change, and no positive general effects of a new name for other groups that renounced a foreign name.

With the exception of List (2004) and to some extent Levitt (2004) and, more recently, Ewens et al. (2012), it is very difficult to disentangle between taste-based and statistical discrimination. As stated above, there can be different reasons for discrimination. Preference-based discrimination, for example, is a situation in which someone evaluating a woman for a job simply does not like women. Statistical discrimination describes a situation in which underlying factors or expectations explain the discrimination; for example, if women on average have lower productivity.

List (2004) was the first to correctly test for the nature of discrimination by employing a number of experiments. List uses a series of field experiments in an actual marketplace: the sports car market. He begins by documenting an interesting pattern of discrimination: there is a strong tendency for dealers to give nondealer minorities (women, nonwhite, and older agents) initial and final offers that are inferior to those received by their majority counterparts. These results hold when nondealers are acting as buyers and sellers, though the degree of discrimination is greater when agents are selling their wares, providing initial evidence that consumer-side discrimination is more pronounced than seller-side discrimination. The differences in the empirical distribution of prices could be due to at least three sources: (i) *taste-based discrimination*, whereby dealers are willing to incur a cost to avoid transacting with a minority; (ii) differences in bargaining ability, that is majorities are superior bargainers and obtain better outcomes in the marketplace; and (iii) statistical discrimination, where minorities have a different distribution of reservation values and in their pursuit of profits dealers use observable variables to make inferences about a relevant but unobservable variable (reservation values). List (2004) finds that, in light of the pattern of discrimination observed in the marketplace, each of the three theories of discrimination provides clear predictions of behavior in the complementary experiments. First, it would be incorrect to conclude that the observed differences in treatment are due to noneconomic tastes for discrimination among dealers or differences in bargaining ability across minorities and majorities. Rather, empirical results from all the experiments suggest that the observed differences in treatment are due to statistical discrimination – dealers use minority membership as a proxy for the distribution of reservation values. Thus, the main conclusion of List (2004) is that the observed discrimination of minority groups is explained by statistical discrimination rather than preference-based discrimination.

In another paper, Hedegaard and Tyran (2011) disentangle taste-based and statistical discrimination in the workplace by using a field experiment. They find that taste-based discrimination is common but remarkably responsive to the price of prejudice, that is to the opportunity cost of choosing a less productive worker on ethnic grounds. In addition, they find that accurate statistical discrimination fails to explain observed choices, and that taking ethnic prejudice into account helps to predict the incidence of discrimination.[5]

So far we have reviewed the literature on discrimination and explained the mechanisms behind the results. Most of the papers reviewed above focused on ethnicity or gender. In the remainder of this section we will expose the existing empirical research on discrimination of other categories of people. Our review here focuses on the groups that are the subjects of empirical investigation in Section 7.3. In Chapter 9 we will review the existing studies and specific theoretical mechanisms for other types of discrimination of certain interest (age discrimination, disability discrimination, housing discrimination).

Table 6.1 summarizes our overview of the empirical studies on the relationship between homosexuality, obesity, and beauty, and the labor market outcomes (earnings and employment) of workers with these traits, differentiating between males and females and between registered data studies and field experiments.

---

[5] There is also a small literature that use job advertisement to study discrimination. This is interesting since advertisement-based indicators of discrimination differ from audit-type indicators in ways that have opposite implications for how much discrimination we should expect to observe (Kuhn and Shen, 2011). The main problem with advertisement-based indicators of discrimination is that it is illegal in most Western countries, so few studies have used it. However, it is not illegal in China. Kuhn and Shen (2011) study firms' advertised gender preferences in a population of advertisement on a Chinese internet job board. They find that higher job skill requirements reduces the tendency to gender-target a job advertisement. This suggests that rising skill demands may be a potent deterrent to explicit discrimination of the job advertisement type. They also find that firms' underlying gender preferences are highly job-specific, with many firms requesting men for some jobs and women for others.

Table 6.1. Overview of the empirical studies

		Earning/ Wages	Employment
Homosexuality	Male	Registered data and field experiments: Lower wages (US and Europe)	Registered data: Less employment (Europe) No effect (US) Field experiments: Lower callback rates (Sweden)
	Female	Registered data and field experiments: No effect and sometimes higher wages (US and Europe)	Registered data: Less employment (Europe) No effect (US) Field experiments: Lower callback rates (Sweden)
Obesity	Male	Registered data: No effect or small effect (US) Field experiments: Lower wages (Sweden)	Registered data: Strong penalty (Europe) Field experiments: 6% lower callback rates (Sweden)
	Female	Registered data: Strong negative effect (US) Field experiments: Lower wages (Sweden)	Registered data: Strong penalty (Europe) Field experiments: 8% lower callback rates (Sweden)
Beauty	Male	Registered data: Higher wages (US) 15% lower wages for unattractive workers (UK)	Registered data: Strong premium (US) Field experiments: Higher callback rates (Argentina, Israel)
	Female	Registered data: Higher wages (US) 11% lower wages for unattractive workers (UK)	Registered data: Premium only in female jobs (US) Field experiments: Higher callback rates (Argentina, Israel)

6.3.2 Homosexuality and Labor Market Outcomes

There is a relative small literature (especially in economics) on discrimination and the labor market outcomes of being homosexual that we would like to review here.

During recent decades economists have used field experiments in order to detect discrimination in labor markets, housing markets, and product markets in different countries (see Riach and Rich (2002) for an overview and Section 6.3.1). Many of these field experiments have focused on females, on immigrants, on the elderly, but less attention has been paid to discrimination against homosexuals.

Psychological and sociological research demonstrates the existence of sexual prejudice. Like other types of prejudice, sexual prejudice is an attitude; it is directed at a social group and its members, and it involves hostility or dislike. There is some literature in psychology furnishing proofs that negative attitudes towards homosexuals do exist (Herek and Capitanio, 1996; Yang, 1997).

Economic research regarding discrimination against homosexuals has so far primarily made use of register data and econometric methods. Focus has been on differences between homo- and heterosexuals in labor market outcomes (see Section 6.3.2.1 for such evidence).

There are very few experiments that try to test discrimination against homosexuals. In Canada, Adam (1981) established discrimination against male as well as female homosexuals who applied for jobs in Canadian law firms, and Weichselbaumer (2003) found that lesbian females were subject to discrimination when they applied for jobs in Austria.

To the best of our knowledge, Ahmed and Hammarstedt (2009)[6] were the first to conduct a field experiment studying discrimination against homosexuals on the housing market in Sweden. They conducted a study of the rental housing market using the internet as a research platform. Two fictitious couples, one heterosexual and one homosexual, both openly signaling their sexual orientation, apply for vacant rental apartments advertised by landlords on the internet in Sweden. Homosexuals are identified as individuals living with partners of the same sex. The authors explore the incidence of discrimination by observing how landlords e-mail back and invite applicants to further contacts and/or to a showing of the housing unit. Their findings show that homosexual males are discriminated against on the Swedish housing market, since the homosexual couple gets far fewer callbacks and fewer invitations to further contacts and to showings of apartments than the heterosexual couple.

6.3.2.1 EVIDENCE ON EARNINGS DIFFERENCES

A number of studies have investigated earnings differences between homosexual and heterosexual people. Most studies have been conducted in the United States and have used data from the General Social Survey (GSS), where sexual orientation is identified through responses to questions regarding sexual behavior, for example their recent sex partners. GSS is often used in combination with complementary data. Badgett (1995) pioneered the study of the wage effects of sexual orientation, where she used the pooled 1989–1991 GSS data. She found that gay males earned from 11 to 27% less than heterosexual males. She found a similar pattern for females, but these results were not significant. Badgett (2001) extended her analysis and continued to find lower earnings for gay males, but not for lesbians. In subsequent work on updated GSS data, Berg and Lien (2002), Black et al. (2003), and Blandford (2003), confirmed Badgett's findings that the earnings of gay males are

---

[6] See also Ahmed et al. (2012).

significantly lower than the earnings of heterosexual males, but in contrast, they found that lesbians earn significantly more than heterosexual females.

Other studies in the United States used the US Census of Population data, which allow the identification of people with same-sex unmarried partners. Using the 1990 US Census, Klawitter and Flatt (1998) found that males in same-sex couples have significantly lower earnings than males in opposite-sex couples. They found no significant differences for females. Allegretto and Arthur (2001) reached similar results in a study of gay males. Carpenter (2005, 2007) and Elmslie and Tebaldi (2007) have used other sources of data to test the robustness of the results in the studies based on the GSS and Census data in the United States. Overall, they present the same pattern of results as their predecessors: gay males suffer from an earnings penalty, while lesbians do not, compared with their heterosexual counterparts.

Research on the earnings of homosexuals outside the United States is limited. Yet the handful of studies that have been conducted in the UK, Netherlands, Canada, and Sweden find similar results to those in the United States. From the UK, Arabsheibani et al. (2004) found the usual pattern that gay males suffer from an income penalty, and lesbians experience an income premium. Similar results are provided by Plug and Berkhout (2004) for the Netherlands.

A recent paper by Ahmed et al. (2011a) studies the earnings differences in Sweden between homosexuals and heterosexuals at the household level. This is important because the individual decision on labor force participation, labor supply, and, thus, individual earnings, is likely to be affected by or even be an outcome of decisions at the household level. As a result, the pattern of earnings differentials found at the individual level may not extend to the household level. This study was made possible by the fact that all homosexuals in Sweden were allowed to enter civil unions in 1995. The authors use the Longitudinal integration database of health insurance and labor market studies at Statistics Sweden since they have access to data on earnings, age, gender, educational attainment, and region of residence for all homosexuals who were living in civil unions, and for all married heterosexual people in Sweden in 2007. In line with previous research, they find that gay males are at an earnings disadvantage compared with heterosexual males, while lesbians earn slightly more than heterosexual females. However, when the authors combine individuals into households, they find very small earnings differentials between gay households and lesbian households. However, lesbian households earn considerably less than both gay and heterosexual households.

These results are similar to previous findings on household earnings. Using US 1990 Census data, Klawitter and Flatt (1998) also found that at the individual level, gay males earned less than male heterosexuals, and lesbians earned more than female heterosexuals, but at the household level, gay households and heterosexual households earned more than lesbian households. Using US 2000 Census data, Black et al. (2007) found that the earnings of lesbian and heterosexual households were alike, and that gay households had the highest earnings.

6.3.2.2 EVIDENCE ON EMPLOYMENT DIFFERENCES

We have seen that there are important differences in terms of earnings between homosexual and heterosexual workers. We would now like to study the difference in the hiring process in the labor market. In this section, we will survey the field experiments in this literature.

Interestingly, the European studies (Drydakis, 2009, 2011, for Greece; Weichselbaumer, 2003, for Austria) find strong evidence of discrimination against gays and lesbians in the hiring process while studies for the US (e.g. Hebl et al., 2002) find no effect. All these studies have some limitations and we will look in detail at the recent study by Ahmed et al. (2011b) for Sweden, which is the "cleanest" study in terms of testing this effect. They constructed written applications consisting of an application letter that describes a fictitious applicant and a résumé suited for applying to ten different occupations. The applications were sent to all employers that were announcing an open vacancy during the period between August 2010 and January 2011. The applicant's gender and sexual orientation were randomly assigned to the application for each employer they contacted. Therefore, each potential employer received only one application, which was either from a heterosexual male or female or from a gay or lesbian person. The authors used distinctive male or female names to signal the gender of the applicant and labeled the applicant as a gay, lesbian, or heterosexual by revealing the gender of the applicant's spouse and by adding information about voluntary work in a homosexual organization (for gay and lesbian) and a neutral help organization (for heterosexual). Interestingly, this is the first nationwide field experiment, even though gays and lesbians tend to live disproportionately in big cities (Black et al., 2007). Ahmed et al. (2011b) find that there is indeed discrimination in the hiring process in the labor market for both gays and lesbians. Gays are discriminated against in typically male-dominated occupations while lesbians are discriminated against in typically female-dominated occupations. The magnitude of the discrimination varies between different occupations and there is discrimination against gays and lesbians only in the private sector. To be more precise, a heterosexual female applicant received 22% more responses from employers than a lesbian applicant, while for a heterosexual male this figure was 14%.[7]

---

[7] For Austria (Weichselbaumer, 2003) and Greece (Drydakis, 2011), a heterosexual female applicant received 31 and 123% more responses from employers than a lesbian applicant, while

So far we have reviewed the empirical literature on homosexuals. Physical appearance is also an aspect that has been studied and which is the subject of discrimination. We would first like to review the literature on obesity, which is one aspect of physical appearance. We will then review the literature on beauty and examine whether people who are not good looking (this could include obese people but in fact includes many more individuals) are discriminated against and have adverse labor market outcomes as compared to better-looking workers.

6.3.3 *Physical Appearance and Labor Market Outcomes*

6.3.3.1 OBESITY

Obesity is a rapidly growing health problem that affects an increasing number of countries worldwide (World Health Organization, 1998). Almost two-thirds of Americans aged 20 and older are classified as overweight in 1999–2000, compared to 46% in 1976–1980 (Flegal et al., 1998, 2002). From 1980 to 1999–2000, for Australian people aged 25–64 years, the proportion of overweight women increased from 27% to 47%, and the proportion of overweight men increased from 47% to 66% (Dixon and Waters, 2003). In England and many other European countries the prevalence of obesity is also rising to epidemic proportions. In 1980, 6% of males and 8% of females in England were obese; by 2003 the prevalence had trebled to 21% and 24% respectively (Department of Health, 2003). The worldwide growth in obesity is a serious cause for concern because as well as being a debilitating condition in its own right, obesity is an important risk factor for a number of major diseases, including coronary heart disease, type II diabetes, osteoarthritis, hypertension, and stroke (NHLBI, 1998).

There are five reasons why obesity and employment may be negatively correlated.

(i) Obesity can be a debilitating health condition (NHLBI, 1998). Therefore, everything else being equal, the obese are likely to be less productive than the non-obese, and therefore less likely to be employed.

(ii) Obese workers may be discriminated against. Based on Balsa and McGuire (2003) this might arise for three reasons. First, there may be prejudice by employers, reflecting their distaste for obese workers and the psychological costs incurred when dealing with them (Moon and McLean, 1980). Second, there may be stereotyping by employers, arising from a belief that the obese are less productive (Everett, 1990). Third, discrimination may arise through uncertainty or a lack of knowledge about the productivity of obese workers (Pagan and Davila, 1997).

---

for a heterosexual male this figure was 186% for Greece, since Weichselbaumer (2003) only studied lesbians.

(iii) Unemployment causes obesity. For example, unemployed individuals, who have lower incomes, are more likely to consume cheaper and more fattening food (Cawley, 2004).

(iv) There are unobserved variables, such as lack of self-confidence, that could cause both obesity and low wages or low employment rates.

(v) Obesity may be measured systematically with error owing to unobserved factors correlated with employment. This might arise if individuals in lower socioeconomic groups are more likely to under or over-report their BMI everything else being equal.

Although much attention has been directed towards the association between (usually bad) health and (bad) labor market outcomes (see Currie and Madrian, 1999, for a review of studies on health and labor market outcomes), there is an important literature on the impact of obesity on labor market outcomes. Currie and Madrian (1999) state that the overall impression from this literature is that the associations between health status and labor market outcomes are mostly positive, but not very strong. From this strand of literature we will, however, only be discussing the results for the obesity penalty.

In laboratory settings, psychologists and sociologists have documented differential treatment by employers toward the obese (see Roehling, 1999). In such experiments, subjects are asked to make hiring decisions about hypothetical employees where the only difference is the subject's weight. The results of these studies show that differential treatment on the basis of a person's weight can be found in a number of employment decisions (including compensation, placement, and promotion). These studies have often found that differential treatment owing to weight is more common for women than for men. However, the extent to which these experimental results have external validity is questionable.

In the economics literature, Cawley (2004) uses the National Longitudinal Survey of Youths (NLSY) in the United States to estimate an obesity effect and ends up with an obesity wage penalty that is sizable and statistically significant for women, while the results for males are more mixed. Cawley correlates mother's weight with child's weight and ends up with obesity wage penalties. Register and Williams (1990) and Averett and Korenman (1996) also use the same data, the NLSY, to estimate an obesity effect. They find similar effects. In other words, these studies find a sizable and statistically significant obesity wage penalty for women, while the results for males are more mixed. Using other US datasets, Biddle and Hamermesh (1994) and Behrman and Rosenzweig (2001) find no effect of weight on wages.[8]

---

[8] In their study, Behrman and Rosenzweig (2001) use data on identical twins from the Minnesota Twins Registry in order to address specifically the issue of endowment heterogeneity.

For Europe, different papers have analyzed the relationship between obesity and employment. Using a 1994 sample of Finnish adults, Sarlio-Lahteenkorva and Lahelma (1999) used a logit model to analyze the impact of current obesity on current employment and long-term unemployment, defined as being unemployed for two years or more in the previous five-year period. Controlling for age, educational attainment, region of residence, and limiting long-standing illness, they found for females that obesity has a significant and positive impact on long-term unemployment and an insignificant effect on current employment. For males, obesity had an insignificant effect on both employment measures. Using data from two rounds of the Health Survey for England, Morris (2007) investigated the impact of obesity on employment. The findings show that obesity has a statistically significant and negative effect on employment for both males and females. The study by Garcia and Quintana-Domeque (2006), for nine European countries using the European Community Household Panel (ECHP), finds a negative correlation between wages and obesity, ranging from −2 to −10% for women; for men, no country estimate is lower than −2%, and five estimates are in fact positive.

Making inferences about differential treatment against obese/unattractive persons from interview data is, however, problematic for a number of reasons. Upon questioning, employers don't necessarily express their true attitudes toward these applicants; and, even if they do, their attitudes are not automatically consistent with their behavior.

To circumvent these difficulties, researchers have relied on field experiments. Correspondence testing has been used, in which the researcher sends two equal applications to advertised job openings with the only difference being the photo attached to the application: one obese and the other of normal weight. This is similar to the methodology used for homosexuals (see e.g. Weichselbaumer, 2003, who also used pictures in the correspondence-testing framework to study sexual orientation discrimination in hiring, and Section 6.3.2). This methodology ensures that productive characteristics on the supply side are held constant. The degree of differential treatment is quantified by the difference between the two groups in the number of callbacks for a job interview. Using this methodology, Rooth (2009) sent fictitious applications for real job openings to find evidence of differential treatment in the hiring of obese individuals in the Swedish labor market. The applications were sent in pairs, where one facial photo of an otherwise identical applicant was manipulated to show the individual as obese. Applications sent with the weight-manipulated photo had a significantly lower call back response for an interview. The call back response rate was six percentage points lower for men and eight percentage points lower for women. Lundborg et al. (2010) also find a statistically significant obesity penalty when analyzing the association between BMI (Body Mass Index) and earnings. Interestingly, this penalty was reduced when cognitive and non-cognitive skills were included in the earnings regression. Non-cognitive skills explained about half of the obesity penalty, while cognitive skills explained around 20%.

6.3.3.2 BEAUTY

Obsesity is one aspect of physical appearance. There are obviously many more aspects of physical appearance that are important in explaining discrimination and labor market outcomes of workers. There is indeed a growing literature analyzing the importance of physical appearance on labor market outcomes. This literature shows that attractive people are believed to possess socially desirable traits. Indeed, Feingold's (1992) meta-analysis of this literature reports a robust association between physical attractiveness and many personality traits, social skills, mental health, and intelligence.

A relatively large body of empirical literature has analyzed the correlation between beauty and labor market outcomes (for a review of this literature, see Hamermesh, 2011). However, the evidence demonstrating a causal relationship is scarce.

Heilman and Saruwatari (1979) provide evidence of a positive correlation between beauty and labor market performance. They asked college students to rate résumés (which included a photograph) of applicants for one of two jobs, a traditionally male managerial job and a traditionally female non-managerial job. Subjects were told that all applicants had recently graduated and had been pre-screened on the basis of educational and background qualifications. An examination of the results showed that attractiveness was consistently an advantage for male applicants but was an advantage only for females seeking traditionally female jobs. Attractive females were perceived as more feminine than unattractive females, and were therefore at a disadvantage when seeking a job that traditionally required masculine characteristics. Biddle and Hamermesh (1994) provide further evidence of the beauty premium. Analyzing self-reported data on respondents' appearance and labor market variables, they find that unattractive people earn 5 to 10% less than average-looking people, who in turn earn less than the good-looking individuals. Harper (2000) studies individuals born in Britain. He finds that the penalty of being unattractive (a self-reported measure) is about 15% lower wages for men and 11% lower wages for women as compared to the attractive applicants. Fink et al. (2007) find attractiveness to be correlated with the subjects' physical strength. Fletcher (2009) uses longitudinal data on wages from the United States and finds that wage returns to (self-reported) attractiveness are large (5 to 10%) relative to the returns to ability (3 to 6%).

The works cited are all non-experimental studies. The identification of a causal link between attractiveness and labor market performance is a complex task; one that becomes particularly questionable in non-experimental settings. Different sources of biases, ranging from the selection into occupations/labor market to the potential reverse causality from income to attractiveness, might contaminate the results obtained from non-experimental settings (Bertrand and Mullainathan, 2004). In an experimental setting, Mobius and Rosenblat (2006) revealed that attractive people received higher wages because they were perceived as more able, conditional on productive skills. They find, however, that beauty is not correlated with labor productivity.

Different field experiments have been conducted in different countries. Using recent research in psychology, anthropology, and graphic design technology, people have been using the following methodology (similar to experiments testing discrimination of obese people). Researchers construct a series of fictitious faces and attaches them to fictitious résumés. While ensuring that the résumés are of equal quality (by controlling for their content), they made the faces progressively more attractive or unattractive through computer manipulation. The researchers then submit these fictitious resumes (including photographs) to real job openings and analyze the responses (callbacks).

For instance, in a randomly selected telephone survey in the US (Kuran and McCaffery, 2004), it was found that most of the participants felt that discrimination based on looks exceeded discrimination based on ethnicity or national background.

López Bóo et al. (2012) conducted a randomized field experiment in Buenos Aires, Argentina, by providing evidence on the existence of discrimination based on physical appearance in an early stage of the job search process. Although they analyze a different question, their experiment design follows the empirical strategy utilized in Bertrand and Mullainathan (2004). Their results indicate that attractive people receive 36% more callbacks than unattractive people. The authors also document that more attractive candidates are not only more likely to be contacted, but that they are contacted sooner than less attractive applicants. Given the experimental setting, the estimated beauty premia can only be attributed to the differences in facial attractiveness of the job candidates. A similar study is that of Ruffle and Shtudiner (2010). These authors analyze the effects of attractiveness on callback rates following a similar experimental strategy in Israel. They find similar effects.

6.4 Concluding Remarks

Our survey of the empirical literature has revealed that homosexual females do not seem to suffer from discrimination in the labor market and, on the contrary, some studies find that they have a premium in terms of wages. Using the taste-based and statistical theories of discrimination, we can probably explain why homosexual males have adverse labor market outcomes but not why we find the opposite result for homosexual females. There is another theory that can explain the latter fact. Becker (1981) has put forward the idea of specialization within families by arguing that heterosexual males specialize in market labor and heterosexual females in household labor because of comparative advantages caused by biological differences. On the contrary, homosexual households are unable to specialize to the same extent as heterosexual households, because the gains from gender differences between spouses in comparative advantages do not exist. Compared to heterosexual females, lesbians acquire more market-related human capital, are more focused on their career, and will therefore have a higher chance of finding a job and higher wages. In contrast, gay males are predicted to have worse labor market outcomes than heterosexual males, because they will invest less in market-related human capital than heterosexual males. Regarding obese and unattractive individuals, the existing (limited) studies suggest the presence of a penalty, both for males and females, although the magnitude varies greatly between the different studies. With the exception of some studies based on field experiments in Sweden and a few other studies using special datasets for one country, the evidence on these topics for most European countries is virtually non-existent.

7

Exploratory Analysis for Europe: Religion and Physical Appearance

Eleonora Patacchini, Giuseppe Ragusa, and Yves Zenou

7.1 Introduction

This chapter provides novel evidence on the employment and labor market participation rates of underweight and overweight people as well as people belonging to different religious groups, using the available cross-country data for Europe. Our results should not be interpreted as causal, but as illustrative of interesting correlations.

Using data from the International Social Survey Program (ISSP), we investigate the relationship between religion and labor market outcomes. We find that, in Europe, Jews are the most educated group, with high employment and participation rates, whereas Muslims are the least educated group with the lowest employment rate. Interestingly, Muslims do not show on average a particularly low average participation rate. Asians appear instead as highly educated individuals (on average only less educated than Jews) and with an employment rate comparable to that of the other European religious groups. Interestingly, in Southern Europe, these differences in terms of education and labor market outcomes across religious groups are more pronounced. Our simple OLS regressions, which control for individual characteristics (including education, age, household size, and marital status) show an employment penalty for Muslim males of about 12%. This is even larger for females (more than 17%). Muslims, however, also tend to participate less in the labor market (especially females, who are about 16% less likely to participate in the labor market than non-religious females). When we distinguish between Northern and Southern Europe, it appears that both Muslim males and females participate more in the labor market in Southern Europe compared with Central Europe but they find it more difficult to find a job, especially females. This seems to suggest that discrimination might be at work against this group in Southern Europe, in particular against Muslim females. In Europe, while

Asians, Muslims, and Jews are always in the minority, Catholics, Protestants, and Orthodox Christians can be in the majority or minority in the country considered. We then perform our analysis distinguishing between strongly Catholic, strongly Protestant, and strongly Orthodox European countries. In particular, accordingly to the conventional wisdom, highly religious, especially Catholic women, tend to have an extremely low participation rate in highly Catholic countries such as Italy or Spain, and this could be the main explanation of their low employment rates. We instead find that, compared to non-religious women, they tend to participate less in Northern countries such as Sweden or Norway, but once in the labor market, they find a job more easily.

Using data from the European Community Household Panel and the European Union Statistics on Income and Living Conditions, we then study the relationship between obesity and labor market outcomes. The results concerning Body Mass Index (BMI) largely differ depending on the gender of the person. In terms of employment, the penalty of underweight individuals is mainly a male problem whereas that of obese individuals is mainly a female issue. The magnitude of the effects is about 3% both for underweight males and obese females. In terms of labor force participation, underweight males also seem to be the most discouraged group (about 9% less likely to participate), whereas both female and male obese individuals participate less in the labor market than "normal" individuals (about 8% and 3% less likely to participate, respectively). We also find that while in Northern Europe obese males have more difficulties in finding a job (more than 2% less likely to find a job compared to normal-weight males), in Southern Europe they are not penalized. On the contrary, they even receive a premium in terms of probability of finding a job. On the other hand, while in Northern Europe underweight males do not seem to be penalized with respect to normal-weight individuals, in Southern Europe they show a strong employment penalty (more than 6%). There are no differences, however, in terms of labor market participation of obese or underweight males between Northern and Southern Europe. Regarding females, we instead find that the most notable difference is in terms of participation rates. In particular, we find that, in Southern Europe, underweight females tend to participate more. This reduces the strong penalty for women that is found in Northern Europe. We begin the chapter by discussing the labor market and antidiscrimination policies that have been implemented in the different European countries.

7.2 Antidiscrimination Policies in Europe: Evidence from the MIPEX Index

The importance given to the protection of human rights and fundamental freedoms in the European Community Treaties has changed considerably since the European venture was first launched. A decisive step towards a formal recognition of human rights was the implementation of antidiscrimination laws and principles in the Treaty of Amsterdam, which are common to all the member states. In 1997, the member states of the European Union (EU) unanimously decided to add a new article to the Amsterdam Treaty (Article 13). The new article enables the European Council to take appropriate actions to combat discrimination based on sex, racial or ethnic origin, religion or belief, disability, age, or sexual orientation. After the implementation of the Amsterdam Treaty on May 1, 1999, the Council adopted measures to implement Article 13. Since then, the Member States have introduced different policies and activities fighting against discrimination based on sex, racial and ethnic origin, religion or belief, disability, age, and sexual orientation along the lines proposed by the Commission. The EU Charter of Fundamental Rights is now formally recognized as legally binding. The EU directives aim at ensuring uniformity in the interpretation and application of Community law. The Amsterdam Treaty, however, did not settle all institutional questions. Work is still in progress on reforming the institutions to make them capable of operating effectively and democratically in a much enlarged EU. In particular, the legal definitions of discrimination and the mechanisms to enforce them are still widely varied across EU member states. Countries also greatly diverge on fields of application and equality policies. The OECD Employment Outlook in 2008 provides a focus on antidiscrimination legislation in Europe, highlighting some of the cross-country differences in worker incentives to bring a case before court and employer incentives to comply with discrimination policies (see also Boeri and Van Ours, 2012, Chapter 4, for an overview). However, while for the employment protection legislations the OECD provides a comprehensive index combining various indicators, such an index is not available for the discrimination policies. To the best of our knowledge, the only quantitative measure capturing the complexity of antidiscrimination laws and principles across European countries is a composite score assigned to each European country for its performance in this policy area that can be extracted from the Migrant Integration Policy Index (MIPEX). We will use this index in our regression analysis in Section 7.3. The use of this quantitative indicator will provide us with a first investigation of the role of antidiscrimination policies in the employment prospects of individuals who might suffer from market discrimination because of religion, sexual orientation, and physical attribute (e.g. obesity).

Let us now describe in detail the MIPEX and provide a descriptive picture of Europe with regard to the antidiscrimination component of this index.

The MIPEX is produced by a consortium of 25 organizations. Amongst them are universities, research institutes, think-tanks, foundations, NGOs, and equality bodies. The MIPEX project was first launched in 2004 with the aim of improving the quality of the debate on migrant integration policy in Europe by providing objective, accessible, and comparable data. The MIPEX index measures policies integrating migrants in 25 EU member states and three non-EU countries. It considers over 140 policy indicators to create a rich, multidimensional picture of migrants' opportunities to participate in European societies. MIPEX covers six policy areas that shape a migrant's journey to full citizenship: labor market access, family reunion, long-term residence, political participation, access to nationality, antidiscrimination. Since policies are measured against the same standards across all member states, MIPEX is a benchmark tool to compare performance. The goal of keeping track of the progress of integration policies in Europe over time is achieved by different editions of the index. Data are now available for 2007 and 2010 (when data on new states were collected).

For our purposes, we will use the antidiscrimination component, hereafter D_MIPEX, of the MIPEX index. The D_MIPEX measures the antidiscrimination law in each country that helps guarantee equal opportunities in economic, social, and public life for all members of society. It also measures whether the law punishes a wide range of actors who discriminate against a migrant because of his/her ethnic origin, race, religion or nationality, among other grounds. It also determines if the state helps individuals seek justice through strong enforcement mechanisms.

More specifically, the D_MIPEX encompasses four aspects of antidiscrimination law and principles: (i) definition and concepts; (ii) fields of application; (iii) enforcement mechanisms; (iv) equality policies. Best practice for each policy indicator is set at the highest European standard, drawn from the Council of Europe Conventions or European Community Directives. The highest European standards for each of these practices are given a score of 100 and the index is then standardized at between 0 and 100 to ease cross-country comparisons. Table 7A.1 shows in detail what a best policy practice (i.e. an index equals 100), a halfway practice (i.e. an index equals 50), and a worst policy practice (i.e. an index equals 0) mean in terms of laws and principles in each policy area. In the case of the D_MIPEX, the best possible case is a country where the law punishes a wide range of actors who discriminate against an individual in many ways and on various grounds. The law applies these definitions to the many aspects of life where the individual participates in his/her community. The state helps him/her seek justice through strong enforcement mechanisms. Protection from victimization empowers him/her to bring forward a case without fear of reprisals in his/her job, school, etc. The court can choose the most appropriate of a wide range of sanctions, such as financial compensation or negative or positive measures, to stop further discrimination. Equality bodies have a robust legal standing to help

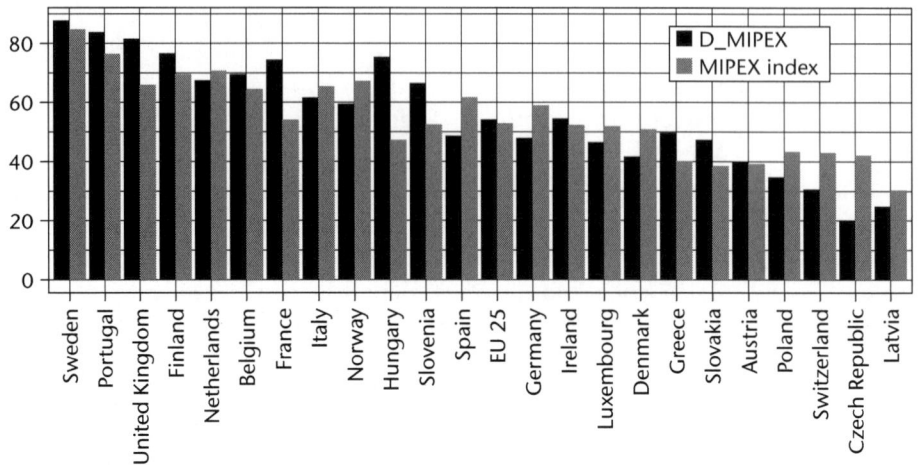

Figure 7.1. Anti-discrimination index (D_INDEX) and total index, 2007 values.
Source: MIPEX, 2007.

all victims. The state takes up its responsibility to lead public dialogue and systematically promote equality in its functions. In the worst possible case (i.e. an index equals 0), perpetrators are free to deny employment, housing, health, welfare, and educational opportunities to a individual based on his/her race, religion, nationality, etc. He/she is left exposed to public incitements to violence, hatred or discrimination, and public insults and threats. Because the definitions in the law are weakly enforced, an individual who feels that he/she is discriminated against is discouraged from bringing forward the case. He/she has limited access to procedures with no access to legal aid or assistance from NGOs (legal entities with a legitimate interest in defending equality). Equality bodies cannot conduct independent investigations or help victims of discrimination. He/she also cannot rely on the state to actively combat discrimination.

Figure 7.1 shows the values of the D_MIPEX and MIPEX for different European countries in 2007. It appears that antidiscrimination policies (D_MIPEX index) are strongly favorable in Sweden (88), Portugal (84), United Kingdom (81.5), and Finland (77). These are also countries with favorable integration policies (MIPEX index). In particular, Sweden and Portugal are the countries with the highest values of the overall index of integration (MIPEX): 84.7 and 76.4, respectively. Note also that France (74.5) and Hungary (75.3) have a quite favorable antidiscrimination policy, although they are only just halfway to best practice in terms of the overall integration policy index (54 and 47.2 respectively). Antidiscrimination policies are instead strongly unfavorable in Latvia (25), the Czech Republic (20), and in Switzerland (30.6).

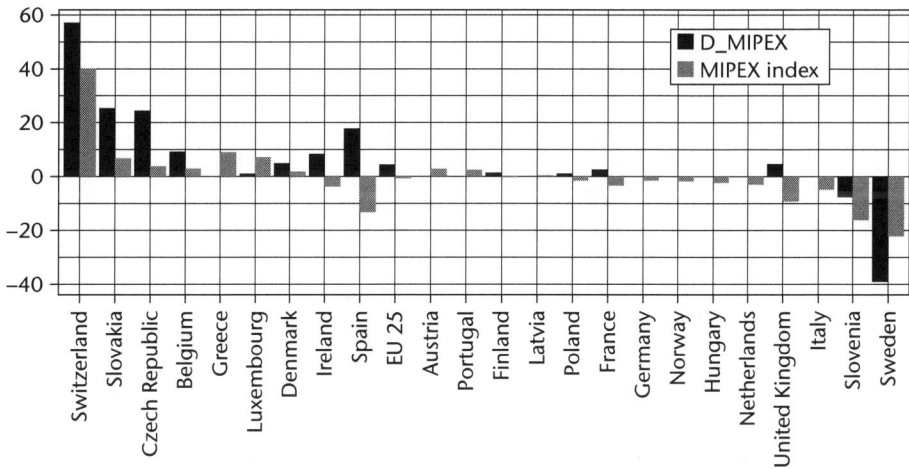

Figure 7.2. Anti-discrimination index (D_INDEX) and total index, 2007–2010 changes.

Source: MIPEX, 2007–2010 changes.

These are countries that also show values of the overall index of integration much below the European average (53). In Italy, the value of the D_MIPEX (61.6) reveals that antidiscrimination policies are only slightly favorable, and the similar value of the overall indicator (65.3) suggests that this area does not receive higher attention than other integration policies.

Figure 7.2 displays the changes that occurred in these indicators between 2007 and 2010. The graph reveals a number of notable features. First, there are important variations in terms of changes of these indicators across European countries. This is true for both the MIPEX and the D_MIPEX. For the MIPEX, positive variations are as large as 40 points (Switzerland) and as small as 0.35 (Latvia), whereas negative variations are as large as 22 points (Sweden) and as small as 0.3 (Finland). For the D_MIPEX, positive variations are as large as 57 points (Switzerland) and as small as virtually 0 (Austria), whereas negative variations are as large as 39 points (Sweden) and as small as virtually 0 (Netherlands). Even more interestingly, variations in one indicator do not always correspond to similar variations for the same country, sometimes not even in sign. For example, we find that Spain has gained almost 18 points in the D_MIPEX (meaning that the country has improved its antidiscrimination policies), whereas the MIPEX has lost more than 13 points in the same time period (meaning that, on the contrary, its integration policies have been worse). A similar pattern is true for the UK, Ireland, France, and Finland. In addition, a number of other countries, such as Belgium, the Czech Republic, Denmark, and Slovakia, have shown improvements in antidiscrimination policies, which are much larger than those registered in the other integration policy areas. On the other hand, we find countries that gave more importance to integration policies other than those against discrimination. This is the case of Luxembourg, Latvia, Portugal, and Greece, where the D_MIPEX shows no or limited change over 2007–2010 while the value of MIPEX largely increased.

The interesting question to investigate is what are the areas of the D_MIPEX that have registered the highest gains or losses.

Table 7.1 collects the values of the D_MIPEX for the different European countries, distinguishing between the different policy areas. We report the values of the index in 2007 (upper panel) and the variations between 2007 and 2010 (lower panel). We also report the values of the D_MIPEX and MIPEX in the last two columns of each panel. It appears that countries greatly diverge on fields of application and equality policies, whereas definition and concepts of discrimination are relatively more homogeneous across European countries. It also appears that, while few countries show similar indices for the different areas (exceptions include Greece and Ireland), most of the countries have very different values in each policy area. For example, for Italy we find a value as large as 100 in terms of field of application and a value as low as 11 in terms of equality policies (the worst practice after the Czech Republic, which has a value equal to 0). This means that Italy has very strong antidiscrimination laws that cover employment and vocational training, education, social protection and access to goods and services for race and ethnicity, religion and belief, and nationality. On the other hand, Italy has weak antidiscrimination laws for equality policies (i.e. positive actions that promote equality). If we look at the European average, we can see that Europe is performing poorly, in particular in terms of equality policies.

7.3 Empirical Analysis

We begin our empirical investigation by providing a first picture of the labor market outcomes of individuals with specific characteristics, using the available cross country data for Europe. More specifically, we investigate the employment and labor market participation rates of obese people as well as people belonging to different religious groups using the existing data for Europe.[1] We will also attempt to relate these findings to the labor market policies and antidiscrimination policies that have been implemented in different countries.

---

[1] In Section 6.3, we did not survey the literature on the impact of religion on labor market outcomes. This is because this literature is very large and involves other theoretical mechanisms than discrimination such as social norms, culture, and social interactions. A good introduction to this literature can be found in Iannaccone (1998).

Table 7.1. MIPEX Index on anti-discrimination policies

| | MIPEX 2007 | | | | | |
	Definition and Concepts	Field of Application	Enforcement Mechanism	Equality Policies	D_MIPEX	MIPEX Total
Austria	57.1	8.3	50.0	44.4	40.0	39.2
Belgium	64.3	83.3	75.0	55.6	69.5	64.4
Cyprus	42.9	100.0	50.0	44.4	59.3	36.1
Czech Republic	42.9	8.3	29.2	0.0	20.1	42.1
Denmark	50.0	50.0	50.0	16.7	41.7	50.9
Finland	78.6	100.0	66.7	61.1	76.6	69.5
France	71.4	100.0	70.8	55.6	74.5	54.0
Germany	50.0	75.0	50.0	16.7	47.9	58.9
Greece	50.0	50.0	54.2	44.4	49.6	40.1
Hungary	50.0	100.0	79.2	72.2	75.3	47.2
Ireland	50.0	66.7	45.8	55.6	54.5	52.3
Italy	64.3	100.0	70.8	11.1	61.6	65.3
Latvia	28.6	8.3	29.2	33.3	24.9	30.4
Luxembourg	50.0	50.0	58.3	27.8	46.5	51.9
Netherlands	71.4	66.7	87.5	44.4	67.5	70.8
Norway	57.1	50.0	58.3	72.2	59.4	67.2
Poland	50.0	16.7	50.0	22.2	34.7	43.3
Portugal	64.3	100.0	87.5	83.3	83.8	76.4
Slovakia	64.3	25.0	66.7	33.3	47.3	38.5
Slovenia	64.3	100.0	62.5	38.9	66.4	52.5
Spain	57.1	50.0	54.2	33.3	48.7	61.7
Sweden	78.6	100.0	83.3	88.9	87.7	84.7
Switzerland	57.1	0.0	37.5	27.8	30.6	43.0
United Kingdom	85.7	100.0	62.5	77.8	81.5	65.8
EU 25	56.9	60.3	57.5	42.0	54.2	52.9

| | MIPEX 2007–2010 Changes | | | | | |
	Definition and Concepts	Field of Application	Enforcement Mechanism	Equality Policies	D_MIPEX	MIPEX Total
Austria	0.0	0.0	0.0	0.0	0.0	2.8
Belgium	14.3	16.7	0.0	5.6	9.1	2.9
Cyprus	0.0	0.0	0.0	0.0	0.0	−0.9
Czech Republic	14.3	41.7	25.0	16.7	24.4	3.7
Denmark	0.0	0.0	8.3	11.1	4.9	1.8
Finland	0.0	0.0	0.0	5.6	1.4	−0.3
France	14.3	0.0	−4.2	0.0	2.5	−3.4
Germany	0.0	0.0	0.0	0.0	0.0	−1.5
Greece	0.0	0.0	0.0	0.0	0.0	8.9
Hungary	0.0	0.0	0.0	0.0	0.0	−2.3
Ireland	0.0	33.3	0.0	0.0	8.3	−3.8
Italy	0.0	0.0	0.0	0.0	0.0	−4.9
Latvia	0.0	0.0	0.0	0.0	0.0	0.3
Luxembourg	0.0	0.0	4.2	0.0	1.0	7.1
Netherlands	0.0	0.0	0.0	0.0	0.0	−3.0
Norway	0.0	0.0	0.0	0.0	0.0	−1.7
Poland	0.0	0.0	4.2	0.0	1.0	−1.6
Portugal	0.0	0.0	0.0	0.0	0.0	2.4
Slovakia	−7.1	75.0	16.7	16.7	25.3	6.7
Slovenia	7.1	−50.0	12.5	0.0	−7.6	−16.2
Spain	7.1	50.0	8.3	5.6	17.8	−13.2
Sweden	−21.4	−50.0	−29.2	−55.6	−39.0	−22.2
Switzerland	21.4	100.0	45.8	61.1	57.1	40.1
United Kingdom	14.3	0.0	4.2	0.0	4.6	−9.2
EU 25	4.1	6.0	4.7	2.9	4.4	−0.7

Notes: The upper panel shows the level in 2007. The bottom panel shows the changes between 2007 and 2010.

7.3.1 Data

Our cross-country analysis is based on data coming from different sources. To analyze the labor market outcomes of individuals with a certain physical appearance (mainly related to BMI), we use data from the European Community Household Panel (ECHP) and the European Union Statistics on Income and Living Conditions (EU-SILC), which are collected under Eurostat (Statistical Office of the European Union) coordination. The ECHP is a longitudinal survey started in 1994 in 15 European Union member states and carried out yearly until 2001. The EU-SILC is a yearly survey started in 2004, which also includes new EU members and some non-EU countries. Both datasets cover a wide range of subjects such as income, labor force, sociodemographics, health, education, housing, poverty, and social exclusion.

The EU-SILC does not contain information on the respondent's weight and height. This information is available in the ECHP data, starting from 1998. Therefore, in our analysis on the labor market outcomes of obese individuals in Europe, we use the Body Mass Index (BMI) that can be constructed from the ECHP data for the years 1998–2001. The BMI is defined as the individual's weight divided by the square of his/her height. As it is standard (see Section 6.3), we use this index to assess how much individuals depart from a normal weight. Following the US National Institute of Health, we consider a BMI smaller than 18.5 as evidence that the individual is underweight, and a BMI above 30 to be an indication of obesity. In our regression analysis we will also use a finer classification. The countries included in our dataset are Denmark, Belgium, Ireland, Italy, Greece, Spain, Portugal, Austria, Finland, and Sweden.

The data provided by Eurostat (including the ECHP and the EU-SILC data) do not contain a breakdown by ethnic group or religion. Indeed, Eurostat collects data coming from the different national institutes for statistics. National legislation and practice in a number of member states prevent the collection and dissemination of information on ethnic group or religion in statistics. Some information might be obtained from indirect questions about nationality or country of birth, but this is far from being satisfactory and tends to cover only foreign-born citizens.

However, individual data on labor market outcomes and religion in Europe can be obtained from the International Social Survey Program (ISSP). In particular, this survey program contains special modules with additional questions on particular topics, including a module devoted to religion. More specifically, the ISSP religion module deals with religious beliefs, religious socialization, past and current religious practices, religion and governmental connections, religion in comparison to other aspects, and secular aspects. The module also contains basic demographic characteristics of the individuals and information on labor market participation and on employment status. The

ISSP religion module consists of three surveys from 1991, 1998, and 2008. We use this data to analyze the labor market outcomes of individuals with different religions in Europe. In our analysis on religion, we combined data from the 1998 and 2008 surveys. The data cover the following countries: Germany, United Kingdom, Hungary, the Netherlands, Italy, Ireland, Norway, Austria, Slovenia, Poland, Sweden, the Czech Republic, Bulgaria, Spain, Latvia, the Slovak Republic, France, Cyprus, Portugal, Denmark, Switzerland, Belgium, and Finland.

In all datasets, we select individuals of between 14 and 64 years. Stylized facts and summary statistics are presented by topic (religion and BMI) in the following subsections.

7.3.2 Religion in Europe

Let us begin our investigation by looking at the labor market outcomes of different religious groups in Europe. Table A.1 in Appendix A shows some descriptive statistics, distinguishing between the North, the Center, and the South of Europe.

Looking at the overall picture, it appears that Jews are, on average, the oldest and most educated group, with high employment and participation rates, whereas Muslims are the youngest and least educated with the lowest employment rate. Interestingly, Muslims do not show a particularly low average participation rate. It is worthwhile to note that Asians appear instead as highly educated individuals (on average less educated than Jews only) and with an employment rate comparable with that of the other European religious groups.[2] Interestingly, Southern Europe is the area where differences in terms of education and labor market outcomes across religious groups are more pronounced. Muslims show a particularly low education level, which does not translate into an extremely low participation rate. The penalty seems to be in the labor market, with extremely low employment rates (only 55% of them are employed).[3] Notably, people belonging to a Christian minority (labeled as Other Christians in the table) are only slightly more educated than Muslims but have a much higher employment rate and a much lower (actually the lowest among all groups) participation rate in Southern Europe. This could be a signal that there is more discrimination against Muslims than against Asians, Jews, or even Christians when they are in a minority.

In Table 7.2 upper panel, we investigate further these results using a simple OLS regression analysis where the different religious groups are coded as different dummies (with no religion as the reference category) and where

---

[2] With the term "Asians" we refer generally to persons of the following four Asian religions: Buddhists, Hindu, Shinto, and Sikh.

[3] For similar results, see Bisin et al. (2008, 2011).

Table 7.2. Religious affiliation and labor market outcomes

	All Employed	Females Employed	Males Employed	All Labor Force	Females Labor Force	Males Labor Force
			Baseline OLS regression results			
Asians	−0.0211	−0.00531	−0.0327	−0.0337	−0.0198	−0.0382
	(0.0191)	(0.0229)	(0.0292)	(0.0211)	(0.0323)	(0.0262)
Catholics	0.0235***	0.0130*	0.0323***	−0.0204***	−0.0387***	−0.00271
	(0.00498)	(0.00737)	(0.00674)	(0.00534)	(0.00840)	(0.00658)
Protestants	0.0189***	0.0241***	0.0121	0.000219	−0.0106	0.00737
	(0.00542)	(0.00786)	(0.00749)	(0.00648)	(0.00970)	(0.00830)
Orthodox	0.000275	−0.0406	0.0409*	−0.0144	−0.0498**	0.0176
	(0.0181)	(0.0273)	(0.0234)	(0.0149)	(0.0222)	(0.0197)
Jewish	−0.00548	−0.0586	0.0597***	0.0399	0.0271	0.0613
	(0.0351)	(0.0646)	(0.0162)	(0.0483)	(0.0743)	(0.0579)
Muslims	−0.131***	−0.175***	−0.120***	−0.0916***	−0.158***	−0.0581**
	(0.0244)	(0.0452)	(0.0291)	(0.0234)	(0.0402)	(0.0271)
Others	0.0161	0.0151	0.0125	−0.0175	−0.0335	−0.0110
	(0.0139)	(0.0174)	(0.0219)	(0.0187)	(0.0266)	(0.0259)
Female	−0.0159***			−0.0152***		
	(0.0037)			(0.0038)		
Constant	0.546***	0.351***	0.608***	−0.365***	−0.533***	−0.399***
	(0.0292)	(0.0537)	(0.0412)	(0.0303)	(0.0430)	(0.0375)
Observations	32,160	15,791	16,369	43,266	23,402	19,864
Country and Time FE	Yes	Yes	Yes	Yes	Yes	Yes
			Additional OLS regression results			
Asians	−0.0210	−0.00575	−0.0325	−0.0337	−0.0200	−0.0381
	(0.0192)	(0.0229)	(0.0293)	(0.0211)	(0.0323)	(0.0262)
Catholics	0.0317***	0.0220***	0.0399***	−0.0208***	−0.0412***	0.00160
	(0.00582)	(0.00809)	(0.00834)	(0.00669)	(0.0100)	(0.00843)
Catholic × strongly Catholic ctry	−0.0197*	−0.0261	−0.0161	−0.00001	0.00450	−0.00865
	(0.0103)	(0.0170)	(0.0132)	(0.0106)	(0.0171)	(0.0129)
Protestants	0.0229***	0.0272***	0.0163*	−0.00233	−0.0151	0.0103
	(0.00645)	(0.00935)	(0.00897)	(0.00734)	(0.0108)	(0.00945)
Protestant × strongly Protestant ctry	−0.0132	−0.00894	−0.0145	0.0135	0.0249	−0.0110
	(0.0103)	(0.0149)	(0.0141)	(0.0152)	(0.0230)	(0.0197)
Orthodox	−0.000395	−0.0417	0.0415*	−0.0161	−0.0479**	0.0126
	(0.0190)	(0.0285)	(0.0247)	(0.0151)	(0.0227)	(0.0197)
Orthodox × strongly orthodox ctry	0.0266	0.0445	−0.00198	0.0301	−0.0889	0.0954
	(0.0219)	(0.0334)	(0.0285)	(0.0831)	(0.0898)	(0.116)
Jewish	−0.00482	−0.0594	0.0608***	0.0404	0.0276	0.0614
	(0.0350)	(0.0644)	(0.0165)	(0.0482)	(0.0741)	(0.0580)
Muslims	−0.133***	−0.177***	−0.121***	−0.0919***	−0.158***	−0.0592**
	(0.0244)	(0.0453)	(0.0291)	(0.0234)	(0.0403)	(0.0271)
Others	0.0150	0.0134	0.0118	−0.0167	−0.0315	−0.0116
	(0.0140)	(0.0175)	(0.0221)	(0.0188)	(0.0266)	(0.0260)
Strongly Catholics	0.0392**	0.0219	0.00850	−0.0819	0.0586**	0.0652***
	(0.0158)	(0.0253)	(0.0192)	(0.0825)	(0.0271)	(0.0226)

(Continued)

Table 7.2. *(Continued)*

	All Employed	Females Employed	Males Employed	All Labor Force	Females Labor Force	Males Labor Force
			Additional OLS regression results			
Strongly Protestants	0.0243	0.0641***	0.0512***	−0.0294	0.0536*	0.0719***
	(0.0163)	(0.0198)	(0.0168)	(0.0826)	(0.0309)	(0.0250)
Strongly Orthodox		0.0570***			0.187**	0.0192
		(0.0218)			(0.0872)	(0.115)
Female	−0.0158***			−0.0152***		
	(0.0037)			(0.0038)		
Constant	0.530***	0.495***	0.610***	−0.393***	−0.604***	−0.465***
	(0.0284)	(0.0436)	(0.0371)	(0.0854)	(0.0410)	(0.0360)
Observations	32,160	15,791	16,369	43,266	23,402	19,864
Country and Time FE	Yes	Yes	Yes	Yes	Yes	Yes

Notes: The dependent variable of the regressions in Columns 1–3 is a dummy variable (employed) taking as value 1 if the individual is in the labor force and employed and zero if the individual is in the labor force but unemployed. The dependent variable of the regressions in columns 4–6 is a dummy variable (labor force) taking as value 1 if the individual is in the labor force and 0 otherwise. Strongly Catholic ctry, strongly Protestant ctry, and strongly Orthodox ctry are dummy variables that take value 1 if the country is strongly Catholic, Protestant, or Orthodox, respectively. Strongly Catholic countries are Italy, Ireland, Austria, Slovenia, Poland, Spain, Portugal, and Belgium. Strongly Protestant countries are Norway, Denmark, Finland. The only strongly Orthodox country is Greece. Robust standard errors in parentheses. "Asians" refers to persons of the following four Asian religions: Buddhism, Hinduism, Shintoism, and Sikhism. Although not reported, all specifications include as regressors: education, age, age squared, household size, marital status indicator, and urban vs. rural indicator. *** $p < 0.01$, ** $p < 0.05$, * $p < 0.1$.
Source: ISSP, 1998, 2008.

the influence of various factors (such as education, age, marital status and household size, country, and year fixed) is controlled for. We perform our analysis for males and females separately. In terms of employment prospects, compared to nonreligious individuals, this table shows that there is a significant premium for being Catholic and Protestant in Europe but a significant penalty for being Muslim. This premium is higher for males if Catholic and for females if Protestant. For Jews, only males have a statistically significant premium in terms of employment, capturing certainly their higher level of education. Interestingly, the penalty for Muslims is higher for females. This may suggest that discrimination is at work for the Muslim group, especially females. Muslims, however, also tend to participate less in the labor market (especially females, who are about 16% less likely to participate to the labor market than nonreligious females), whereas for the other religious groups we only find a penalty for Catholic and Orthodox women. This is not surprising as highly religious women, in particular Catholics, tend to stay more at home than participating in the labor market.

An interesting issue to investigate is whether the labor market outcomes are different when a religion is in the minority or majority. In Europe, while Asians, Muslims, and Jews are always in a minority, Catholics, Protestants, and Orthodox Christians can be in the majority or minority in the country considered. We distinguish between the strongly Catholic countries (such as Italy, Spain, Ireland, Poland), the strongly Protestant countries (such as Norway, Denmark, Finland),[4] and strongly Orthodox countries (mainly Greece). We then investigate whether the relationship between being Catholic, Protestant, or Orthodox Christian and labor market outcomes varies when these religions are in the minority (e.g. Catholic in Norway or Protestant in Italy) or majority. For this purpose, in the lower panel of Table 7.2, we define and include an interaction term with the correspondent religion dummies. Quite surprisingly, we find that Catholics and Protestants tend to have a higher probability of being employed in countries where they are in a minority with respect to nonreligious individuals. This is also true for Orthodox Christians, but only for males. Instead, we do not find notable differences with respect to participation rates, with the exception of Catholic and Orthodox Christian females who tend to participate less in countries where they are in a minority. This evidence is interesting. Accordingly to the conventional wisdom, highly religious, especially Catholic women, tend to have an extremely low participation rate in highly Catholic countries such as Italy or Spain, and this is the main source of their low employment rates. We find instead that they tend to participate less in Northern countries such as Norway or Finland (compared wih nonreligious women), but once in the labor market they find a job more easily. The strong penalty that accrues to Muslims (both to males and females and both in terms of employment and participation rates), however, is again a notable feature.

In the remaining part of our analysis, we devote our attention to further investigate the adverse labor market outcomes of Muslims in Europe. Table 7.3 investigates the penalty when distinguishing between Northern, the Central, and Southern Europe. Most notably, it appears that both Muslim males and females participate more in the labor market in Southern Europe compared to Central Europe but they find more difficulties in finding a job, especially females. This finding seems to suggest that discrimination might be at work against this group in Southern Europe, in particular against Muslim females. Gaining a conclusive understanding of the reasons underlying these differences is an extremely difficult task. Cultural attitudes about gender roles, poor socioeconomic background, and discrimination are possible explanations. In addition, discrimination might be due to factors other than religion per se, such as skin color or ethnic religion. Disentangling the different causes of discrimination is beyond the purpose of this chapter.

Let us attempt to investigate the effects of antidiscrimination (defined by the D_MIPEX in Section 7.2) and labor market policies on the negative

---

[4] The complete list of strongly Catholic and strongly Protestant countries are given in the note of Table 7.2. A country is strongly Protestant (Catholic) if the fraction of persons in the ISSP data that identify themselves as Protestant (Catholic) is above 75%.

Table 7.3. Muslim religion and labor market outcomes

	Focus on Muslims					
	All Employed	Females Employed	Males Employed	All Labor Force	Females Labor Force	Males Labor Force
Muslims	−0.0920***	−0.0644	−0.104*	−0.157**	−0.185**	−0.143**
	(0.0302)	(0.0451)	(0.0530)	(0.0569)	(0.0803)	(0.0513)
Muslim × north	−0.0111	−0.230**	0.0677	−0.0501	−0.210*	0.0785
	(0.0500)	(0.0863)	(0.0608)	(0.0902)	(0.114)	(0.0670)
Muslim × south	−0.165	−0.240**	−0.141	0.233***	0.265**	0.185***
	(0.0998)	(0.111)	(0.0985)	(0.0673)	(0.118)	(0.0582)
Asians	−0.00355	0.0105	−0.0149	−0.0360*	−0.0340	−0.0310
	(0.0208)	(0.0285)	(0.0291)	(0.0209)	(0.0287)	(0.0241)
Catholics	0.0134	0.00807	0.0173	−0.0203*	−0.0380*	−0.00179
	(0.0153)	(0.0199)	(0.0132)	(0.0106)	(0.0204)	(0.00687)
Protestants	0.0294**	0.0258*	0.0312**	0.0102	0.0122	0.00449
	(0.0118)	(0.0139)	(0.0121)	(0.0149)	(0.0247)	(0.0123)
Orthodox	0.0163	0.00828	0.0236	0.0423**	0.0329	0.0519**
	(0.0508)	(0.0611)	(0.0419)	(0.0168)	(0.0240)	(0.0214)
Jewish	0.00693	−0.0420	0.0693***	0.0500	0.0322	0.0696
	(0.0362)	(0.0676)	(0.0224)	(0.0438)	(0.0738)	(0.0546)
Others	0.0275**	0.0248	0.0292	−0.0190	−0.0347	−0.00361
	(0.0106)	(0.0163)	(0.0182)	(0.0166)	(0.0243)	(0.0235)
North	0.0193	0.0216	0.0159	0.0253	0.0323	0.0142
	(0.0176)	(0.0201)	(0.0187)	(0.0220)	(0.0375)	(0.0160)
South	−0.0124	−0.0269	−0.000338	0.00390	0.0110	−0.00275
	(0.0282)	(0.0365)	(0.0231)	(0.0203)	(0.0314)	(0.0185)
Female	−0.0147*			−0.152***		
	(0.00765)			(0.0138)		
Constant	0.514***	0.467***	0.555***	−0.469***	−0.632***	−0.436***
	(0.0632)	(0.0759)	(0.0628)	(0.111)	(0.138)	(0.0960)
Observations	32,160	15,791	16,369	43,266	23,402	19,864
R-squared	0.042	0.048	0.044	0.250	0.218	0.269
Country FE	No	No	No	No	No	No
Time FE	No	No	No	No	No	No

Notes: Pooled OLS regression results. The dependent variable of the regressions in columns 1–3 is a dummy variable (employed) taking as value 1 if the individual is in the labor force and employed and zero if the individual is in the labor force but unemployed. The dependent variable of the regressions in columns 4–6 is a dummy variable (labor force) taking as value 1 if the individual is in the labor force and 0 otherwise. Although not reported, all specifications include as regressors: education, age, age squared, household size, marital status indicators, and urban vs. rural indicator. Robust standard errors in parentheses. *** $p < 0.01$, ** $p < 0.05$, * $p < 0.1$.
Source: ISSP, 1998, 2008.

relationship between being Muslim and their labor market outcomes. We consider three main labor market policies in Europe: minimum wage, strictness of employment protection legislation, and trade union density. In Appendix B, we describe in detail these labor market policies. Table 7.4 shows that more regulated labor markets are favorable to Muslim males in terms of regular contracts, whereas Muslim females seem to show higher employment rates in countries with a higher minimum wage. We also find that an higher trade union density is associated with higher participation rates for Muslims.

Table 7.4. Muslim religion and labor market policies

	Policy investigation					
	All Employed	Females Employed	Males Employed	All Labor Force	Females Labor Force	Males Labor Force
Muslims	−0.294	−0.266	−0.260	−0.368*	−0.346**	−0.251
	(0.172)	(0.191)	(0.280)	(0.187)	(0.152)	(0.511)
Muslim × anti-discriminatory policy	−0.00260	−0.00121	−0.00575	−0.00473*	−9.16e-05	−0.0126
	(0.00338)	(0.00340)	(0.00488)	(0.00254)	(0.00203)	(0.00828)
Muslim × minimum wage	0.343**	0.400***	0.191	0.445**	0.251	0.824*
	(0.125)	(0.120)	(0.284)	(0.179)	(0.152)	(0.471)
Muslim × regular contracts	0.0495**	0.00401	0.145**	0.0920*	0.0658**	0.116
	(0.0202)	(0.0266)	(0.0611)	(0.0438)	(0.0291)	(0.0839)
Muslim × temporary contracts	−0.000206	−0.0107	0.00190	0.0158	0.0234	−0.0630
	(0.0259)	(0.0262)	(0.0872)	(0.0405)	(0.0337)	(0.0961)
Muslim × union density	0.00413	0.00417	0.00263	0.00586*	0.000824	0.0146***
	(0.00308)	(0.00303)	(0.00363)	(0.00279)	(0.00284)	(0.00378)
Anti-discrimination policy	0.000309	0.000482	−5.77e-06	−0.000139	−1.01e-05	−0.000327
	(0.000378)	(0.000454)	(0.000345)	(0.000377)	(0.000362)	(0.000775)
Minimum wage	−0.0173	−0.0712*	0.0596	0.0443	−0.0173	0.103
	(0.0420)	(0.0391)	(0.0492)	(0.0267)	(0.0423)	(0.0614)
Regular contracts	0.0148**	0.0122	0.0203**	0.0280***	0.00546	0.0492***
	(0.00687)	(0.00788)	(0.00779)	(0.00797)	(0.0106)	(0.0148)
Temporary contracts	−0.0192**	−0.00782	−0.0352***	−0.00219	−0.0122	0.00775
	(0.00748)	(0.00698)	(0.00925)	(0.00620)	(0.00770)	(0.0117)
Trade union density	0.000911**	0.000584	0.00145***	0.00132***	3.33e-05	0.00251***
	(0.000423)	(0.000482)	(0.000417)	(0.000408)	(0.000543)	(0.000851)
Asians	−0.0203	−0.0286	−0.00669	−0.0458*	−0.0512**	−0.0312
	(0.0247)	(0.0289)	(0.0302)	(0.0262)	(0.0231)	(0.0440)
Catholics	0.0228	0.0243*	0.0206	−0.0243	0.00405	−0.0562*
	(0.0150)	(0.0130)	(0.0200)	(0.0159)	(0.00720)	(0.0305)
Jewish	0.0479	0.0662***	0.0368	0.0504	0.00392	0.0851
	(0.0292)	(0.0191)	(0.0542)	(0.0713)	(0.0479)	(0.126)
Protestants	0.0102	0.00587	0.0131	0.00313	0.00709	−0.00804
	(0.0172)	(0.0157)	(0.0197)	(0.0188)	(0.0119)	(0.0330)
Orthodox	−0.0257	0.00204	−0.0686**	0.0167	−0.00205	0.0435
	(0.0246)	(0.0321)	(0.0313)	(0.0454)	(0.0383)	(0.0661)
Others	0.0284*	0.0171	0.0423*	−0.0123	−0.000493	−0.0307
	(0.0135)	(0.0186)	(0.0203)	(0.0180)	(0.0240)	(0.0297)
Female	−0.0157			−0.174***		
	(0.0104)			(0.0182)		
Constant	0.460***	0.517***	0.391***	−0.454***	−0.375***	−0.679***
	(0.0803)	(0.0788)	(0.0932)	(0.131)	(0.106)	(0.164)
Observations	30,312	15,865	14,447	42,043	19,472	22,571
R-squared	0.041	0.044	0.050	0.254	0.263	0.223
Country FE	No	No	No	No	No	No
Time FE	No	No	No	No	No	No

Notes: Pooled OLS regression results. The dependent variable of the regressions in columns 1–3 is a dummy variable (employed) taking as value 1 if the individual is in the labor force and employed and zero if the individual is in the labor force but unemployed. The dependent variable of the regressions in columns 4–6 is a dummy variable (labor force) taking as value 1 if the individual is in the labor force and 0 otherwise. Although not reported, all specifications include as regressors: education, age, age squared, household size, marital status indicator, and urban vs. rural indicator. Robust standard errors in parentheses. *** $p < 0.01$, ** $p < 0.05$, * $p < 0.1$.
Source: ISSP, 1998, 2008.

This finding may signal a change in trade union policies. Indeed, in the past some unions have actively lobbied for racist policies to guard their special interests. The interpretation of these correlations is, however, quite difficult. For example, a high density of trade union members does not always signal high trade union power. In France, Germany, and also in Italy, although the density of trade union members is relatively low, trade unions are very powerful, and this might discourage minorities from entering the labor market. The indicator used in the regressions does not capture this aspect. In addition, there is a high correlation between employment protection for temporary and regular contracts and it might be difficult to disentangle the effect of one form of rigidity from the other. Furthermore, these indicators can capture a variety of other country-specific factors. These results, therefore, should be taken with caution. Turning our attention to antidiscrimination policy effects, one can see that the antidiscrimination policy index does not seem to be a crucial factor in shaping employment prospects of Muslims.

However, as explained in Section 7.2, the antidiscrimination policies implemented in different countries vary widely. We thus attempt to shed some light on the antidiscrimination policy areas which appear to be more effective in affecting the labor market outcomes of Muslims. Table 7.5 shows a negative coefficient only for definition and concepts, whereas enforcement mechanisms and equality policies show positive and statistically significant effects in terms of employment prospects. While a favorable policy with respect to enforcement mechanisms seems to benefit females, equality policies seem to benefit mostly males. Strong enforcement mechanisms also appear to be associated with higher participation rates for males.

7.3.3 *Obesity in Europe*

Let us now turn our attention to the relationship between obesity and labor market outcomes in Europe. As explained before, using data from the ECHP, a BMI smaller than 18.5 is evidence that an individual is underweight, and a BMI above 30 is an indication of obesity. Figure 7.3 displays the BMI for different European countries, which, on average, have a similar BMI of roughly 25. Interestingly, the main differences between these countries are in the upper tail of the distribution, since southern countries such as Italy, Greece, and Spain have a lot of outliers, that is individuals with BMI above 40, while in Northern Europe (e.g. Denmark, Sweden, Austria) this is less the case. Figure 7.4-(a) displays the average BMI by gender. One can see that, on average, the BMI are the same but the dispersion is much higher for males, especially for those with a very high BMI. If we look at the BMI by level of education, as shown in Figure 7.4-(b), we see that less educated people

Table 7.5. Muslim religion and anti-discrimination policies

	Policy Investigation					
	All Employed	Females Employed	Males Employed	All Labor Force	Females Labor Force	Males Labor Force
Muslims	0.0349 (0.116)	−0.0454 (0.232)	0.109 (0.112)	−0.121 (0.201)	−0.127 (0.301)	−0.198 (0.126)
Muslim × definition and concepts	−0.00603** (0.00251)	−0.00983 (0.00682)	−0.00487** (0.00219)	−0.00560 (0.00348)	−0.00400 (0.00548)	−0.00416 (0.00276)
Muslim × fields of application	1.49e-05 (0.000686)	0.00104 (0.000779)	−0.000326 (0.000829)	0.000854 (0.00145)	0.000869 (0.00236)	0.000894 (0.00101)
Muslim × enforcement mechanisms	0.00151 (0.00197)	0.00946*** (0.00213)	−0.00241 (0.00225)	0.00528** (0.00232)	0.00429 (0.00327)	0.00493** (0.00200)
Muslim × equality policies	0.00356** (0.00133)	−0.00158 (0.00427)	0.00590*** (0.00125)	−0.000666 (0.00196)	−0.00367 (0.00321)	0.000722 (0.00117)
Definitions and concepts	0.000734 (0.000525)	0.000256 (0.000560)	0.00117** (0.000553)	0.000122 (0.000934)	−0.000400 (0.00115)	0.000689 (0.000816)
Fields of application	−0.000303 (0.000345)	−0.000451 (0.000370)	−0.000172 (0.000364)	−0.000175 (0.000347)	−0.000247 (0.000539)	−0.000108 (0.000315)
Enforcement mechanisms	−0.000305 (0.000678)	−0.000117 (0.000820)	−0.000474 (0.000660)	−0.000676 (0.000878)	−0.000415 (0.00147)	−0.000907 (0.000584)

	(1)	(2)	(3)	(4)	(5)	(6)
Equality policies	0.000791**	0.00115***	0.000483	0.000615	0.00102	0.000125
	(0.000343)	(0.000397)	(0.000348)	(0.000451)	(0.000780)	(0.000304)
Asians	-0.00997	0.00323	-0.0211	-0.0343	-0.0294	-0.0329
	(0.0204)	(0.0245)	(0.0296)	(0.0207)	(0.0297)	(0.0244)
Catholics	0.00862	-0.00103	0.0162	-0.0230**	-0.0411*	-0.00365
	(0.0142)	(0.0179)	(0.0119)	(0.0110)	(0.0205)	(0.00724)
Jewish	-0.000810	-0.0529	0.0628**	0.0503	0.0344	0.0673
	(0.0372)	(0.0693)	(0.0233)	(0.0417)	(0.0699)	(0.0569)
Protestants	0.0323**	0.0293*	0.0329***	0.0145	0.0156	0.00862
	(0.0126)	(0.0151)	(0.0113)	(0.0127)	(0.0227)	(0.00983)
Orthodox	0.0547*	0.0359	0.0704***	0.0478*	0.0297	0.0676***
	(0.0306)	(0.0439)	(0.0230)	(0.0238)	(0.0399)	(0.0173)
Others	0.0245***	0.0206	0.0246	-0.0227	-0.0390*	-0.00915
	(0.00760)	(0.0156)	(0.0152)	(0.0165)	(0.0216)	(0.0245)
Female	-0.0137*			-0.152***		
	(0.00757)			(0.0142)		
Constant	0.496***	0.449***	0.533***	-0.439***	-0.602***	-0.410***
	(0.0552)	(0.0718)	(0.0508)	(0.107)	(0.137)	(0.0943)
Observations	31,572	15,512	16,060	42,438	22,972	19,466
R-squared	0.038	0.044	0.041	0.246	0.216	0.264
Country FE	No	No	No	No	No	No
Time FE	No	No	No	No	No	No

Notes: Pooled OLS regression results. The dependent variable of the regressions in columns 1–3 is a dummy variable (employed) taking as value 1 if the individual is in the labor force and employed and zero if the individual is in the labor force but unemployed. The dependent variable of the regressions in columns 4–6 is a dummy variable (labor force) taking as value 1 if the individual is in the labor force and 0 otherwise. Although not reported, all specifications include as regressors: education, age, age squared, household size, marital status indicator, and urban vs. rural indicator. Robust standard errors in parentheses. *** p < 0.01, ** p < 0.05, * p < 0.1.
Source: ISSP, 1998, 2008.

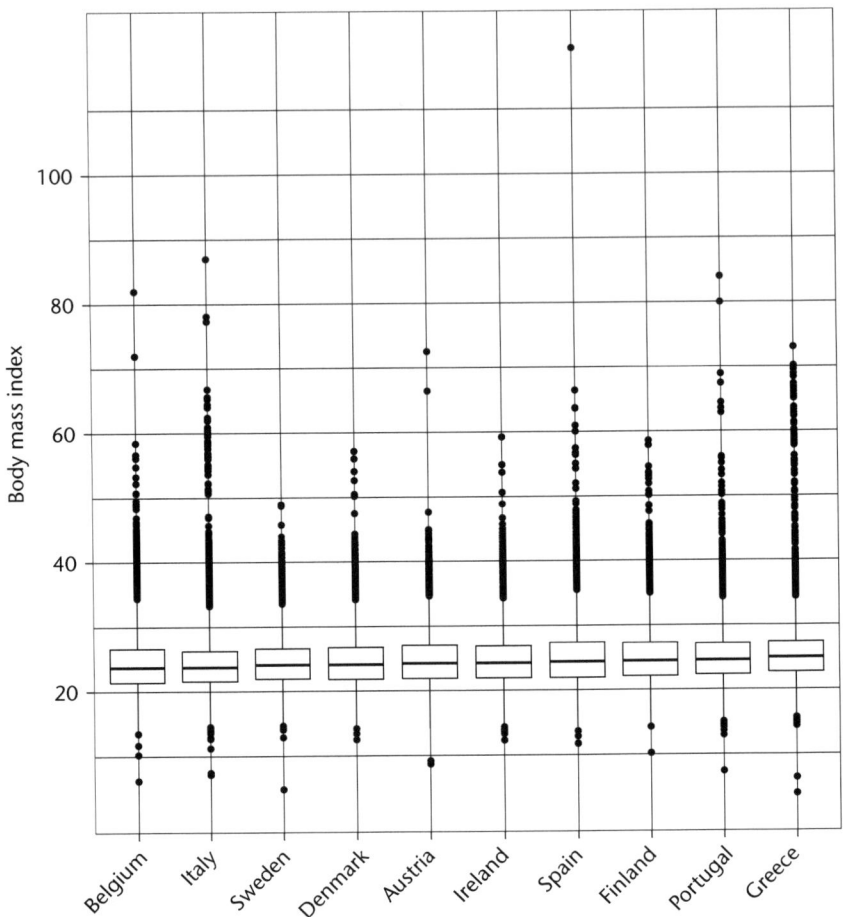

Figure 7.3. Distribution of Body Mass Index (BMI) by European countries.

Notes: The graph shown here and in the next two figures depicts features of the emprical distribution of BMI using a series of box-plots. In these plots, the outer lines of the "box" are the lower quartile and upper quartile of the data; the horizontal thicker line is the median. The points plotted represent outlying observations, that is, observations that are larger than 1.5 times the interquartile range.

Source: ECHP, 1998, 1999, 2000, 2001.

tend to be more overweight. This negative relationship between education and obesity (or more generally health) is relatively well known (Hammond, 2002, Groot and Maassen van den Brink, 2007). For example, Webbink et al. (2010) analyze the causal effect of education on the probability of being overweight by using longitudinal data of Australian identical twins. Their study confirms this well-known negative association between education and the probability of being overweight. For men, they find that education also

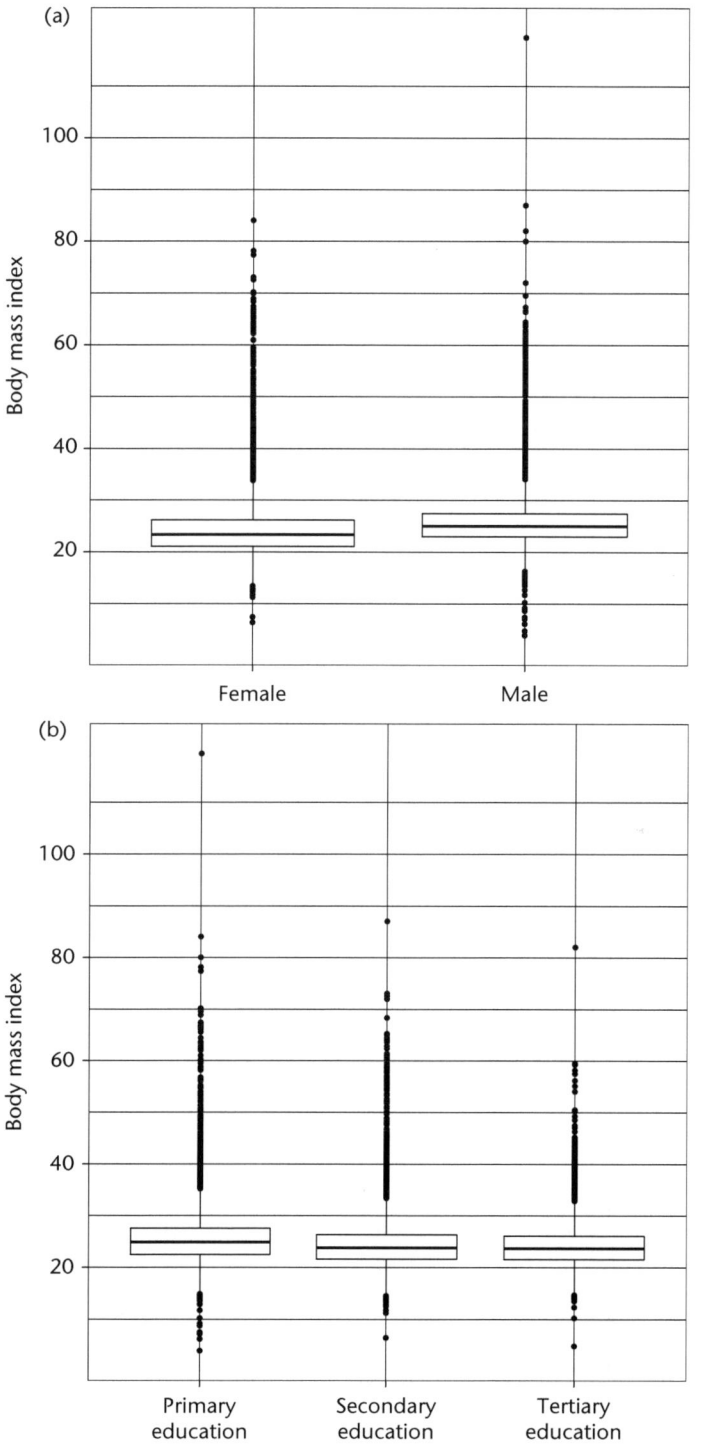

Figure 7.4. Distribution of Body Mass Index (BMI) by gender (a) and education (b).
Source: ECHP, 1998, 1999, 2000, 2001.

reduces the probability of being overweight within pairs of identical twins. Remarkably, for women they find no negative effect of education on body size when fixed family effects are taken into account. Identical twin sisters who differ in educational attainment do not systematically differ in body size. If we look at the relationship between education and BMI by country (Figure A.1 in Appendix A), we see that there are large variations between countries but the tendency is the same: the higher the education level, the lower the average BMI. One can also see that Southern European countries are the ones with a larger fraction of obese, especially among less educated individuals. Take, for example, Greece. Most people with a BMI above 40 have a low level of education. For Nordic countries this is still true, but the differences are less pronounced.

In Figure A.2 in Appendix A, we report on the relationship between BMI and age where the median is given as a continuous line. It appears that the relationship is increasing for all countries, in other words people tend to put on weight as they grow older. We also see that this relationship tends to be more linear or convex for women (women tend to increase their weight steadily over time) and more concave for men (i.e. men tend to put on weight between 30 and 50 and then keep the same weight).

In Table 7.6, we investigate the relationship between BMI and the probability of being employed and of participating in the labor force using a regression analysis, distinguishing underweight and obese people (i.e. with BMI smaller than 18.5 and larger than 30, respectively) with respect to a now broadly defined "normal" category. We find that the results greatly differ depending on the gender of the person. Indeed, in terms of employment, the penalty of underweight individuals occurs among males, whereas that of obese individuals occurs among females. The magnitude of the effects is remarkably similar: about 3% both for male underweight individuals and female obese individuals. In terms of labor force participation, underweight males also seem to be the most discouraged group (about 9% less likely to participate), whereas both female and male obese individuals participate less than "normal" individuals (about 8% and 3% less likely to participate, respectively).

This is in accordance with the studies described in Section 6.3 and the literature overview of Currie and Madrian (1999). However, our results reveal that the penalty in terms of employment only remains for females. This evidence might suggest that discrimination on physical appearance is stronger for females. As highlighted in Section 6.3, it is also possible that employers statistically discriminate against the very obese by believing that they are less productive than the non-obese.

In Table 7.6, we investigate whether these results differ between Northern and Southern Europe. Interestingly, we find that while in Northern Europe

Table 7.6. Body Mass Index and labor market outcomes

	All Employed	Females Employed	Males Employed	All Labor Force	Females Labor Force	Males Labor Force
			Baseline OLS regression results			
Underweight	−0.0168**	−0.00601	−0.0360*	0.00163	−0.00634	−0.0905***
	(0.00693)	(0.00755)	(0.0184)	(0.00720)	(0.00782)	(0.0174)
Obese	−0.0163**	−0.0328**	−0.00585	−0.0636***	−0.0802***	−0.0330***
	(0.00740)	(0.0132)	(0.00810)	(0.00907)	(0.0135)	(0.0100)
Female	−0.0371***			−0.203***		
	(0.00182)			(0.00220)		
Constant	0.662***	0.626***	0.734***	−0.660***	−0.543***	−0.773***
	(0.0131)	(0.0204)	(0.0170)	(0.0146)	(0.0202)	(0.0198)
Observations	172,400	74,070	98,330	250,670	127,129	123,541
R-squared	0.065	0.078	0.055	0.271	0.240	0.289
Country FE	Yes	Yes	Yes	Yes	Yes	Yes
Year FE	Yes	Yes	Yes	Yes	Yes	Yes
			Additional OLS regression results			
Obese	−0.0329***	−0.0419***	−0.0251*	−0.0501***	−0.0853***	−0.00598
	(0.0103)	(0.0147)	(0.0141)	(0.0129)	(0.0180)	(0.0170)
Obese × southern	0.0375**	0.0225	0.0418**	0.0168	0.0189	0.0356
	(0.0147)	(0.0265)	(0.0168)	(0.0198)	(0.0283)	(0.0237)
Underweight	0.00448	0.00172	−0.0160	−0.0847***	−0.0798***	−0.226***
	(0.00875)	(0.00933)	(0.0227)	(0.0121)	(0.0133)	(0.0274)
Underweight × southern	−0.0449***	−0.0181	−0.0650*	0.0475***	0.0547***	0.0367
	(0.0131)	(0.0140)	(0.0369)	(0.0156)	(0.0170)	(0.0382)
Southern	−0.0829***	−0.0465***	−0.0180***	−0.0335***	−0.252***	−0.0436***
	(0.00405)	(0.00603)	(0.00440)	(0.00606)	(0.00847)	(0.00771)
Female	−0.0367***			−0.213***		
	(0.00183)			(0.00239)		
Constant	0.862***	0.823***	0.933***	0.971***	1.035***	1.144***
	(0.00617)	(0.0101)	(0.00744)	(0.00927)	(0.0135)	(0.0123)
Observations	172,429	74,084	98,345	250,717	127,152	123,565
R-squared	0.060	0.073	0.050	0.145	0.144	0.090
Country FE	Yes	Yes	Yes	Yes	Yes	Yes
Time FE	Yes	Yes	Yes	Yes	Yes	Yes

Notes: Pooled OLS regression results. The dependent variable of the regressions in columns 1–3 is a dummy variable "employed" taking value 1 if the individual is in the labor force and employed and zero if the individual is in the labor force but unemployed. The dependent variable of the regressions in columns 4–6 is a dummy variable "labor force" taking value 1 if the individual is in the labor force and 0 otherwise. The dependent variable "underweight" is 1 if BMI is less or equal to 18.5 and 0 otherwise; "obese" is 1 if BMI is larger than 35 and 0 otherwise. Southern countries are: Italy, Greece, Spain, and Portugal. Although not reported, all specifications include as regressors education, age, age squared, household size, marital status indicator, and urban vs. rural indicator. Robust standard errors in parentheses. *** $p < 0.01$, ** $p < 0.05$, * $p < 0.1$.
Source: ECHP, 1998, 1999, 2000, 2001.

obese males have more difficulties in finding a job (more that 2% less likely to find a job compared to normal weight males), in Southern Europe they are not penalized. On the contrary, they even receive a premium. On the other hand, while in Northern Europe underweight males do not seem to penalized with respect to normal weight individuals, in Southern Europe they show a strong employment penalty (more than 6%). There are instead no differences in terms of labor market participation of obese or underweight males between Northern and Southern Europe. Regarding females, we instead find the most notable difference in terms of participation rates. In particular, we find that in Southern Europe underweight females tend to participate more. This reduces the strong penalty for women which is found in Northern Europe.

As we did for Muslims (see Table 7.4), we now attempt to investigate how the antidiscrimination and labor market policies implemented in Europe (see Appendix B for a description of these policies) affect the relationship between weight and labor market outcomes. We interact our indicators of antidiscrimination and labor market rigidity with our indicator of obese and underweight individuals in Table 7.7. Looking first at the results on our indicators of labor market rigidity, the upper panel of Table 7.7 shows that the signs of the estimated coefficients of the interaction terms when considering employment prospects are negative and statistically significant for most of the labor market rigidity indicators. This suggests that obese individuals are less penalized in the labor market in countries that have more flexible labor markets. The only exception is a positive and statistically significant effect for the regulation on temporary contracts for males, signaling that obese males seem to be hampered by a more flexible regulation in terms of temporary contracts. Observe that more rigid labor markets can be found in Southern Europe, where our previous results signal a premium for obese men. In this case, better employment prospects for obese men can be also associated with cultural rather than institutional reasons. When looking at the results for labor market participation, one can also see that a more flexible regulation in terms of temporary contracts is associated with higher participation rates of obese males. The lower panel of Table 7.7 shows instead that the employment penalty of underweight individuals seems to be reduced in countries that have a more flexible regulation in terms of temporary contracts. Again, we find an opposite effect for the regulation on regular contracts for males. In addition, Table 7.7 also shows some beneficial effects of a higher labor market flexibility in terms of participation rates, especially for females. As mentioned before, these indicators are highly correlated, and can capture other country-specific factors. Therefore, these differences should be taken with caution. Nevertheless, these results suggest that different labor market policies might affect differently underweight and obese individuals and that their effects can vary by gender.

Turning our attention to the effects of antidiscrimination policies, we find that more favorable antidiscrimination policies are associated with better employment prospects for obese individuals and worse employment prospects for underweight individuals, especially males.

Table 7.7. Body Mass Index and labor market policies

	All Employed	Females Employed	Males Employed	All Labor Force	Females Labor Force	Males Labor Force
			Policy investigation – Obese			
Obese	0.0406* (0.0210)	0.0334* (0.0173)	0.0427 (0.0413)	-0.167*** (0.0311)	-0.311*** (0.0753)	0.0118 (0.0400)
Obese × anti discrimination policy	0.00154** (0.000535)	0.00141 (0.000805)	0.00154** (0.000525)	0.000156 (0.000965)	-0.000281 (0.00193)	0.000854 (0.000482)
Obese × minimum wage	-0.115*** (0.0184)	-0.0929** (0.0343)	-0.114*** (0.0248)	0.0251 (0.0259)	0.0552 (0.0573)	0.0502 (0.0333)
Obese × regular contracts	-0.0283** (0.00875)	-0.0217** (0.00845)	-0.0303*** (0.0127)	0.0389** (0.0144)	0.0517 (0.0312)	0.0259** (0.0112)
Obese × temporary contracts	0.00974 (0.00713)	-0.000684 (0.0163)	0.0119* (0.00625)	-0.00329 (0.00474)	0.0143 (0.0119)	-0.0265** (0.00839)
Obese × union density	-0.00185*** (0.000314)	-0.00177*** (0.000428)	-0.00172** (0.000530)	0.000578 (0.000670)	0.00208 (0.00121)	-0.00171*** (0.000412)
Underweight	-0.0227* (0.0117)	-0.00925 (0.0113)	-0.0481* (0.0251)	-0.0551** (0.0196)	-0.0427*** (0.0122)	-0.213*** (0.0216)
Anti discrimination policy	-0.00155** (0.000544)	-0.00182** (0.000667)	-0.00136** (0.000461)	-0.00157* (0.000744)	-0.00181* (0.000877)	-0.00149* (0.000678)
Minimum wage	0.105** (0.0391)	0.162*** (0.0495)	0.0670* (0.0324)	-0.0227 (0.0176)	-0.0405 (0.0242)	-0.00368 (0.0240)
Regular contracts	0.0507*** (0.0126)	0.0666*** (0.0154)	0.0387*** (0.0107)	0.0830*** (0.0123)	0.122*** (0.0151)	0.0436*** (0.0109)

(Continued)

Table 7.7. (Continued)

	All Employed	Females Employed	Males Employed	All Labor Force	Females Labor Force	Males Labor Force
			Policy investigation – Obese			
Temporary contracts	−0.0368** (0.0131)	−0.0605*** (0.0171)	−0.0204* (0.0105)	−0.0402*** (0.00470)	−0.0494*** (0.00647)	−0.0302*** (0.00685)
Trade union density	0.000864* (0.000397)	0.00119** (0.000500)	0.000610 (0.000336)	0.00152** (0.000644)	0.00268** (0.000857)	0.000503 (0.000509)
Female	−0.0363** (0.0124)			−0.213*** (0.0296)		
Constant	0.842*** (0.0363)	0.805*** (0.0476)	0.915*** (0.0291)	0.803*** (0.0585)	0.724*** (0.0624)	1.117*** (0.0794)
Observations	172,429	74,084	98,345	250,717	127,152	123,565
Country FE	No	No	No	No	No	No
Year FE	Yes	Yes	Yes	Yes	Yes	Yes
			Policy investigation – Underweight			
Underweight	0.0819 (0.0535)	0.0557 (0.0532)	0.216*** (0.0557)	0.142** (0.0488)	0.197** (0.0617)	0.0180 (0.0792)
Underweight × anti discrimination policy	−0.000564 (0.000695)	0.000126 (0.000682)	−0.00271*** (0.000720)	−0.00118 (2.000732)	−0.000584 (0.000620)	−0.00423 (0.00265)
Underweight × minimum wage	0.0329 (0.0389)	−0.0225 (0.0327)	0.0733 (0.0514)	−0.108** (0.0345)	−0.119*** (0.0310)	0.117 (0.0776)
Underweight × regular contracts	0.0169 (0.0155)	−0.00169 (0.0138)	0.0362* (0.0176)	−0.00261 (0.00891)	−0.0375*** (0.0104)	0.0524 (0.0339)

	(1)	(2)	(3)	(4)	(5)	(6)
Underweight × temporary contracts	-0.0483***	-0.0207*	-0.0830***	-0.0122	-0.00109	-0.0509**
	(0.0107)	(0.0111)	(0.0153)	(0.0135)	(0.0125)	(0.0180)
Underweight × union density	-0.000237	-0.000460	-0.000667	-0.00184**	-0.00249**	-0.000204
	(0.000560)	(0.000635)	(0.000704)	(0.000766)	(0.000867)	(0.00187)
Anti discrimination policy	-0.00152**	-0.00183**	-0.00132**	-0.00154*	-0.00181*	-0.00144*
	(0.000526)	(0.000648)	(0.000453)	(0.000745)	(0.000924)	(0.000661)
Minimum wage	0.103**	0.162***	0.0650*	-0.0188	-0.0329	-0.00386
	(0.0381)	(0.0485)	(0.0318)	(0.0174)	(0.0252)	(0.0234)
Regular contracts	0.0500***	0.0667***	0.0381***	0.0836***	0.125***	0.0433***
	(0.0122)	(0.0149)	(0.0105)	(0.0124)	(0.0159)	(0.0106)
Temporary contracts	-0.0355**	-0.0595***	-0.0195*	-0.0399***	-0.0492***	-0.0299***
	(0.0129)	(0.0170)	(0.0104)	(0.00468)	(0.00677)	(0.00666)
Trade union density	0.000849**	0.00120**	0.000598	0.00158**	0.00284**	0.000491
	(0.000389)	(0.000489)	(0.000338)	(0.000644)	(0.000897)	(0.000503)
Obese	-0.0128	-0.0295**	-0.00254	-0.0418***	-0.0732***	0.0104
	(0.00817)	(0.0114)	(0.00918)	(0.00975)	(0.0112)	(0.0153)
Female	-0.0363**			-0.213***		
	(0.0125)			(0.0296)		
Constant	0.840***	0.802***	0.913***	0.795***	0.709***	1.114***
	(0.0353)	(0.0461)	(0.0288)	(0.0581)	(0.0637)	(0.0793)
Observations	172,429	74,084	98,345	250,717	127,152	123,565
Country FE	No	No	No	No	No	No
Year FE	Yes	Yes	Yes	Yes	Yes	Yes

Notes: Pooled OLS regression results. Dependent variable in columns 1–3: dummy variable "employed" taking value 1 if the individual is in the labor force and employed and zero if the individual is in the labor force but unemployed. Dependent variable in columns 4–6 is a dummy variable "labor force" taking value 1 if the individual is in the labor force and 0 otherwise. Variable underweight is 1 if BMI is less or equal to 18.5 and 0 otherwise; obese is 1 if BMI is larger than 35 and 0 otherwise. All specifications include education, age, age squared, household size, marital status indicator, and urban vs. rural indicator. Robust standard errors in parentheses. *** $p < 0.01$, ** $p < 0.05$, * $p < 0.1$.
Source: ECHP, 1998, 1999, 2000, 2001.

When we look more closely at the different policy areas embedded in the antidiscrimination index, Table 7.8 shows that obese individuals seem to benefit in terms of employment prospects in countries where the antidiscrimination legislation applies to wider fields and, in terms of labor market participation, in countries that have stronger enforcement mechanisms (especially males) and perform better in terms of equality policies. Table 7.8 also reveals that no type of antidiscrimination policy seems to be associated with better employment prospects for underweight individuals. It only shows some positive effects in having strong enforcement mechanisms in terms of participation rates.

Taken as a whole, the picture that emerges from the evidence in this section suggests that individuals with specific characteristics might be discriminated against in the European labor markets. The scarcity of cross-country data for Europe on these topics prevents us from providing detailed evidence on other important dimensions of discrimination, such as age discrimination, disability discrimination, and housing discrimination.[5] Because of the importance of these issues for policy purposes, further research and in particular further data are needed to enlighten the political debate. This motivates the field experiment that we have performed in Italy and that we cover in Chapter 8.

7.4 Concluding Remarks

In this chapter we have provided a first picture of the labor market outcomes of individuals with specific characteristics using the available cross-country data for Europe, and also attempted to relate our results to labor market and antidiscrimination policies that have been implemented in different European countries. After the implementation of the Amsterdam Treaty (May 1, 1999), all the EU member states have introduced different policies and activities that fight against discrimination based on sex, racial and ethnic origin, religion or belief, disability, age, and sexual orientation. However, while for the employment protection legislations the OECD provides a comprehensive index combining various indicators, such an index is not available for antidiscrimination policies. To the best of our knowledge, the only quantitative measure capturing the complexity of antidiscrimination laws and principles across European countries is a composite score assigned to each European country for their performance in this policy area that

---

[5] The ECHP and EU-SILC data do not contain information on labor market tenure and/or experience, but only potential experience that is a linear function of age. As a result, in an employment regression age would capture the effect of experience rather than being a signal of discrimination.

Table 7.8. Body Mass Index and anti-discrimination policies

	All Employed	Females Employed	Males Employed	All Labor Force	Females Labor Force	Males Labor Force
			Panel A			
Obese	−0.0484 (0.0412)	−0.0870 (0.0974)	−0.0113 (0.0577)	−0.0801 (0.0524)	−0.0851 (0.146)	0.0333 (0.0761)
Obese × definition	0.000366 (0.000582)	6.92e−05 (0.00127)	0.000621 (0.00114)	−0.00171** (0.000721)	−0.00221 (0.00199)	−0.00386*** (0.00111)
Obese × fileds of applications	0.000281 (0.000183)	3.02e−05 (0.000494)	0.000549** (0.000232)	0.000442 (0.000298)	0.00157 (0.00102)	−0.000646 (0.000441)
Obese × enforcement	0.000650 (0.000559)	0.00152 (0.00110)	−0.000384 (0.00108)	0.00113 (0.000971)	−0.000342 (0.00230)	0.00366*** (0.00107)
Obese × equality policy	−0.000987*** (0.000181)	−0.000909* (0.000421)	−0.000919*** (0.000318)	0.000758** (0.000301)	0.00104 (0.000863)	0.000609 (0.000426)
Definition	−0.00236 (0.00142)	−0.0313 (0.00183)	−0.00191 (0.00118)	0.000445 (0.00173)	0.00240 (0.00273)	−0.00128 (0.000873)
Fileds of applications	−0.000389 (0.000590)	−0.000234 (0.000885)	−0.000510 (0.000373)	−0.000247 (0.000601)	−0.000592 (0.000822)	2.06e−05 (0.000372)
Enforcement	0.00111 (0.000870)	0.000764 (0.00119)	0.00135* (0.000725)	0.000928 (0.000978)	0.00160 (0.00142)	0.000154 (0.000678)
Equality policy	0.000990*** (0.000247)	0.00159*** (0.000368)	0.000572** (0.000185)	0.000842* (0.000373)	0.00128* (0.000567)	0.000402 (0.000242)

(Continued)

Table 7.8. (Continued)

	All Employed	Females Employed	Males Employed	All Labor Force	Females Labor Force	Males Labor Force
				Panel A		
Underweight	-0.0249*	-0.0125	-0.0474*	-0.0600**	-0.0510***	-0.212***
	(0.0121)	(0.0124)	(0.0246)	(0.0214)	(0.0150)	(0.0243)
Female	-0.0350**			-0.213***		
	(0.0124)			(0.0296)		
Constant	0.906***	0.894***	0.962***	0.777***	0.643***	1.141***
	(0.0669)	(0.0960)	(0.0436)	(0.141)	(0.196)	(0.0986)
Observations	172,429	74,084	98,345	250,717	127,152	123,565
Country FE	No	No	No	No	No	No
Year FE	Yes	Yes	Yes	Yes	Yes	Yes
				Panel B		
Underweight	-0.0214	-0.0975	0.260	0.104	0.107	0.323**
	(0.138)	(0.114)	(0.165)	(0.0949)	(0.122)	(0.106)
Underweight × definition	7.89e-05	0.00188	-0.00577*	-0.00415*	-0.00281	-0.0109***
	(0.00245)	(0.00230)	(0.00307)	(0.00193)	(0.00239)	(0.00218)
Underweight × fileds of applications	-0.000307	-0.000364	-0.000726	-0.00100	-0.00103	-0.000114
	(0.00106)	(0.000767)	(0.00130)	(0.000547)	(0.000588)	(0.000535)
Underweight × enforcement	0.000118	0.000194	0.00117	0.00352**	0.00259	0.00217
	(0.000213)	(0.00185)	(0.00260)	(0.00116)	(0.00152)	(0.00146)
Underweight × equality policy	0.000151	-0.000376	0.000415	-0.00153***	-0.00192***	0.000261
	(0.000585)	(0.000472)	(0.000891)	(0.000398)	(0.000567)	(0.000511)

	(1)	(2)	(3)	(4)	(5)	(6)
Obese	-0.0124	-0.0278**	-0.00215	-0.0438***	-0.0750***	0.00953
	(0.00776)	(0.0108)	(0.00877)	(0.0115)	(0.0161)	(0.0147)
Definition	-0.00236	-0.00319	-0.00188	0.000492	0.00243	-0.00124
	(0.00139)	(0.00177)	(0.00118)	(0.00173)	(0.00277)	(0.000865)
Fileds of applications	-0.000378	-0.000220	-0.000499	-0.000218	-0.000531	7.34e − 06
	(0.000568)	(0.000858)	(0.000363)	(0.000588)	(0.000800)	(0.000371)
Enforcement	0.00112	0.000762	0.00134*	0.000870	0.00150	0.000200
	(0.000839)	(0.00114)	(0.000731)	(0.000964)	(0.00142)	(0.000680)
Equality policy	0.000974***	0.00160***	0.000560**	0.000895**	0.00138**	0.000406
	(0.000238)	(0.000354)	(0.000186)	(0.000376)	(0.000585)	(0.000241)
Female	-0.0349**			-0.213***		
	(0.0124)			(0.0296)		
Constant	0.905***	0.896***	0.960***	0.773***	0.638**	1.137***
	(0.0648)	(0.0930)	(0.0432)	(0.141)	(0.198)	(0.0979)
Observations	172,429	74,084	98,345	250,717	127,152	123,565
Country FE	No	No	No	No	No	No
Year FE	Yes	Yes	Yes	Yes	Yes	Yes

Notes: Pooled OLS regression results. The dependent variable of the regressions in columns 1–3 is a dummy variable "employed" taking as value 1 if the individual is in the labor force and employed and zero if the individual is in the labor force but unemployed. The dependent variable of the regressions in columns 4–6 is a dummy variable "labor force" taking as value 1 if the individual is in the labor force and 0 otherwise. The dependent variable "underweight" is 1 if BMI is less or equal to 18.5 and 0 otherwise; "obese" is 1 if BMI is larger than 35 and 0 otherwise. vs. rural indicator. Robust standard errors in parentheses. *** $p < 0.01$, ** $p < 0.05$, * $p < 0.1$.
Source: ECHP, 1998, 1999, 2000, 2001.

can be extracted from the MIPEX. We use this index in our regression analysis to describe the antidiscrimination laws and principles implemented in different European countries and to provide a first investigation of the role of antidiscrimination policies in the employment prospects of individuals who might suffer from market discrimination because of religion, sexual orientation, and physical appearance (e.g. obesity).

We find that more regulated labor markets seem to be favorable to Muslims, in particular in terms of participation. In terms of antidiscrimination policies, it appears that a favorable policy with respect to enforcement mechanisms seems to benefit females, while equality policies seem to benefit mostly males. Strong enforcement mechanisms also appear to be associated with higher participation rates for males. For obesity, we instead find that more flexible labor markets are associated with lower employment penalties for obese individuals. They are also associated with higher participation rates for obese males and underweight females. We also find that more favorable antidiscrimination policies are associated with better employment prospects for obese individuals and worse employment prospects for underweight individuals, especially males. In particular, obese individuals seem to benefit in terms of employment prospects in countries where the antidiscrimination legislation applies to wider fields. In terms of labor market participation, countries that have stronger enforcement mechanisms favor obese individuals (especially males). On the other hand, no type of antidiscrimination policy seems to be associated with better employment prospects for underweight individuals. It only shows positive effects of strong enforcement mechanisms in terms of participation rates.

The interpretation of these correlations, however, is quite difficult. The different indicators can capture a variety of other country-specific factors that are often highly correlated. It might thus be difficult to understand the effect of a specific antidiscrimination policy or to disentangle the effect of one form of labor market rigidity from another. Nevertheless, these results suggest that different labor market policies and different antidiscrimination policies might affect differently individuals with specific traits (e.g. obesity), and that their effects can vary by gender.

Appendix to Chapter 7

Eleonora Patacchini, Giuseppe Ragusa, and Yves Zenou

7A Additional Figures and Tables

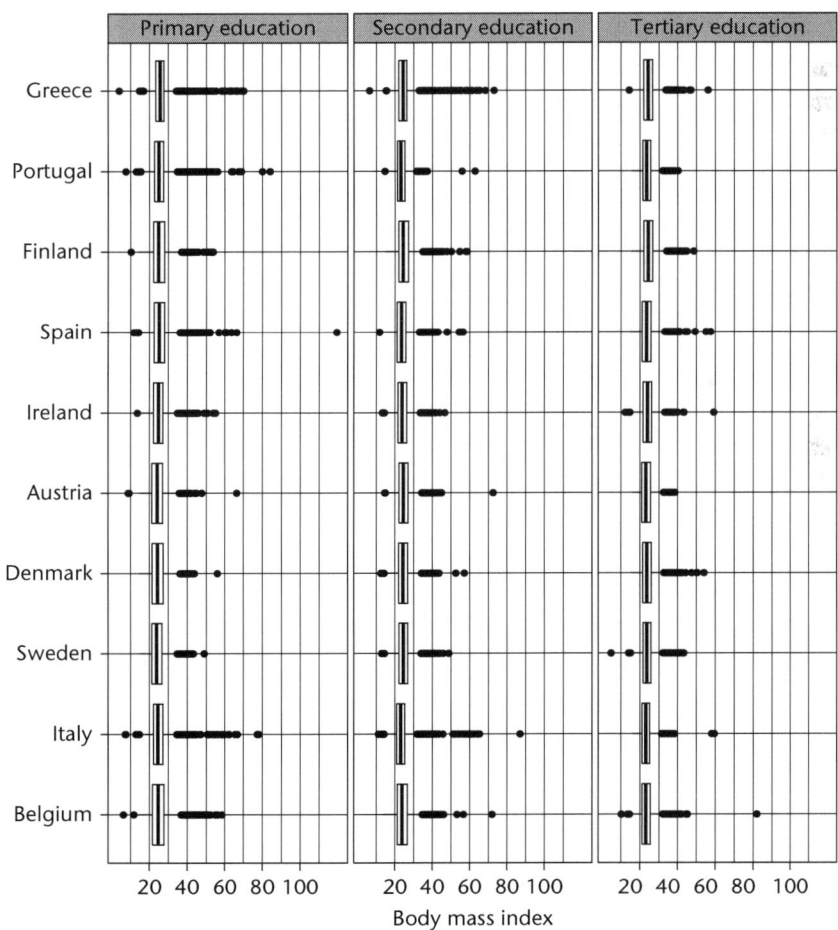

Figure A.1 Distribution of BMI by European countries and education levels.
Source: ECHP, 1998, 1999, 2000, 2001.

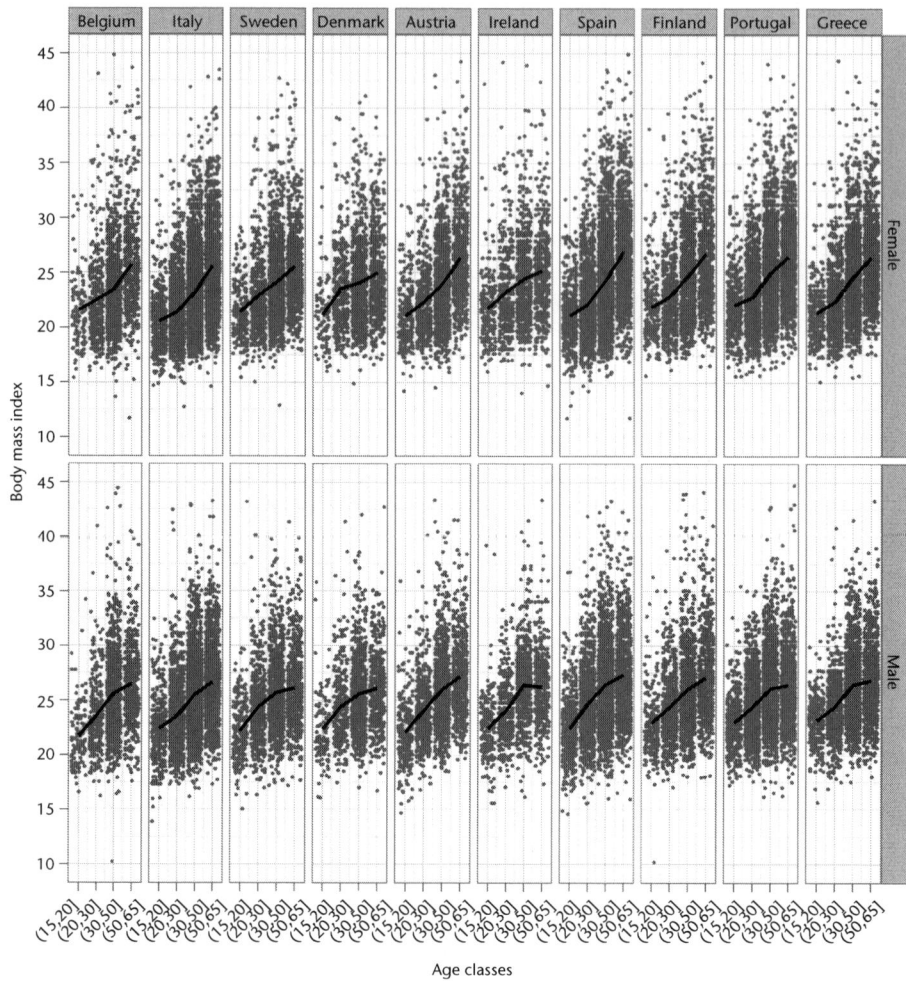

Figure A.2 Distribution of BMI by countries and age classes.

Notes: The points represent individual observations for each age class. For each country, the dark line depicts the age-class specific means.

Source: ECHP, 1998, 1999, 2000, 2001.

Table 7A.1. Summary statistics by geographical area

Religion	Age Mean	Age Sd	Female Mean	Female Sd	Education Mean	Education Sd	Employed Mean	Employed Sd	Labor Force Mean	Labor Force Sd
all										
No religion	41.11	12.67	0.52	0.50	12.95	3.42	0.91	0.29	0.79	0.41
Catholics	43.35	12.94	0.43	0.50	11.62	3.88	0.91	0.29	0.71	0.46
Protestants	43.96	12.81	0.44	0.50	12.66	3.49	0.95	0.22	0.77	0.42
Orthodox	41.59	12.79	0.47	0.50	12.05	3.50	0.91	0.29	0.79	0.41
Other Chr.	40.82	13.04	0.39	0.49	12.55	3.36	0.94	0.25	0.75	0.43
Jewish	44.55	13.72	0.42	0.50	13.75	2.98	0.91	0.29	0.77	0.43
Muslims	38.85	10.98	0.56	0.50	10.52	4.31	0.70	0.46	0.74	0.44
Asians	41.14	11.85	0.47	0.50	13.01	3.85	0.91	0.29	0.75	0.43
northern										
No religion	40.64	12.55	0.51	0.50	12.96	3.32	0.92	0.27	0.81	0.39
Catholics	42.26	12.65	0.42	0.49	12.87	3.42	0.93	0.26	0.73	0.44
Protestants	43.74	12.88	0.44	0.50	12.88	3.52	0.96	0.20	0.79	0.41
Orthodox	42.61	13.14	0.35	0.48	12.31	2.99	0.86	0.35	0.81	0.39
Other Chr.	40.74	12.52	0.37	0.48	13.19	3.07	0.95	0.23	0.78	0.41
Jewish	45.09	13.11	0.47	0.51	13.97	3.01	1.00	0.00	0.75	0.44
Muslims	39.80	10.86	0.49	0.50	13.21	4.17	0.84	0.37	0.63	0.49
Asians	40.38	11.35	0.49	0.50	13.50	3.81	0.91	0.28	0.79	0.41
central										
No religion	41.57	12.68	0.51	0.50	12.63	3.18	0.90	0.30	0.77	0.42
Catholics	43.67	12.80	0.43	0.50	11.85	3.04	0.92	0.28	0.71	0.45
Protestants	44.58	12.61	0.43	0.50	12.14	3.31	0.93	0.26	0.72	0.45
Orthodox	43.44	12.16	0.58	0.50	11.03	2.82	0.84	0.37	0.82	0.39
Other Chr.	40.57	13.59	0.43	0.50	12.06	3.11	0.93	0.26	0.72	0.45
Jewish	43.92	15.36	0.46	0.52	13.08	2.53	0.78	0.44	0.69	0.48
Muslims	38.70	10.60	0.57	0.50	10.85	3.77	0.80	0.40	0.70	0.46
Asians	41.77	12.13	0.48	0.50	12.74	3.79	0.93	0.26	0.71	0.45
southern										
No religion	40.59	12.78	0.56	0.50	13.77	3.97	0.89	0.31	0.79	0.41
Catholics	43.30	13.24	0.44	0.50	10.78	4.86	0.89	0.32	0.69	0.46
Protestants	40.78	12.87	0.44	0.50	12.09	4.75	0.89	0.32	0.70	0.46
Orthodox	41.42	12.76	0.48	0.50	12.04	3.57	0.92	0.28	0.79	0.41
Other Chr.	44.05	14.35	0.32	0.48	9.09	5.75	0.86	0.36	0.64	0.49
Jewish	43.93	14.47	0.27	0.46	13.87	3.36	0.83	0.39	0.87	0.35
Muslims	38.53	11.48	0.58	0.49	8.79	4.15	0.55	0.50	0.84	0.37
Asians	39.55	11.44	0.36	0.49	13.38	4.18	0.83	0.38	0.89	0.31

Note: Northern countries are UK, Ireland, Norway, Sweden, Latvia, Denmark, and Finland. Central countries are Austria, Belgium, Czech Republic, Germany, Hungary, the Netherlands, Poland, the Slovak Republic, and Slovenia. Southern countries are Bulgaria, Cyprus, France, Italy, Spain, and Portugal.
Source: ISSP 1998, 2008.

7B Labor Market Policies

We consider three main policies in Europe: minimum wage, strictness of employment protection legislation, and trade union density.

Using data from OECD, we first collect for each European country the minimum wage relative to the median wage of full-time workers, that is, the ratio of minimum wages to median earnings of full-time employees – excluding overtime and bonus payments.[6] Indeed, for cross-country comparisons, data on minimum wage levels are further supplemented with data on average or median wages. Median rather than mean earnings provide a better basis for international comparisons as they account for differences in earnings dispersion across countries. A country such as France has a very high minimum wage relative to median wages while other countries such as Luxembourg and Spain have a much lower ratio. Other countries, for example those in Scandinavia, have no legislation on a national minimum wage. For these countries the value of the indicator is set to 0.[7] Countries with high minimum wages should be less favorable to immigrants since the latter tend to be less educated and thus paid at the minimum wage. Indeed, higher minimum wages implies higher labor costs for employers and thus a lower chance of being hired.

We then use the OECD employment protection indicators, which are compiled from 21 items, including: (1) Individual dismissal of workers with regular contracts: this index incorporates three aspects of dismissal protection: (i) procedural inconveniences that employers face when starting the dismissal process, such as notification and consultation requirements; (ii) notice periods and severance pay, which typically vary by tenure of the employee; and (iii) difficulty of dismissal, as determined by the circumstances in which it is possible to dismiss workers, as well as the repercussions for the employer if a dismissal is found to be unfair (such as compensation and reinstatement); (2) Regulation of temporary contracts: this index quantifies regulation of fixed-term and temporary work agency contracts with respect to the types of work for which these contracts are allowed and their duration. This measure also includes regulation governing the establishment and operation of temporary work agencies and requirements for agency workers to receive the same pay and/or conditions as equivalent workers in the

---

[6] A national minimum wage is the minimum rate which by collective agreement must be paid in all circumstances for certain work or to employees of a certain category.

[7] Observe that wage floors can exist even in absence of statutory minimum wages. For example, in Sweden, there exist personal contracts which are concluded between individual employees and employers specifying such a minimum rate. An employer who pays rates below the minimum incurs liability for breach of the collective agreement concerned. However, these agreements largely vary between economic sectors and depend on employer characteristics. Negotiated wage floors are thus not considered here.

user firm, which can increase the cost of using temporary agency workers relative to hiring workers on permanent contracts. It is important to note that employment protection refers here to only one dimension of the complex set of factors that influence labor market flexibility.

All these indices range between 0 (least restrictions) and 6 (most restrictions). Different countries have different employment protection legislations. For example, when considering individual dismissal of workers with regular contracts, countries such as Portugal and to a lesser extent the Netherlands have stricter legislations while countries such as the UK and Ireland have very weak ones. Looking at the legislation on the regulation of temporary contracts, which is another important aspect of labor market flexibility, again the UK and Ireland have very weak legislations. This should not come as a surprise because these Anglo-Saxon countries are well known to have very flexible labor markets. On the other hand, countries such as Belgium and to a lesser extent Italy and France have much more regulated labor markets.

Finally, we consider trade union density, which corresponds to the ratio of wage and salary earners that are trade union members, divided by the total number of wage and salary earners. Not surprisingly, Scandinavian countries have very high rates of trade union density while countries such as France, Spain, and Germany have much lower rates, even though trade unions are very powerful.

8

Do Employers Discriminate Against Physical Appearance and Sexual Preference? A Field Experiment

Eleonora Patacchini, Giuseppe Ragusa, and Yves Zenou

8.1 Introduction

Estimating the effect of sexual preferences and personal appearances is difficult because it is practically impossible to deal with potential unobserved traits
that are likely to be correlated with both sexuality and appearances. Unlike
ethnicity and gender, which are both easily observable, the sexual orientation
of individuals is not generally an *observable characteristic*; its exposure can
happen either voluntarily or involuntarily. If it occurs voluntarily it is an
endogenous action. According to economic theory, rational individuals
should experience at least some benefits arising from such an action, which
might bias the results.

To circumvent these problems, we conducted a field experiment that builds
on the correspondence testing methodology that has been primarily used in
the past to study minority outcomes in the United States, notably by Bertrand
and Mullainathan (2004).[1]

We studied the effect of perceived homosexuality and of physical appearances in the labor market by sending fictitious résumés to help-wanted
advertisements in Rome and Milan.[2] These are the two Italian cities with
the biggest labor markets. We expected it to be easier to find an online help-
wanted advertisement and to receive a callback. As a matter of fact, most
of the help-wanted advertisements on websites commonly used to advertise
job vacancies are for jobs in Milan and in Rome. As in the studies surveyed

---

[1] See Section 6.3.

[2] Doris Weichselbaumer conducted a similar experiment on discrimination by sexual orientation in Berlin and Munich (Weichselbaumer, 2012).

in Section 6.3, we experimentally manipulated perceived homosexuality by randomly modifying résumés, adding items that reveal sexual preferences. At the same time, we randomly attached to the résumés pictures that had been previously ranked in terms of beauty to study the effect of appearance on labor market outcomes.

8.2 Description of the Experiment

The first step of the experimental design was to restrict the advertisements to which résumés were sent. We restricted the field experiment to seven occupations: administrative clerk, bookkeeper, call center operator, receptionist, sales clerk, secretary, and shop assistant. These occupations were selected by looking at the distribution of help-wanted advertisements on specialized websites. These seven occupations were the most frequent among those not requiring very specific skills, for which it would have been difficult to create standard profiles of job applicants.

The second step was to create templates for the résumés that were to be sent. To generate those templates, we collected résumés of actual job seekers by posting advertisements on the most used Italian websites for job search.[3] From the résumés that we received, we extracted information concerning the distribution of educational attainment, including names of schools and colleges attended and types of experience including names of previous employers. More specifically, we constructed databases containing names of high schools in Milan and in Rome (within an area of 30 km), names of colleges in Milan and in Rome, names of companies, and description of work experiences. This information was then used as building blocks for generating the résumés.

Résumés were generated through an ad-hoc software that randomly chose some characteristics from these ad-hoc datasets.

For each city and occupation, we used six different identities, three males and three females. Some of their characteristics remained constant among résumés for the same city and occupation. First and last names for these identities were selected among the most common Italian names. For each occupation, we associated a specific name–surname pair. By doing so, we could easily understand the occupation and profile considered in case of callbacks. For example, "Giulia Villa" was always an administrative clerk in Milan, while "Francesco Ricci" was always a bookkeeper in Rome. The addresses of residence were chosen in such a way that they didn't give any additional information about the socioeconomic status of the applicants.

---

[3] In order to avoid generating false hope, candidates were notified by mail that the job vacancy they were applying for had already been filled.

The year of birth of the applicants was randomly set between 1977 and 1992. Education and work experience were coherently set with the age of a particular applicant. We used six phone numbers, each of them associated with one name in Milan and one in Rome. This means that each number was associated with 14 different identities, two for each of the seven occupations (then identified by the name–surname pairs).

The résumé items revealing *homosexual preferences* were periods of internship in pro-gay advocacy groups that are real, well known by the public at large, and city-specific; in any case their names were very explicit about the nature of the group, for example, Arcilesbica Roma, Centro di Iniziativa Gay-Arcigay or DGP – Di Gay Project. Applicants in the control group had instead worked as interns for a period of similar length in a non-gay/non-lesbian cultural association or in a company. In order to better match the occupation, tasks performed during internships were different across applicants. For each city and for each occupation, one of the three types of internship was associated with two identities, one male and one female.

For *physical appearance*, we randomly assigned to each résumé a picture chosen from 89 previously collected photos of individuals aged between 20 and 35 years old. The photo was chosen in such a way that it minimized differences between the age declared in the résumé and the real age of the person depicted in the picture.

For each city and for each occupation, we created 1,200 fake résumés.[4] To understand how the program generates a fake résumé, consider a specific identity. Name, surname, home address, phone number, e-mail address, date and place of birth, and type of internship are fixed. First of all, the program randomly chooses the year of birth from 1977 to 1992. Then, depending on the age, it picks a picture. The program associates pictures to identities that have +/- 2 years from the age of the person in the picture. Secondly, the program randomly chooses the highest level of education attained. If it has selected a degree, then it randomly chooses a senior high school from the second dataset. Thirdly, the program fixes the length of the work period according to the following formula: length of work period = age − 19 − years of the degree − 6 months of internship. Then, on the basis of the years of work, the program assigns one, two, or three work experiences, according to the following rules:

- work period ≤ 3 years: one work experience
- work period > 3 years: two work experiences (each experience lasts "work period/2")

[4] The size is relatively small. For instance, Bertrand and Mullainathan (2004) sent about 5,000 resumes. We justify our smaller sample because of ethical considerations that prevented us flooding the Italian job market (which is smaller in Rome/Milan than in Boston/Chicago) with fake résumés.

- work period > 10 years: three work experiences (each experience lasts "work period/3")

Lastly, the program chooses a level of language skills and a level of computer skills. If the program has selected a senior high school or a degree specializing in modern languages, it then assigns to the résumé the knowledge of two foreign languages, one with excellent proficiency. For the computer skills, there are no constraints.

The beauty of the person portrayed in the picture was assessed by an independent panel formed by 24 people. Members of this panel had never seen in real life the people in the pictures. Some of the members of the panel were employees of an employment agency that specializes in matching résumés to open vacancies.

The field experiment started on January 17, 2012 and ended on February 21, 2012. During this period, for each city and occupation, we selected the most recent employment advertisements published on two websites: Job Rapido and Monster. They are the most popular websites among actual jobseekers. We answered 531 advertisements, 336 in Milan and 195 in Rome. We typically sent four résumés in response to each advertisement; two from the treatment group and two from the control group. In total, we sent 2,320 résumés.

8.3 Results

Table 8.1 reports the recall rates by sex and cities. The overall response rate was about 11%, with a minor difference between males and females (10.83% and 11.24%, respectively). Looking at the percentages by city, the response rate is higher in Rome (about 16%), where males were more likely to be called back than females (17.48% vs. 14.96%). On the contrary, in Milan the overall response is roughly divided by two (about 8%), and males were less likely to be called back than females (7.19% vs. 9.10%).

Table 8.2 shows that the call center operator job was the occupation which received the highest rate of callbacks (also by gender), followed by receptionist and sales clerk. Interestingly, people who sent their résumés to a secretary or a shop assistant job got a very low callback rate, 4.66% and 2.95%, respectively.

We continue our data analysis by showing some evidence of the validity of our experiments in answering our main research question. Table 8.3 shows the association between our treatment variables and characteristics of the résumés and the advertisements (treatment variable "homosexual" and "beauty scores" in panel a and b, respectively). We provide this table as a randomization check to examine whether random assignment has succeeded, thus enabling us to assess the internal validity of the experiment results. The beauty score is associated with a "gay" internship and with age. As a result, it

Table 8.1. Callback rates by city and gender

	callback	All sample		Females		Males	
		count	freq.	count	freq.	count	freq.
All	yes	256	**11.03%**	130	**11.24%**	126	**10.83%**
	no	2,064	88.97%	1,027	88.76%	1,037	89.17%
Rome	yes	135	**16.21%**	63	**14.96%**	72	**17.48%**
	no	698	83.79%	358	85.04%	340	82.52%
Milan	yes	121	**8.14%**	67	**9.10%**	54	**7.19%**
	no	1,366	91.85%	669	90.90%	697	92.81%

Table 8.2. Callback rates by type of job

Occupation	callback						
	yes	no	yes	no	yes	no
	All sample		Females		Males	
administrative clerk	19	284	12	134	7	150
	6.27%	93.73%	8.22%	91.68%	4.46%	95.54%
bookkeeper	20	287	10	144	10	143
	6.51%	93.49%	6.49%	93.51%	6.54%	93.46%
call center	120	248	51	131	69	117
	32.61%	67.39%	28.02%	71.98%	37.10%	62.90%
receptionist	32	256	18	125	14	131
	11.11%	88.89%	12.59%	87.41%	9.66%	90.34%
sales clerk	39	320	24	166	15	154
	10.86%	89.14%	12.63%	87.37%	8.88%	91.12%
secretary	15	307	10	151	5	156
	4.66%	95.34%	6.21%	93.79%	3.11%	96.89%
shop assistant	11	362	5	176	6	186
	2.95%	97.05%	2.76%	97.24%	3.12%	96.88%

is important in our following regression analysis to control for picture beauty and age when assessing the premium/penalty of being homosexual in the labor market. Notice that we also control for other covariates as it is well known that their inclusion increases the precision of the estimates.

We start with Table 8.4 to investigate the relationship between response rate (callback) and homosexual preferences in panel a and between response rate and picture beauty in panel (b), with basic controls and distinguishing between males and females. We use linear probability models where the dependent variable takes value 1 if the identity of the person is called back (denoted "callback" in the table). Our target variable in panel a is a dummy taking value 1 if the identity is associated with periods of internship in pro-gay advocacy groups and 0 otherwise (denoted by "homosexual"). In panel (b), it is a variable containing the beauty scores received by the picture associated

Table 8.3. Randomization check

	Panel (a) Dep. var: homosexual			Panel (b) Dep. var: beauty score		
	All sample	Females	Males	All sample	Females	Males
beauty score	0.13***	0.12*	0.11*			
	(0.04)	(0.06)	(0.06)			
homosexual				0.12***	0.10*	0.10*
				(0.04)	(0.05)	(0.06)
bookkeeper	0.01	0.10	−0.08	0.06	−0.05	0.16
	(0.16)	(0.23)	(0.23)	(0.08)	(0.11)	(0.11)
call center	0.13	0.20	0.07	0.02	−0.03	0.08
	(0.16)	(0.22)	(0.22)	(0.07)	(0.10)	(0.11)
receptionist	0.06	0.14	−0.01	−0.06	−0.08	−0.01
	(0.17)	(0.23)	(0.24)	(0.08)	(0.10)	(0.12)
sales clerk	0.03	0.19	−0.15	−0.01	0.02	−0.05
	(0.16)	(0.22)	(0.22)	(0.07)	(0.10)	(0.11)
secretary	0.03	0.10	−0.06	−0.02	−0.14	0.08
	(0.16)	(0.23)	(0.23)	(0.08)	(0.10)	(0.11)
shop assistant	0.00	0.06	−0.07	0.07	0.02	0.10
	(0.16)	(0.22)	(0.23)	(0.07)	(0.10)	(0.11)
rome	0.06	0.10	0.02	0.00	−0.03	0.03
	(0.09)	(0.12)	(0.13)	(0.04)	(0.06)	(0.06)
age	0.02**	0.01	0.04***	−0.05***	−0.08***	−0.02***
	(0.01)	(0.01)	(0.01)	(0.00)	(0.01)	(0.01)
degree	0.14	0.19	0.13	0.10*	0.16*	0.06
	(0.12)	(0.17)	(0.17)	(0.06)	(0.08)	(0.08)
sex	−0.12			0.69***		
	(0.90)			(0.03)		
[3pt] Constant	−1.44***	−1.09*	−1.81***	5.73***	6.53***	5.63***
	(0.39)	(0.59)	(0.54)	(0.14)	(0.18)	(0.20)
N	2320	1163	1157	2320	1163	1157

Notes: Panel (a) reports logit regression results, where the dependent variable is "homosexual." Panel (b) reports OLS regression results, where the dependent variable is "beauty score."

with the identity (denoted by "beauty score"), as assessed by the jury panel. The scores range between 0 and 10, where 10 indicates the most attractive individual. Figure 8.1 shows the distribution of beauty scores in our sample of job applicants. The distribution is broken into five intervals, each containing approximately 20% of the sample.

Results in panel (a) reveal a statistical significant penalty (in terms of callback rates) associated to homosexual males of about 3%, whereas homosexual females do not seem to show a significant difference in callback rate with respect to heterosexual females, even though the sign is positive. Observe that the 3% penalty for homosexual males is quite high since the callback rate for males is 10% (see Table 8.1), which means that compared to heterosexual males, they have 30% less chance of being called back.

Table 8.4. Response rate, homosexual preferences, and beauty scores

Dependent: call back	Panel (a)			Panel (b)			Panel (c)		
	All sample	Females	Males	All sample	Females	Males	All sample	Females	Males
homosexual	-0.008 (0.012)	0.015 (0.018)	-0.031* (0.017)				-0.009 (0.012)	0.014 (0.018)	-0.030* (0.017)
beauty score				0.005 (0.006)	0.018** (0.009)	-0.008 (0.009)	0.005 (0.006)	0.018* (0.009)	-0.007 (0.009)
bookkeeper	0.004 (0.020)	-0.014 (0.030)	0.021 (0.025)	0.004 (0.020)	-0.018 (0.030)	0.020 (0.025)	0.004 (0.020)	-0.018 (0.030)	0.021 (0.025)
call center	0.255*** (0.028)	0.192*** (0.041)	0.316*** (0.038)	0.255*** (0.028)	0.190*** (0.040)	0.314*** (0.038)	0.255*** (0.028)	0.190*** (0.040)	0.315*** (0.038)
receptionist	0.051** (0.023)	0.047 (0.036)	0.054* (0.029)	0.051** (0.023)	0.047 (0.036)	0.053* (0.029)	0.051** (0.023)	0.046 (0.036)	0.054* (0.029)
sales clerk	0.042* (0.022)	0.043 (0.034)	0.038 (0.028)	0.042* (0.022)	0.042 (0.034)	0.036 (0.028)	0.042* (0.022)	0.043 (0.034)	0.038 (0.028)
secretary	-0.020 (0.018)	-0.020 (0.030)	-0.023 (0.022)	-0.020 (0.018)	-0.022 (0.030)	-0.025 (0.021)	-0.020 (0.018)	-0.022 (0.030)	-0.024 (0.022)
shop assistant	-0.040** (0.017)	-0.058** (0.026)	-0.024 (0.021)	-0.040** (0.017)	-0.060** (0.026)	-0.024 (0.021)	-0.040** (0.017)	-0.060** (0.026)	-0.024 (0.021)
age	0.039** (0.020)	0.028 (0.029)	0.044 (0.027)	0.038* (0.020)	0.023 (0.029)	0.038 (0.027)	0.039** (0.020)	0.020 (0.029)	0.040 (0.027)
age2	-0.001** (0.000)	-0.001 (0.001)	-0.001* (0.000)	-0.001** (0.000)	0.000 (0.001)	-0.001 (0.000)	-0.001** (0.000)	0.000 (0.001)	-0.001 (0.000)
rome	0.066*** (0.014)	0.048** (0.020)	0.085*** (0.020)	0.066*** (0.014)	0.048** (0.020)	0.084*** (0.020)	0.066*** (0.014)	0.048** (0.020)	0.085*** (0.020)
Constant	-0.443* (0.267)	-0.305 (0.394)	-0.505 (0.368)	-0.461* (0.269)	-0.330 (0.391)	-0.392 (0.377)	-0.475* (0.269)	-0.293 (0.394)	-0.408 (0.376)
R^2	0.11	0.07	0.17	0.11	0.07	0.16	0.11	0.07	0.17
adj. R^2	0.11	0.06	0.16	0.11	0.07	0.16	0.11	0.07	0.16
N	2320	1157	1163	2320	1157	1163	2320	1157	1163

Notes: OLS regression results. Robust standard errors in parentheses. *** $p < 0.01$, ** $p < 0.05$, * $p < 0.1$.

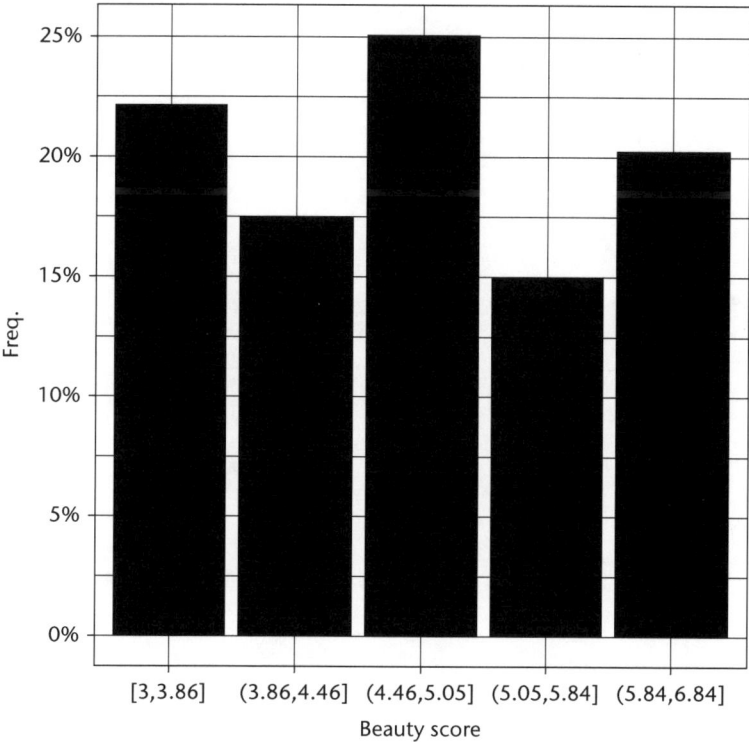

Figure 8.1. Distribution of Beauty scores into intervals.

Note: Each interval contains approximately 20% of the sample of job applicants.

This confirms previous studies on the relationship between homosexuality and labor market outcomes (see Section 6.3) where there is strong evidence of discrimination against gays in the hiring process. For example, Ahmed et al. (2011b) for Sweden, who also construct fake résumés, find that a heterosexual male applicant received 14% more responses from employers than a homosexual applicant (see also Weichselbaumer, 2003, for Austria, and Drydakis, 2011, for Greece).

When we instead look at differences in response rates by picture beauty, panel (b) shows a significant premium for attractive females of about 2% and no significant difference between handsome and less attractive men. This is in line with the beauty premium highlighted in Section 6.3. Panel (c) shows that these results remain unchanged when both our variables of interest (homosexuality and beauty) are included as regressors.

In Table 8.5 panel a we use the same specification as in Table 8.4 panel (c) and add as controls all the other characteristics that were collected in our experiment. They include type of secondary schools (e.g. schools specializing

Table 8.5. Response rate, homosexual preferences, and beauty scores – different specifications

Callback	Panel (a)			Panel (b)		
	All sample	Females	Males	All sample	Females	Males
homosexual	−0.008	0.014	−0.028*	−0.008	0.014	−0.029*
	(0.012)	(0.018)	(0.017)	(0.012)	(0.019)	(0.017)
beauty score	0.007	0.019**	−0.006			
	(0.006)	(0.009)	(0.009)			
beauty score ∈ (3.86,4.46]				0.019	0.043	0.016
				(0.019)	(0.033)	(0.025)
beauty score ∈(4.46,5.05]				0.027	0.052*	0.017
				(0.018)	(0.030)	(0.023)
beauty score ∈(5.05,5.84]				0.008	0.036	−0.009
				(0.019)	(0.029)	(0.034)
beauty score ∈(5.84,6.84]				0.021	0.077**	−0.036
				(0.020)	(0.032)	(0.026)
bookkeeper	0.012	−0.008	0.028	0.013	−0.007	0.029
	(0.020)	(0.031)	(0.026)	(0.020)	(0.031)	(0.027)
call center	0.256***	0.193***	0.317***	0.255***	0.192***	0.318***
	(0.030)	(0.045)	(0.040)	(0.030)	(0.045)	(0.040)
receptionist	0.040	0.037	0.045	0.040	0.038	0.046
	(0.026)	(0.041)	(0.035)	(0.026)	(0.041)	(0.035)
sales clerk	0.050**	0.049	0.051	0.049**	0.047	0.049
	(0.024)	(0.036)	(0.031)	(0.024)	(0.037)	(0.031)
secretary	−0.010	−0.020	−0.002	−0.010	−0.020	−0.001
	(0.021)	(0.034)	(0.027)	(0.021)	(0.034)	(0.027)
shop assistant	−0.041**	−0.069**	−0.014	−0.041**	−0.069**	−0.015
	(0.019)	(0.030)	(0.025)	(0.019)	(0.031)	(0.025)
age	0.069**	0.038	0.077**	0.072**	0.038	0.078**
	(0.028)	(0.041)	(0.038)	(0.028)	(0.040)	(0.038)
age2	−0.001**	−0.001	−0.001**	−0.001***	−0.001	−0.001**
	(0.000)	(0.001)	(0.000)	(0.000)	(0.001)	(0.000)
rome	0.052***	0.040*	0.062***	0.052***	0.040*	0.062***
	(0.015)	(0.022)	(0.021)	(0.015)	(0.022)	(0.021)
Constant	−0.943**	−0.574	−0.959	−0.963**	−0.511	−1.006*
	(0.451)	(0.641)	(0.609)	(0.446)	(0.631)	(0.607)
R^2	0.13	0.10	0.20	0.13	0.10	0.20
adj. R^2	0.12	0.07	0.17	0.12	0.07	0.18
N	2320	1157	1163	2320	1157	1163
Additional controls	Yes	Yes	Yes	Yes	Yes	Yes

Notes: Panel (a) shows the OLS regression results of the same specification in Table 8.4. Panel (c) plus additional controls describing the applicant's characteristics and the requirements of the job posting. Controls of the first kind are years of working experience, dummies for type of secondary school attended, dummies for foreign languages proficiency, and dummies for different types of computer skills. Controls of the second kind are dummies for whether the posting required a picture and/or a cover letter, and whether the posting targeted applicants of a given gender and/or is good looking. In Panel (b), besides including these additional controls, we code beauty score using the quantiles of its empirical distribution. Robust standard errors in parentheses. *** $p < 0.01$, ** $p < 0.05$, * $p < 0.1$.

in math or in literature), the years of experience of the candidate, whether he/she has a college degree or not, and characteristics of each advertisement, namely if it targeted a specific gender, if it mentioned the equal opportunity (non discriminatory) act, if a picture was required, if a cover letter was required (if so, we sent a cover letter), if it was posted by an employment agency or directly by a company, if the knowledge of one or more foreign languages was required, and if computer knowledge was specified. As was expected given the randomized nature of our experiment, the results remain unchanged. In Table 8.5 panel (b) we instead investigate possible non-linearities in the relationship between response rate and picture beauty by coding the beauty scores with a set of dummy variables capturing various beauty ranges. These ranges are those plotted in Figure 8.1. The main results remain mainly unchanged, in other words attractive females are the group that seem to receive a premium whereas attractive males do not. However, these results show that this premium for females seems to be mainly driven by highly attractive women (in the extreme upper tail of the beauty score distribution), who appear to receive a premium of almost 8%.

We continue our analysis in Table 8.6 by using the same specification as in Table 8.5, panel (b) and add an interaction term between our dummy capturing homosexual preferences ("homosexual") and a dummy variable ("good CV"), taking value 1 if the individual is depicted in the résumé as having a college degree with excellent English proficiency and excellent computer skills and 0 otherwise. Our aim is to investigate if the penalty associated with homosexual preferences is mitigated for high-skilled indi-viduals. Interestingly, we find the opposite result. Indeed, Table 8.6 reveals that the penalty actually seems to be higher for high-skilled homosexual individuals, with an associated magnitude of more than 8% for homosexual males. No penalty or premium is associated with high-skilled homosexual females, confirming that only males are penalized in the labor market for their homosexuality. This suggests that high-skilled homosexuals are more discriminated against than low-skilled homosexuals, although our experiment only considers jobs with low-skilled profiles.

In Table 8.7, we also investigate whether the beauty premium for women varies by skills. We find that high-skilled attractive women are called back less often than low-skilled attractive women. This may indicate that beauty might not be an advantage for high-skilled women.

A possible concern, however, can be that employers are discriminating between internships in cultural associations and in companies, as the control group includes identities reporting internships both in non-gay/non-lesbian cultural associations and companies. If employers prefer to employ people who had experience in companies rather than in cultural associations, then

Table 8.6. High-skilled vs low-skilled individuals – homosexuality

Dep. var: call back	All sample	Females	Males
homosexual	−0.001	0.020	−0.019
	(0.013)	(0.020)	(0.018)
homosexual × good cv	−0.059*	−0.057	−0.081*
	(0.036)	(0.056)	(0.047)
good cv	0.044	0.073	0.012
	(0.034)	(0.050)	(0.048)
beauty ∈ (3.86,4.46]	0.019	0.046	0.015
	(0.019)	(0.033)	(0.025)
beauty ∈ (4.46,5.05]	0.027	0.052*	0.016
	(0.018)	(0.030)	(0.023)
beauty ∈ (5.05,5.84]	0.008	0.036	−0.008
	(0.019)	(0.029)	(0.035)
beauty ∈ (5.84,6.84]	0.021	0.078**	−0.037
	(0.020)	(0.032)	(0.026)
bookkeeper	0.012	−0.009	0.029
	(0.020)	(0.031)	(0.027)
call center	0.256***	0.191***	0.319***
	(0.030)	(0.045)	(0.040)
receptionist	0.040	0.039	0.046
	(0.026)	(0.042)	(0.035)
sales clerk	0.050**	0.046	0.050
	(0.024)	(0.037)	(0.031)
secretary	−0.009	−0.020	0.000
	(0.021)	(0.034)	(0.026)
shop assistant	−0.041**	−0.069**	−0.015
	(0.019)	(0.031)	(0.025)
age	0.073**	0.037	0.079**
	(0.028)	(0.040)	(0.038)
age^2	−0.001***	−0.001	−0.001**
	(0.000)	(0.001)	(0.000)
rome	0.052***	0.039*	0.061***
	(0.015)	(0.022)	(0.021)
Constant	−0.980**	−0.506	−1.022*
	(0.447)	(0.631)	(0.611)
R^2	0.13	0.10	0.20
adj. R^2	0.12	0.07	0.18
N	2320	1157	1163
Additional controls	Yes	Yes	Yes

Notes: OLS estimation results. Robust standard errors in parentheses. *** $p < 0.01$, ** $p < 0.05$, * $p < 0.1$.

the penalty associated with pro-gay/pro-lesbian cultural associations can simply capture the penalty associated with experience in a cultural association rather than in a company.

We investigate this issue in Table 8.8. In the first panel, we display the results when excluding individuals from the control group that had

Table 8.7. Robustness checks

Dep. var: call back	All sample	Females	Males
beauty	0.01	0.03***	0.00
	(0.01)	(0.01)	(0.01)
beauty × good cv	−0.03**	−0.08***	−0.02
	(0.02)	(0.03)	(0.02)
good cv	0.16*	0.42**	0.09
	(0.09)	(0.17)	(0.11)
homosexual	−0.01	0.01	−0.03*
	(0.01)	(0.02)	(0.02)
bookkeeper	0.01	−0.01	0.03
	(0.02)	(0.03)	(0.03)
call center	0.25***	0.18***	0.31***
	(0.03)	(0.04)	(0.04)
receptionist	0.04	0.03	0.04
	(0.03)	(0.04)	(0.03)
sales clerk	0.04*	0.05	0.04
	(0.02)	(0.04)	(0.03)
secretary	−0.02	−0.03	−0.01
	(0.02)	(0.03)	(0.02)
shop assistant	−0.05**	−0.08***	−0.02
	(0.02)	(0.03)	(0.02)
age	0.03	0.03	0.04
	(0.02)	(0.04)	(0.03)
age2	0.00**	0.00	0.00*
	(0.00)	(0.00)	(0.00)
rome	0.06***	0.04**	0.08***
	(0.01)	(0.02)	(0.02)
Constant	−0.30	−0.49	−0.34
	(0.28)	(0.63)	(0.40)
R^2	0.12	0.10	0.18
adj. R^2	0.12	0.08	0.16
N	2320	1157	1163

Notes: OLS estimation results. Robust standard errors in parentheses. *** $p < 0.01$, ** $p < 0.05$, * $p < 0.1$.

internships in companies. Our target variable is thus now a dummy taking value 1 if the résumé reports an internship in a pro-gay/pro-lesbian cultural association and 0 if the intership is a non pro-gay/pro-lesbian cultural association (labeled as "homosexual association"). One can see that the results are virtually the same as those reported in Table 8.8, with even a slightly higher penalty for homosexual males (about 3.5% in Table 8.8 vs. about 3% in Table 8.4). As a further robustness check, we investigate in the second panel of Table 8.8 if employers actually discriminate between internships in cultural associations and in companies. The results show that this is not the case. When excluding from our sample individuals with homosexual preferences and coding our target as 1 if the internship was in cultural associations and

Table 8.8. OLS regression results. The first panel displays the results when excluding individuals from the control group having internships in companies. The second panel excludes instead individuals having internship in pro-gay/prolesbian cultural association. Although not reported, all specifications include as regressors: age, age^2, dummies for type of job, and city dummy. Robust standard errors in parentheses. *** $p < 0.01$, ** $p < 0.05$, * $p < 0.1$.

Dep. var: call back	Gay/Lesbians vs. general associations			General association vs. companies		
	All sample	Females	Males	All sample	Females	Males
homosexual	−0.009	0.015	−0.035*	−0.003	−0.009	0.001
	(0.015)	(0.021)	(0.021)	(0.017)	(0.024)	(0.024)
beauty score	0.009	0.028**	−0.016	−0.001	0.008	−0.009
	(0.007)	(0.011)	(0.010)	(0.008)	(0.012)	(0.014)
bookkeeper	0.003	−0.002	0.000	0.037	0.006	0.074*
	(0.024)	(0.039)	(0.029)	(0.025)	(0.034)	(0.038)
call center	0.236***	0.192***	0.281***	0.307***	0.237***	0.393***
	(0.034)	(0.051)	(0.047)	(0.040)	(0.056)	(0.055)
receptionist	0.031	0.027	0.035	0.083**	0.098*	0.096**
	(0.031)	(0.050)	(0.040)	(0.034)	(0.053)	(0.047)
sales clerk	0.048*	0.034	0.062*	0.052*	0.055	0.057
	(0.028)	(0.043)	(0.037)	(0.029)	(0.043)	(0.040)
secretary	−0.016	−0.032	−0.002	0.020	0.027	0.027
	(0.025)	(0.039)	(0.031)	(0.026)	(0.042)	(0.032)
shop assistant	−0.044*	−0.091**	−0.004	−0.018	−0.031	0.009
	(0.023)	(0.035)	(0.031)	(0.024)	(0.039)	(0.030)
age	0.096***	0.078	0.091**	0.042	0.026	0.039
	(0.034)	(0.048)	(0.046)	(0.038)	(0.055)	(0.052)
age2	−0.001***	−0.001	−0.001**	−0.001	−0.001	0.000
	(0.000)	(0.001)	(0.001)	(0.000)	(0.001)	(0.001)
rome	0.046**	0.042	0.046*	0.063***	0.044	0.081***
	(0.018)	(0.027)	(0.024)	(0.020)	(0.027)	(0.030)
Constant	−1.379***	−1.297*	−1.111	−0.493	−0.260	−0.475
	(0.533)	(0.779)	(0.712)	(0.598)	(0.842)	(0.843)
R^2	0.12	0.11	0.18	0.15	0.13	0.23
adj. R^2	0.11	0.07	0.15	0.13	0.08	0.20
N	1684	840	844	1272	640	632

0 if instead it was in a company (labeled as "Non homosexual association"), Table 8.8 shows no statisticall differences in response rates between the two groups. This further robustness check increases our confidence in the estimated penalty of 3% for homosexuals in the labor market and the fact that employers tend to discriminate against homosexuals in the labor market.

8.4 Concluding Remarks

This chapter describes a field experiment that we conducted in two Italian cities, Rome and Milan, to study the relationship between homosexuality or beauty and labor market outcomes as measured by the difference in the percentage of callback rates between the reference group (homosexuals or less attractive persons) and the control group (heterosexuals or good looking persons). For that, we sent fake résumés, which clearly indicated participation in a gay or lesbian organization for homosexuals and different pictures to highlight how handsome the candidate was. We randomly assigned résumés so that some belonged to homosexuals and others to heterosexuals. We used the same procedure for the beauty of the person. The design of the experiment allowed us to control for all possible nuisances that might bias the assessment of the relationship between labor market outcomes and sexual orientation in the first case and beauty in the second.

We find that there is a statistical significant penalty (in terms of callback rates) associated with homosexual males of about 3%, whereas homosexual females do not seem to show any significant difference with respect to heterosexual females. To be more precise, since the callback rate for males is about 10%, this means that, compared to heterosexual males, homosexuals have 30% less chance of being called back. We also find that this penalty is higher for high-skilled homosexual individuals, with an associated magnitude of more than 8% for homosexual males. No penalty or premium is associated with high-skilled homosexual females, confirming that only males are penalized in the labor market for their homosexuality.

When we then investigate differences in callback rates by picture beauty, we find that there is a significant premium for attractive females of about 2% and no significant difference between handsome and less attractive men. We also investigate whether the beauty premium for women varies by skills. We find that high-skilled attractive women are called back less often than low-skilled attractive women, which may indicate that beauty might not be an advantage for high-skilled women.

9

Other Dimensions of Discrimination

Eleonora Patacchini, Giuseppe Ragusa, and Yves Zenou

9.1 Introduction

This chapter is devoted to the analysis of other (under-researched) dimensions of discrimination: age discrimination, disability discrimination, and housing discrimination. Although the existing cross-country data for Europe does not allow us to present a detailed analysis on these topics, we revise the specific theoretical mechanisms in each area and present an overview of the existing empirical studies. For age discrimination, we use a special module of the European Social Survey to provide some evidence on attitudes towards ageing and experiences with prejudice because of age in Europe. Although Europe has a steadily ageing population, ageism has never been the subject of a comprehensive cross-national study. However, the fourth round of the European Social Survey that was conducted in 2008 contains a special module entitled "Experiences and Expressions of Ageism", which examines several key components of ageism: age stereotypes, attitudes towards ageing, intergenerational contact, intergenerational attitudes, and experiences of ageism. It appears, for example, that while in all European countries (with the exception of Romania) having a 30-year-old boss is widely accepted, in more than half of the countries having a qualified 70-year-old boss is not commonly accepted. Remarkably, the percentage of people who experienced prejudice because of age is above 20% for all countries, and it peaks to values larger than 40% in countries such as the Czech Republic, Finland, the Netherlands, and Belgium.

9.2 Age Discrimination

The American workforce is becoming older, and some workers face certain discriminatory challenges when seeking or maintaining employment. In the

United States, Holliday (2010, p. 1) reported that the US Senate Special Committee on Aging reported that between the years 2010 and 2030, the elderly, that is people aged 65 and over, will comprise an estimated 21.8% of the total population. A growing proportion of older adults do not have the option of retiring from work. Instead, many continue working because their personal savings and/or Social Security pensions are not sufficient. Others remain on the job to obtain health care coverage because they are not old enough for Medicare or poor enough to qualify for Medicaid. Reversing previous trends, the labor force participation rates and full-time employment of older men and women, especially those 65 years or older, have increased in the last decade. According to the US Census Bureau, nearly a quarter of adults between the ages of 65 and 74 (23.2%) were employed or looking for work in 2006, nearly a 20% increase since 2000. Similarly, the Bureau of Labor Statistics (BLS) indicated that in the United States between 1977 and 2007, employment of workers 65 years of age and over increased by 101%, compared to a smaller increase of 59% for total employment (age 16 and over). The number of employed men aged 65 and over increased by 75%; however, the employment of women aged 65 and over rose substantially to 147%. The BLS, therefore, concludes that a larger portion of people aged 65 and over is remaining or returning to the workforce (either working or looking for work). Another interesting BLS statistic is that in 2007 older workers with less than a high school education accounted for 13% of that group's employment (down from 21% in 1997), compared to 9% for younger workers.

Europe is facing similar problems. For example, if we take the case of Italy, after the baby boom of the 1960s and early 1970s, the total fertility rate declined sharply, falling below the replacement rate of 2.1 at the beginning of the 1980s, and reaching 1.24 in 2000 (Rymkevitch and Villosio, 2007). At the same time, life expectancy is amongst the highest in the world (approximately 79 years). This new demographic structure will have a profound impact on the labor market in Italy. According to the Italian National Statistical Office (ISTAT) forecasts, in the next two decades, the baby boom generations will reach retirement age, and they will be replaced by new cohorts roughly half the size. The employment rate for those aged 55–64 in Italy was 31.4% in 2005, about ten percentage points below the European average and far below the Stockholm target of 50%. The situation is even worse for older women, for whom the employment rate is 20.8%, the lowest in the EU. Age discrimination in the labor market presents itself in various ways. Some are explicit, such as the exclusion of older workers from training or the inclusion of age limits in recruitment advertisements. Other ways are more subtle, such as dealing with job redundancies by means of early retirement.

9.2.1 *What is Age Discrimination?*

Age discrimination is the process by which qualified persons are excluded from employment opportunities because they are older in calendar age. The assumption is made that an older employee may very well possess the necessary background and job skills, but that he/she will be much more likely to resist new and supposedly better methods or procedures. Also, there is some concern that the older employee will not be able to provide a term of service that will last long enough for the company to recoup expenses associated with job training. When age limitation is based on criteria like this, the company stands to lose access to what may have been a valuable asset for the ongoing health of the company, as well as running the risk of being charged with age discrimination and encountering severe legal issues. On a personal level, an older person may be told that he or she is too old to engage in certain physical activities. On an institutional level, there are policies and regulations in place that limit opportunities to people of certain ages and deny them to all others. There are, for example, government regulations that determine when a worker may retire. Currently, in the US, a worker must be 67 years old before becoming eligible for Social Security retirement benefits, but some company pension plans begin benefits at earlier ages.

Like racial and gender discrimination, age discrimination can result in unequal pay for equal work. Unlike racial and gender discrimination, however, age discrimination in wages is often enshrined in law. While older workers benefit more often from higher wages than do younger workers, they face barriers in promotions and hiring. Employers also encourage early retirement or layoffs disproportionately more for older or more experienced workers.

Age discrimination in hiring has been shown to exist in the United States. Lahey (2005) found that firms are more than 40% more likely to interview a young adult job applicant than an older job applicant.

In a survey for the University of Kent, England, 29% of respondents stated that they had suffered from age discrimination. This is a higher proportion than for gender or racial discrimination. Dominic Abrams, social psychology professor at the university, concluded that ageism is the most pervasive form of prejudice experienced in the UK population.

For American corporations, age discrimination can lead to significant expenses. In the fiscal year 2006, the US Equal Employment Opportunity Commission received nearly 17,000 charges of age discrimination, resolving more than 14,000 and recovering $51.5 million in monetary benefits. Costs from lawsuit settlements and judgments can run into the millions, most notably with the $250 million paid by the California Public Employees' Retirement System (CalPERS) under a settlement agreement in 2003.

9.2.2 *Impact on the Labor Market*

Older workers are particularly vulnerable to job dislocations. (Dislocated workers are defined as adults who lose their jobs either because their company or plant closes or moves, there is insufficient work to keep them employed, or their shift or position is eliminated.) Since 1980, the rate of job displacement among workers over the age of 50 has risen sharply compared to younger workers (Elder, 2004). In past decades, older workers were less likely than younger workers to lose their jobs. Now older workers are actually more likely than younger workers to be displaced.

A study (Rodriguez and Zavodny, 2000) comparing dislocation rates by age between two time frames (1983–1987 and 1993–1997) found that the average age of displaced workers has increased over time. Older workers now make up a greater percentage of job losers relative to their proportion of the labor market. The authors calculated that about two-thirds of the shift in age distribution of displaced workers can be attributed to the ageing of the labor force. The probability of displacement has increased over time for older workers compared to younger ones.

When older workers lose jobs, they are less likely to get another one quickly and experience greater earnings losses than younger workers, according to BLS data. In 2004, for example, the average period of joblessness for older workers was 26 weeks, compared with 19 weeks for younger job seekers. Dislocated workers with 20 years' experience find jobs that pay, on average, between 20% and 40% less than their previous jobs. Rodriguez and Zavodny (2000) concluded that older displaced workers (45–75) who found other employment suffered average wage losses of roughly 19%. One-quarter of older men laid off from long-term jobs experienced hourly wage loss of at least 50%. Chan and Stevens (2001) report that a worker who is laid off at the age of 55 has a 61% chance of being back at work two years later if male and a 55% chance if female.

Workers under 50 years of age are 42% more likely to be called for an interview than those aged 50 and older (Lahey, 2005). In addition, older workers re-entering the workforce face fewer employment opportunities than younger workers and are likely to be employed in a narrower range of industries and occupations than younger workers. Moreover, dislocated workers in regions with declining industries may be forced to leave their communities to find work, something that may be extremely difficult for older workers who own homes and have roots in a community (US Department of Labor, 2008).

Another indication that older unemployed workers face difficult challenges is their overrepresentation among the long-term unemployed. While long-term unemployment (lasting more than six months) has been rising over the past several decades, workers over the age of 45 are more likely to be found in this group relative to their proportion in the workforce. Workers aged 45 or older represent 26% of the workforce but 35% of the long-term unemployed. Older workers, particularly older men laid off in the male-dominated manufacturing industries, are disproportionately represented in that group (Allegretto and Stettner, 2004).

Economic research also provides a variety of indirect evidence that dis-crimination against older workers continues to operate in the contemporary American labor market. For example, while younger workers' earnings tend to increase with experience, those of older workers tend to decline (Wanner and McDonald, 1983). Periods of unemployment for involuntarily unemployed older workers average about twice as long as those of their younger counterparts (Bendick, 1983). When unemployed older workers find jobs, they do so in a narrower range of occupations and industries than their younger counterparts (Hutchens, 1988). Older workers who perceive themselves to be victims of age discrimination are separated from their jobs at a higher rate than those who do not (Johnson and Neumark, 1997).

Research that investigates such discrimination directly is much less com-mon. In one of the few studies of this kind (Bendick et al., 1996), pairs of résumés, one for a 57 year old and one for a 32 year old, were mailed to 775 large firms and employment agencies across the United States. Although the résumés presented equal qualifications for both job seekers, the older applicant received a less favorable employer response 26.5% of the time when a position was vacant. That study left many questions unanswered, however. It only examined differences in treatment between older and younger applicants in the initial contact stage of the job-seeking process. What would have occurred during subsequent stages, including interviews and job offers, remained unexplored. Additionally, employers' responses were measured only through telephone messages and letters; such responses encompassed only a fraction of the ways in which older and younger applicants could be treated differently.

Another study of Bendick et al. (1999) extends that earlier research by examining these additional dimensions of the job-seeking process. Pairs of testers, one aged 57 and one aged 32, applied for 102 entry-level sales or management jobs in the Washington DC metropolitan area. Although their credentials described them as equally qualified, the older applicants received less favorable responses from employers 41.2% of the time. Three-quarters of these differences occurred before older applicants could fully present their qualifications. The negative employer assumptions about older workers implied by these differences in outcome were seldom explicitly stated.

9.2.3 Mechanisms

Why do older workers face more adverse labor market outcomes?

These low outcomes can be attributed to the fact that older workers:

(i) have a low intensity of job search; (ii) have a higher reservation wage (the lowest wage rate at which a worker will accept a job); (iii) suffer a negative health shock, or experience a positive budget shock (defined as an increase in either total household non-labor income or total non-pension wealth).

Among the obstacles that older job seekers may encounter is employers' reluctance to hire them. The negative perceptions and stereotypes as barriers to hiring and retaining older workers are:

(i) older workers are more expensive, including their compensation, the rising cost of their health insurance, and the costs to train them; (ii) older workers are both less productive and produce lower-quality work than younger workers; (iii) older workers are resistant to change.

Even if older job seekers do not experience age discrimination, they may experience other impediments to re-employment. Among the more significant obstacles for older unemployed workers are:

(i) limited access to training and skills retraining programs; (ii) limited job search skills; (iii) health problems, disabilities, or physical limitations; (iv) few opportunities for flexible work arrangements; (v) lack of information about starting a business; (vi) retirement laws and regulations that may discourage employers from hiring older workers.

In a study of the age structure of hires into different occupations, Hirsch et al. (2000) conclude that employment opportunities for older workers are restricted. Older workers are least likely to be hired into occupations requiring substantial computer use or where the return to job tenure is high, and most likely to be hired into lower-wage occupations. Lahey (2008) documents evidence of statistical age discrimination against older female job applicants in an experimental study of employer hiring practices.

In the context of a theoretical job search model, Maestas and Li (2006) examine the decision to search for a job and the probability of transitioning to employment using a large sample of non-workers from the Health and Retirement Study in the US. The effects of both supply-side factors (individual characteristics) and demand-side factors (local labor market conditions) are estimated with a set of reduced form econometric models. They find employment transition rates are relatively low for older searchers: only half of older searchers successfully attain jobs. They examine various explanations for this result, including variation in search intensity, reservation wages, and the possibility of intervening health shocks. They conclude that about 13% of older job searchers become discouraged workers, in the sense of being willing to work at the prevailing wage, but unable to find a job.

9.2.4 Ageism and the European Social Survey

Although Europe has a steadily ageing population, ageism has never been the subject of a comprehensive cross-national study. In this section, we provide some evidence on age discrimination using data from the European Social Survey (ESS). The ESS is a European Union-funded survey conducted in most European countries every two years, starting from 2002. In particular, the ESS has data on 23 of the 25 EU25 countries, with Estonia and Italy being the missing countries. The questionnaire comprises core items (which are repeated in all rounds), aiming at monitoring change and continuity in a wide range of socioeconomic, sociopolitical, sociopsychological, and sociodemographic variables, and rotating items (which vary from round to round), aiming instead at deepening the understanding of some special topics. In particular, the fourth round of the ESS which was conducted in 2008 contains a special module entitled "Experiences and Expressions of Ageism" which examines several key components of ageism: age stereotypes, attitudes towards ageing, intergenerational contact, intergenerational attitudes, and experiences of ageism. The observations available for each countries vary, but the survey is designed to be representative of each country's population. Figure 9.1 reports how individuals answered the following question: "On

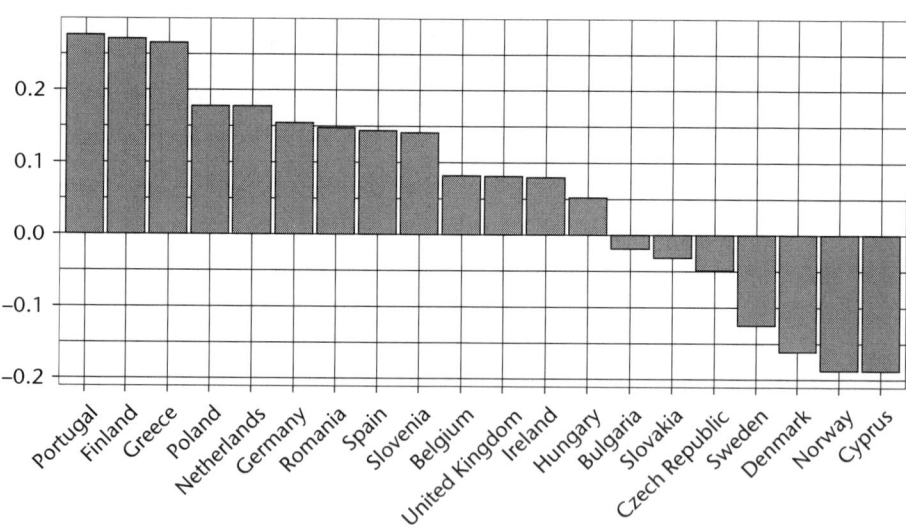

Figure 9.1. Attitudes towards ageism in the EU.

Notes: Index constructed on the question "How worried are you that employers prefer people in their 20s rather than 40 or older?". The answer is a value from 0 to 10. The graph plots the average of the index in percentage deviation from 5, the median value of the possible values.

Source: European Social Survey, 2008.

a score of 0–10 how worried are you that employers might prefer to give jobs to people in their 20s rather than to people in their 40s or older?" For each country, we show the (weighted) mean of the answers[1] in percentage deviation from the median value of the possible values (i.e. 5), which is the zero line. Countries with positive values are thus those where people are more worried than average about the fact that employers might prefer to give jobs to younger people. Southern European countries, such as Greece, Spain, and Portugal, are in this category.[2] Countries with negative values instead are those where people are not too worried about this age-related issue. This is the case, for example, in Norway, Sweden, Denmark, and some of the Eastern European countries (Bulgaria, Slovakia, and the Czech Republic). Figure 9.2 is constructed using the same procedure. It shows the extent to which people consider acceptable the fact that (i) a qualified 30 year old is appointed as their boss (Figure 9.2(a)) and (ii) a qualified 70 year old is appointed as their boss (Figure 9.2(b)). It appears that while in all European countries (with the exception of Romania) it is widely acceptable to have a 30-year-old boss, in more than half the countries having a qualified 70-year-old boss is not commonly accepted. Figures 9.3 and 9.4 provide some evidence about experiences with prejudice because of age. Figure 9.3 depicts country by country the distribution of answers to the following question: "How often in the past year have you been treated with prejudice because of age?", coded as 0 (never) to 4 (very often). Figure 9.4 reports for each country the percentage of people who experienced prejudice because of age, in other words those answering 1 to 4 to the above question. Remarkably, this percentage is above 20% for all countries and it peaks to values larger than 40% in countries such as the Czech Republic, Finland, the Netherlands, and Belgium.

9.3 Disability Discrimination

Across the EU as a whole some 16% of those aged 16–64 reported that they had a long-standing health problem or disability (Table 1 and Fig. 1 in APPLICA et al., 2007). This proportion, however, varied markedly across EU member states, ranging from 32% in Finland, 27% in the UK, around 25% in the Netherlands and France, and just under 24% in Estonia to 8–9% in Spain, Lithuania, Malta, and Slovakia and just under 7% in Italy, while in Romania it was only around 6%.

The type of restriction on the ability to work resulting from a long-standing health problem or disability (LSHPD) is more likely to concern the kind of

---

[1] The weighted mean is obtained simply by multiplying each values (1 to 10) by the number of individuals that chose that value and then dividing by the total number of individuals that answered that question.

[2] Italy is not included in this special module.

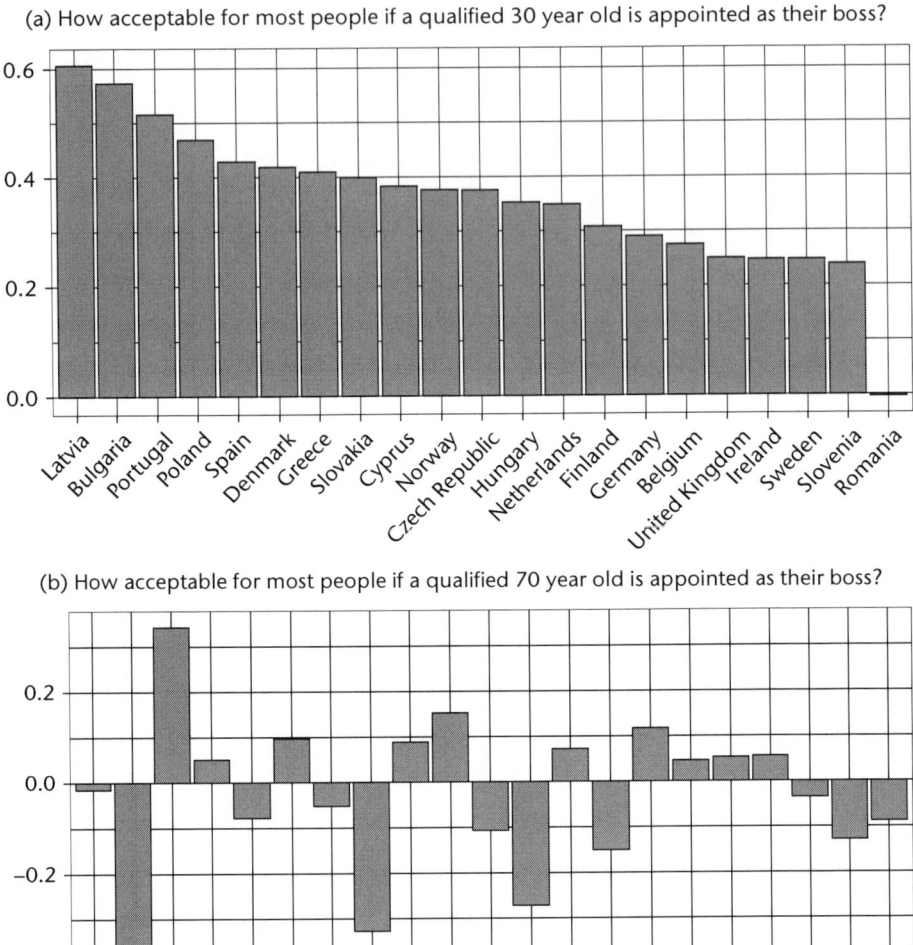

Figure 9.2. The figure (a) plots the index constructed on the basis of the question "How acceptable is for most people that a qualified 30 year old is appointed as their boss?" The figure (b) plots the index constructed on the basis of the question "How acceptable is for most people that a qualified 70 year old is appointed as their boss?" The answers to both questions are values from 0 to 10. The graph plots the average of the index in percentage deviation from 5, the median value of the possible values.

Source: European Social Survey, 2008.

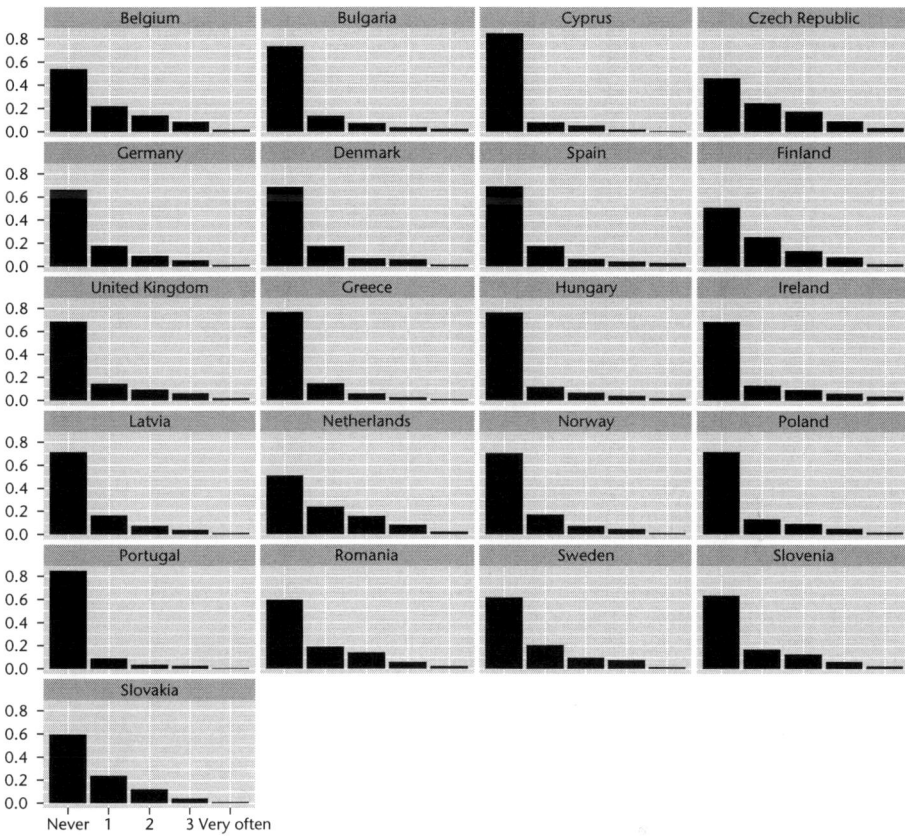

Figure 9.3. Experiences of age discrimination in the EU, by country frequencies.

Notes: The figure plots by-country frequencies of the four possible answers to the question "How often in the past year have you been treated with prejudice because of age?".

Source: European Social Survey, 2008.

work which a person can do or the amount of work than their ability to travel to and from work. Just over 57% of those in the EU reporting an LSHPD, therefore, declared that this restricted the kind of work they could carry out, whether considerably or to some extent, while just under 55% declared that it restricted the amount of work they could do. On the other hand, only around 30% reported that it restricted their mobility to and from work. At the EU level, women were slightly more likely than men to suffer each of these types of restriction.

In the United States, also, a large segment of the population reports some level of disability related to functional activities or activities in daily living (McNeil, 1997; DeLeire, 2000). The Americans with Disabilities Act of 1990 (ADA) is the first federal legislation to provide civil rights protections

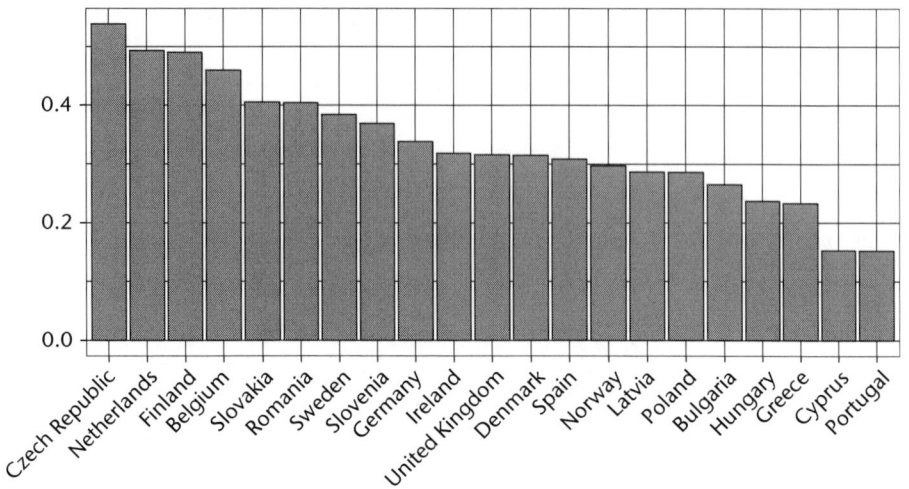

Figure 9.4. Experiences of age discrimination in the EU, total frequencies of people.

Notes: Fraction of individuals who have experienced prejudice because of age.

Source: European Social Survey, 2008.

to persons with disabilities. The Act's supporters promised that it would increase the employment and wages of persons with disabilities and reduce their dependency on public programs. The ADA does not grant a right to employment to all persons with disabilities. It requires that persons with disabilities be able to perform the jobs they seek, subject to "reasonable accommodations" by employers. The ADA's provisions assume that low wages and low employment rates for persons with disabilities are the result of discrimination caused by prejudice. Prejudice against persons with disabilities is well documented, but so are the limiting effects of physical impairments on workplace productivity (Hahn, 1987; Clogston, 1990). The core of the debate concerning the value of the ADA is whether the poor labor market outcomes of persons with disabilities are the result of discrimination or the limiting effects of health conditions.

Disability refers to activities, such as working, rather than attributes, such as gender or race. It is important to distinguish "disability" from "impairment" and "functional limitation," two terms that are often used incorrectly as synonyms for disability. An impairment is a "physiological or anatomical loss or other abnormality." An impairment may or may not cause a functional limitation, that is, a restriction of sensory, mental, or physical capacities. A disability occurs when functional limitations restrict the ability to perform activities such as working or attending school.

Consider, for example, a worker with a neurological impairment, such as epilepsy. Epilepsy causes a functional limitation, namely the inability to walk and to perform physical tasks during severe seizures. Seizures can restrict the person's ability to work, creating a work disability. If seizures are controlled by medication, a typical situation for most persons with epilepsy, the worker's job performance is not affected and the worker is not disabled. Workers with epilepsy are, however, still subject to discrimination.

In Europe, as many as 52% of people with disabilities are economically inactive compared with only 28% of non-disabled people, and only 42% of people with disabilities are employed compared with almost 65% of non-disabled people (European Commission, 2001). An important finding is that, at EU level, people with disabilities who participate in the labor market are only slightly more likely to be unemployed than economically active non-disabled people (12% compared to 10%). However this modest difference at EU level hides the serious problems that exist in individual countries. In most member states the unemployment rates of disabled people are substantially higher, the major exceptions being Spain and Italy, and to a lesser extent Greece and Finland.

Disability has a negative effect on labor market participation and on unemployment. An important question is to what extent differences in socio demographic characteristics such as age and education account for the relatively weak labor market position of people with disabilities. In its report, the European Commission (2001) shows that the probability of being in employment is lower for almost all age categories and for all educational levels. These effects reinforce each other: the labor market position of older people with disabilities is worse than the sum of the effects of being old and being disabled.

Disability affects the participation rate more than the unemployment rate. Consequently, the main labor market problem for people with disabilities is their low participation rate, that is entry into the labour market, rather than the unemployment rate, that is the problem of accessing a job.

The low unemployment rate for people with disabilities may be partly explained by a discouraged worker effect: because chances of getting a job are perceived to be low, they do not enter the labor market at all. In this case, a lack of job opportunities might be reflected in low participation rates rather than in high unemployment rates. The situation is likely to be reinforced by institutional factors and disincentives related to benefit systems (benefit traps). In other words, relatively low unemployment rates among disabled people do not fully capture the extent of their labor market disadvantage.

9.3.1 *Testing for Disability Discrimination*

The design of tests to detect disability discrimination is very challenging. In many jobs there are clear and objective human capital and employment cost differences between the disabled and the able bodied, and therefore differential treatment may well not be discrimination. Nevertheless it is important to ascertain whether the disabled do encounter discrimination when human capital and employment cost differences are either non-existent or negligible; also the extent to which differential treatment is prompted by various disabilities.

There have been three studies, two in England (Fry, 1986; Graham et al., 1990), one in the Netherlands (Gras et al., 1996), that have used written approaches to test for discrimination on the basis of disability. While the Dutch study tested for various types of disability, being confined to a wheelchair, epileptic, or deaf, the English studies only tested for one type of disability, an applicant with cerebal palsy who was confined to a wheelchair.

The first study conducted was in England in 1986 with a follow-up in 1989–1990, and both involved secretarial positions. These tests found statistically significant levels of net discrimination against the disabled applicant of roughly the same magnitude (37.6% in 1986 compared with 33% in 1990). As in other studies using written approaches, no effect was found from type of letter in the English tests.

The study in the Netherlands found a statistically significant level of net discrimination of 24% against the disabled applicant, with no significance attaching to the type of handicap or the occupation (professionals in administrative, commercial, and secretarial areas).

9.3.2 Impact on the Labor Market

Different researchers have examined trends in labor market outcomes according to disability status, concluding that the ADA resulted in lower employment rates for disabled persons (DeLeire, 2000; Acemoglu and Angrist, 2001).

For example, Baldwin and Johnson (2000) estimate the extent of wage discrimination against men with disabilities in 1990, providing a reference that can be used to evaluate the impact of the ADA, which provides civil rights protections to persons with disabilities. The results show large productivity-standardized wage differentials between disabled and non-disabled men that are weakly correlated with the strength of prejudice against different impairments. Physical limitations explain part, but not all, of the wage differentials. The results also show that low employment rates are a more serious problem than wage discrimination for workers with disabilities.[3]

Kruse and Schur (2002), however, find both increases and decreases in disabled employment rates associated with the ADA, depending on how disability is defined. A fundamental problem with these and similar studies of

---

[3] See also Charles (2003) who examines the dynamic effects of disability and finds a small decline in earnings and hours following disability onset, even for those who have positive disability reports for each of the next ten years, and Meyer and Mok (2006) who find a much larger loss in earnings and a greater decline in hours.

public policies with such broad coverage (e.g. the Civil Rights Act of 1964) is that because the policy was implemented at the federal level and covers nearly all disabled persons, it is difficult to identify a comparison group of disabled individuals that can be used to control for changes in the relative outcomes of the disabled that are unrelated to the legislation. For example, if the relative employment of disabled workers was falling prior to the passage of the ADA, then estimating the impact of the ADA requires a comparison of the relative employment levels for disabled individuals in the same time period who are and are not covered by the Act, a technique that is unworkable given the before and after framework available by focusing solely on the passage and implementation of the ADA.

Beegle and Stock (2003) take a different approach that allows them to identify groups of disabled workers in the same period who are and are not covered by legislation prohibiting discrimination against the disabled. Specifically, they exploit variation in state-level legislation that existed prior to the passage of the ADA. At the time of the passage of the ADA, only two states, Alabama and Mississippi, did not have legislation in place prohibiting discrimination against the disabled by private employers. In addition to allowing them to identify a comparison group, this approach explicitly captures the impact of legislation where none previously existed. With the exception of the two aforementioned states, evaluation of the ADA implicitly captures an incremental effect since legislation already existed at the state level. By ignoring the impact of this preexisting state-level legislation, measures of the incremental effect of the ADA will understate its impact when considered against a counterfactual of the ADA introduced into a world with no previous disability discrimination laws.

Using data from the 1970–1990 decennial US Censuses of Population, Beegle and Stock (2003) find that disability discrimination laws are associated with marginally lower labor force participation rates and lower relative earnings for the disabled, but find no systematic relationship between the laws and disabled employment rates. Their results are potentially more appealing than earlier research that focuses on the impact of the ADA, in that they are generated from a quasi-experimental empirical framework and account for the applicable laws, whereas the earlier time-series studies of the federal law assume the ADA is the only applicable legislation.

9.4 Housing Discrimination

9.4.1 *Testing for Housing Discrimination*

During recent decades, field experiments have been conducted in order to detect ethnic discrimination in housing markets. Such field experiments have made use of personal approaches. Generally, two testers are matched and trained so that they make equivalent enquiries when speaking to prospective landlords or real estate agents. The results from previous experiments essentially point in the same direction: ethnic minority groups are discriminated against in the sense that they are shown and offered fewer housing units on audits in the housing market in the United States as well as in European countries (for an overview, see Riach and Rich, 2002).

Indeed, *audit studies* were the first to experimentally examine racial discrimination in housing markets. Examples include Yinger (1986), Ondrich et al. (1999), and Page (1995). However, the use of in-person audit method limits the researcher's ability to restrict information, especially those unobserved to the researchers or actors, available to the subjects.

More recently, researchers have been carrying out experiments using written applications instead of making applications through personal approaches.

Carpusor and Loges (2006) and Ahmed and Hammarstedt (2008) pioneered the use of *e-mail correspondence design* to study whether ethnic discrimination was present in the rental apartment markets.

In particular, Ahmed and Hammarstedt (2008) present a field experiment on the Internet in order to study ethnic discrimination in the housing market. They apply their experimental method to the Swedish rental housing market. In the experiment, three fictitious testers, one with a typical male Swedish name, one with a typical female Swedish name, and one with a typical male Arabic/Muslim name applied for vacant rental apartments advertised by landlords on the Internet. By assigning testers with seemingly different ethnic backgrounds to apply for vacant rental apartments advertised on the Internet, the authors are able to identify the effect of discrimination on the housing market. Sweden is a suitable testing ground for an Internet experiment regarding ethnic discrimination in the housing market, since using the Internet is a relatively common way in that country of advertising vacant apartments and of searching for housing.

Ahmed and Hammarstedt (2008) found convincing evidence that Swedish landlords discriminate. When searching for an apartment, the fictitious Arabic/Muslim male faced different treatment from the fictitious Swedish male and the fictitious Swedish female. They also found that the Swedish female received far more callbacks and invitations to showings of vacant apartments than the Swedish male.

Ahmed et al. (2010) attempted to further these findings by studying the extent to which discrimination is driven by a lack of information about the applicants (statistical information) or by prejudice. They found that all of the applicants gained by providing more information about themselves, but the amount of discrimination against the Arab/Muslim applicants remained unchanged. This evidence suggests that increasing the amount of information about the applicants will not reduce discrimination.

9.4.2 Mechanisms

All the studies mentioned above that examine the real estate and housing markets in the US or Europe, such as Ahmed and Hammarstedt (2008), Bosch et al. (2010), and Hanson and Hawley (2010), find significant racial or ethnic discrimination against minority buyers or applicants, but do not provide clear evidence on the sources of discrimination.

Indeed, although most e-correspondence studies in the housing and real-estate markets are effective in controlling for unobservable factors, it was unclear whether the way that landlords or real estate agents' responses varies with information is driven by statistical discrimination or prejudice. For instance, Bosch et al. (2010) argued that statistical discrimination implied reduced discrimination against minorities with increased positive information, but they found that the racial gap in positive response rates remained unchanged when positive information was introduced. Their finding is similar to those by Bertrand and Mullainathan (2004), where the marginal return to credential for minority is lower than or equal to that for majority. On the other hand, Hanson and Hawley (2010) argued that they showed evidence of statistical discrimination in the US rental apartment market because the reply differences between white and African American applicants are smaller in high-class inquiry e-mails than in low-class inquiry e-mails, where class is determined by the quality of prose used in the e-mails. However, because reply rates decrease with class, their results may be driven by the higher fraction of negative replies to low-class e-mails. This issue highlights the importance of accurate coding of landlords' responses.

Similarly, Altonji and Pierret (2001) and Bertrand and Mullainathan (2004) found significant racial gaps in wages and job interview callback, respectively, but weak support for statistical discrimination. On the other hand, the related literature on racial profiling in the context of police searches, such as Knowles et al. (2001) and Antonovics and Knight (2009), provide a model without racial prejudice and differential treatment by race.

Employing *an e-mail correspondence experiment* in the rental apartment market, Ewens et al. (2012) test whether statistical discrimination is the primary explanation for differential treatment by race. They extend the Aigner and Cain (1977) model of statistical discrimination to provide testable implications for two features of statistical discriminators: differential treatment of signals by race and heterogeneous experience that shapes perception. They contrast the testable implications of the statistical discrimination model with those of a general taste-based model with competing implications. The authors use vacancy listings on Craigslist.org (Craigslist) across 34 US cities and roughly 5,000 neighborhoods (census tracts). They send e-mails with two key components to 14,000 landlords. They use the common racial-sounding first names of Bertrand and Mullainathan (2004) to associate applicants with race, and the email contains differing, but limited, pieces of information: positive, negative, and no signals beyond race. The dependent variable codes landlords' responses to capture an invitation to the fictional inquiry for future contact. Although the outcome reflects only a positive response during the initial inquiry phase of a screening process, any differential treatment in screening will likely influence final outcomes in the same direction. An ideal research environment to test for statistical discrimination has distant communication between agents with imperfect information and also avoids the confounding factors inherent in audit studies. The use of Craigslist for e-mail correspondence gives such an environment. Craigslist is the dominant source of online classifieds in the US, especially for apartment listings, and is frequented by one-third of the white and black US adult population. The website provides control of information and an ability to manipulate signals available to agents. Further, Craigslist allows the authors to accurately track responses and scale the experiment to thousands of heterogeneous neighborhoods.

Their experiment provides four major results. First, they present e-mails to landlords with racial-sounding names as the only signal and confirm that applicants with African American-sounding names are 16% less likely to receive a positive response from a landlord than those with white-sounding names. However, the observed differential treatment can be consistent with both statistical discrimination and prejudice.

Second, the statistical discrimination model posits that landlords differ in their perceptions of signals owing to past experience in the screening and, rental process and, in turn, incorporate race and signals into decisions differently. To test this hypothesis, the authors introduce additional information in some e-mails. In the "positive information" inquiry, the fictional applicant states her name and informs the landlord she is a non-smoker with a respectable (and paying) job. In the "negative information" inquiry, the applicant states her name and tells the landlord she has a below average credit rating and smokes. Using a difference-in-differences estimator, the authors show that the average landlord weights the same signal relatively more when it comes from an applicant with a white-sounding name than one with an African American-sounding name. This shows that this relationship also follows from a taste-based model where the average landlord derives lower marginal utility from a black applicant than a white applicant.

Third, consistent with statistical discrimination, the empirical results show that a surprising positive signal does not widen the racial gap.

Finally, they exploit neighborhood sorting to examine a source of heterogeneity consistent with the shaping of signal perception. By allowing a signal's noise to depend on race, their model presents another testable hypothesis: a landlord's relative experience with a given race increases the relative weight she places on the signal from that group. They find that as the share of black residents in a neighborhood increases, a positive surprise closes the racial gap observed in the base case, while a negative surprise does little to close it. More importantly, the base-case racial gap persists across all types of neighborhood and contradicts the prediction of the taste-based model.

9.5 Concluding Remarks

The last four chapters of this book contribute to the political debate on discrimination in Europe by considering unexplored dimensions of discrimination. Using the available survey data for Europe, we first provide cross-country results about the labor market outcomes of people with different religions, homosexuals, and individuals with specific outlooks. We find that Muslims, homosexuals, obese, and underweight individuals are in general penalized in the labor market, with interesting differences between males and females and between Northern and Southern Europe. Strong enforcement mechanisms and better equality policies seem to be the more beneficial anti-discrimination policies that can reduce these penalties. Notably, these are the anti-discrimination policy areas where the different European countries differ the most and where Europe on average performs worst.

We then conduct a field experiment in Rome and Milan and find that there is a strong penalty for homosexuals. Indeed, homosexuals have 30% less chance to be called back compared to heterosexuals and even more so if they are highly skilled. On the contrary, no penalty exists for homosexual females. We also found a beauty premium for females only, but this premium is much lower when the "pretty" woman is skilled.

Different economic arguments can be considered to explain our results. Following Becker (1957), employers may dislike the lifestyle of gay men but not of lesbians and then act on this bias. Research in social psychology has indeed shown that attitudes towards gay men are much more hostile than attitudes towards lesbians (see e.g. Kite and Whitley, 1996; Herek, 2000). The results could also be explained by an argument based on statistical discrimination (Arrow, 1973; Phelps, 1972). For gay men, an often-mentioned reason for statistical discrimination is HIV/AIDS since this is often the source of negative attitudes towards gay men (Badgett, 2001; Elmslie and Tebaldi, 2007). Statistical discrimination may then occur if employers believe that HIV/AIDS infection decreases workers' productivity and increases absenteeism. In contrast to gay men, most people think that lesbians are more focused on their careers, not on husbands or children, and that they have a strong aggressive style (Peplau and Fingerhut, 2004).

We can also apply the standard economic theories of discrimination (tasted base and statistical) to explain the negative impact on the labor market outcomes of obese and less-attractive individuals. For obese people (especially the very obese), it is clear that statistical discrimination prevails since severe obesity is often associated with low productivity. Furthermore, since previous experimental research indicates that beauty is not correlated with labor productivity (Mobius and Rosenblat, 2006), our finding may suggest the existence of labor market discrimination against the less attractive workers, especially women. The fact that high-skilled pretty women obtain less beauty premium than low-skilled pretty women may indicate the fear of competition with these women for certain types of jobs. Importantly, we show that the beauty results are particularly relevant for occupations requiring the interaction with customers as secretaries, receptionists, and general customer service.

The scarcity of cross-country data for Europe on these topics prevents us from providing detailed evidence on other important dimensions of discrimination, such as age discrimination, disability discrimination, and housing discrimination. In this chapter, we revise the specific theoretical mechanisms in each area and present an overview of the existing empirical studies. For age discrimination, we also use a special module of the European Social Survey to provide some evidence on attitudes towards ageing and experiences with prejudice because of age in Europe.

All these issues are really complex and the mechanisms behind them are difficult to identify. More work should be done, both from a theoretical and empirical viewpoint, and we leave that for future research.

Part II References

Acemoglu, D. and Angrist, J. (2001). "Consequences of employment protection? The case of the Americans with Disabilities Act," *Journal of Political Economy* 109: 915–957.

Adam, B. (1981). "Stigma and employability: Discrimination by sex and sexual orientation in the Ontario legal profession," *Canadian Review of Sociology and Antropology* 18: 216–222.

Ahmed, A.M., Andersson, L., and Hammarstedt, M. (2011a). "Inter- and intra-household earnings differentials among homosexual and heterosexual couples," *British Journal of Industrial Relations* 49: 258–278.

Ahmed, A.M., Andersson, L., and Hammarstedt, M. (2011b). "Are homosexuals discriminated against in the hiring process?," IFAU Working Paper No. 2011: 21.

Ahmed, A.M., Andersson, L., and Hammarstedt, M. (2012). "Are gay men and lesbians discriminated against in the hiring process?," *Southern Economic Journal* 79/3.

Ahmed, A. and Hammarstedt, M. (2008). "Discrimination in the rental housing market: A field experiment on the Internet," *Journal of Urban Economics* 64: 362–372.

Ahmed, A. M. and Hammarstedt, M. (2009). "Detecting discrimination against homosexuals: Evidence from a field experiment on the internet," *Economica* 76: 588–597.

Aigner, D. J. and Cain, G. (1977). "Statistical theories of discrimination in labormarkets," *Industrial and Labor Relations Review* 30: 749–776.

Allegretto, S. A. and Arthur, M. M. (2001). "An empirical analysis of homosexual/heterosexual male earnings differentials: Unmarried or unequal?," *Industrial and Labor Relations Review* 54: 631–646.

Allegretto, S. A. and Stettner, A. (2004). "Educated, experienced, and out of work," Employment Policy Institute, Washington, DC, Issue Brief No. 198.

Altonji, J. G. and Blank, R. M. (1999). "Race and gender in the labor market." In: O. Ashenfelterand D. Card (Eds.), *Handbook of Labor Economics*, vol. 3. Amsterdam: Elsevier, pp. 3143–3259.

Altonji, J.G. and Pierret, C. R. (2001). "Employer learning and statistical discrimination," *Quarterly Journal of Economics* 116: 313–350.

Anderson, L., Fryer, R., and Holt, C. (2006). "Discrimination: Experimental evidence from psychology and economics." In: W. Rogers (Ed.), *Handbook on Economics of Discrimination*. Cheltenham.

Edward Elgar. Antonovics, K. and Knight, B. (2009). "A new look at racial profiling: Evidence from the Boston police department," *Review of Economics and Statistics* 91: 163–175.

Arabsheibani, G. R., Marin, A., and Wadsworth, J. (2004). "In the pink. Homosexual-heterosexual wage differentials in the UK," *International Journal of Manpower* 25: 343–354.

Arai, M. and Skogman, Thoursie P. (2009). "Renouncing personal names: An empirical examination of surname changes and earnings," *Journal of Labor Economics* 27: 127–147.

Arrow, K. J. (1973). "The theory of discrimination." In: O. Ashenfelter and A. Rees (Eds.), *Discrimination in Labor Markets*. Princeton: Princeton University Press, pp. 3–33.

Averett, S. and Korenman, S. (1996). "The economic reality of the beauty myth," *Journal of Human Resources* 31/2: 304–330.

Ayres, I. and Siegelman, P. (1995). "Race and gender discrimination in bargaining for a new car," *American Economic Review* 85: 304–321.

Badgett, M. V. L. (1995). "The wage effects of sexual orientation discrimination," *Industrial and Labor Relations Review* 48: 726–739.

Badgett, M. V. L. (2001).*Money, Myths, and Change: The Economic Lives of Lesbians and Gay Men.* Chicago: University of Chicago Press.

Baldwin, M. L. and Johnson, W. G. (2000). "Labor market discrimination against men with disabilities in the year of the ADA," *Southern Economic Journal* 66: 548–566.

Balsa, A. I. and McGuire, T. G. (2003). "Prejudice, clinical uncertainty and stereotyping as sources of health disparities," *Journal of Health Economics* 22: 89–116.

Becker, G. (1957). *The Economics of Discrimination.* Chicago: University of Chicago Press.

Becker, G. (1981).*Treatise on the Family*. Cambridge, MA: Harvard University Press.

Beegle, K. and Stock, W. A. (2003). "The labor market effects of disability discrimination laws," *Journal of Human Resources* 38: 806–859.

Behrman, J. R. and Rosenzweig, M. R. (2001). "The returns to increasing body weight," University of Pennsylvania Working Paper No. 01–052.

Bendick, M. (1983). "The role of public programs and private markets in reemploying displaced workers," *Policy Studies Review* 2: 715–733.

Bendick, M., Brown, L. E., and Wall, K. (1999). "No foot in the door," *Journal of Aging and Social Policy* 10: 5–23.

Bendick, M., Jackson, C., and Romero, J. (1996). "Employment discrimination against older workers: An experimental study of hiring practices," *Journal of Aging and Social Policy* 8: 25–46.

Berg, N. and Lien, D. (2002). "Measuring the effect of sexual orientation on income: Evidence of discrimination?," *Contemporary Economic Policy* 20: 394–440.

Bertrand, M. and Mullainathan, S. (2004). "Are Emily and Greg more employable than Lakisha and Jamal? A field experiment on labor discrimination," *American Economic Review* 94: 991–1014.

Biddle, J. and Hamermesh, D. (1994). "Beauty and the labor market," *American Economic Review* 84: 174–194.

Bisin, A., Patacchini, E., Verdier, T., and Zenou, Y. (2008). "Are Muslim immigrants different in terms of cultural integration?," *Journal of the European Economic Association* 6: 445–456.

Bisin, A., Patacchini, E., Verdier, T., and Zenou, Y. (2011). "Ethnic identity and labor-market outcomes of immigrants in Europe," *Economic Policy* 26: 57–92.

Black, D. A., Makar, R. H., Sanders, S. G., and Taylor, L. J. (2003). "The earnings effects of sexual orientation," *Industrial and Labor Relations Review* 56: 449–469.

Black, D. A., Sanders, S., and Taylor, L. (2007). "The economics of lesbian and gay families," *Journal of Economic Perspectives* 21: 53–70.

Blandford, J. M. (2003). "The nexus of sexual orientation and gender in the determination of earnings," *Industrial and Labor Relations Review* 56: 622–642.

Boeri, T. and van Ours, J. (2012). *The Economics of Imperfect Labor Markets*, 2nd ed. Princeton: Princeton University Press.

Bosch, M., Farre, L., and Carnero, M. A. (2010). "Information and discrimination in the rental housing market: Evidence from a field experiment," *Regional Science and Urban Economics* 40: 11–19.

Carpenter, S. C. (2005). "Self-reported sexual orientation and earnings: Evidence from California," *Industrial and Labor Relations Review* 58: 258–273.

Carpenter, S.C. (2007). "Revisiting the income penalty for behaviourally gay men: Evidence from NHANES III," *Labour Economics* 14: 25–34.

Carpusor, A. G. and Loges, W. E. (2006). "Rental discrimination and ethnicity in names," *Journal of Applied Social Psychology* 36: 934–952.

Cawley, J. (2004). "The impact of obesity on wages," *Journal of Human Resources* 39: 451–474.

Chan, S. and Stevens, A. H. (2001). "Job loss and employment patterns of older workers," *Journal of Labor Economics* 19: 484–521.

Charles, K. K. (2003). "The longitudinal structure of earnings losses among work-limited disabled workers," Journal of Human Resources 38: 618–646.

Clogston, J. S. (1990). *Disability Coverage in 16 Newspapers*. Louisville, KY: Avocado Press.

Coate, S. and Loury, G. C. (1993). "Will affirmative-action policies eliminate negative stereotypes?," *American Economic Review* 83: 1220–1240.

Cornell, B. and Welch, I. (1996). "Culture, information and screening discrimination," *Journal of Political Economy* 104: 542–571.

Currie, J. and Madrian, B. (1999). "Health, health insurance and the labor market." In: O. Ashenfelter and D. Card (Eds.), *Handbook of Labor Economics*. Amsterdam: Elsevier, pp. 3309–3416.

DeLeire, T. (2000). "The wage and employment effects of the Americans with Disabilities Act," *Journal of Human Resources* 35: 693–715.

Department of Health (2003). *Health Survey for England, 2001: A Survey Carried Out on Behalf of the Department of Health*. London: The Stationery Office.

Dixon, T. and Waters, A. M. (2003). "A growing problem: Trends and patterns in over-weight and obesity among adults in Australia, 1980 to 2001," AIHW, Canberra, Bulletin No. 8. AIHWCat. No. AUS 36.

Drydakis, N. (2009). "Sexual orientation discrimination in the labour market," *Labour Economics* 16: 364–372.

Drydakis, N. (2011). "Women's sexual orientation and labor market outcomes in Greece," *Feminist Economics* 17: 89–117.

Elder, T. E. (2004). "Reemployment patterns of displaced older workers," Northwestern University Unpublished Manuscript.

Elmslie, B. and Tebaldi, E. (2007). "Sexual orientation and labor market discrimination," *Journal of Labor Research* 28: 436–453.

Everett, M. (1990). "Let an overweight person call on your best customers? Fatchance," *Sales and Marketing Management* 142: 66–70.

Ewens, M., Tomlin, B., and Wang, L. C. (2012). "Statistical discrimination or prejudice? A large sample field experiment," Monash University Unpublished Manuscript.

Feingold, A. (1992). "Good-looking people are not what we think," *Psychological Bulletin* 111: 304–341.

Fink, B., Neave, N., and Seydel, H. (2007). "Male facial appearance signals physical strength to women," *American Journal of Human Biology* 19: 82–87.

Flegal, K. M., Carrol, M. D., Kucmarski, R. J., and Johnson, C. L. (1998). "Overweight and obesity in the United States: Prevalence and trends, 1960–1994," *International Journal of Obesity* 22: 39–47.

Flegal, K. M., Carrol, M. D., Ogden, C. L., and Johnson, C. L. (2002). "Prevalence and trends in obesity among US adults, 1999–2000," *Journal of American Medical Association* 288: 1723–1727.

Fletcher, J. (2009). "Beauty vs. brains: Early labor market outcomes of high school graduates," *Economics Letters* 105: 321–325.

Fry, E. (1986). *An Equal Chance for Disabled People?* London: The Spastics Society, Campaigns and Parliamentary Department.

Fryer, R. G. and Levitt, S. D. (2004). "The causes and consequences of distinctively black names," *Quarterly Journal of Economics* 119: 767–805.

Galster, G. C. (1990). "Neighborhood racial change, segregationist sentiments, and affirmative marketing policies," *Journal of Urban Economics* 27: 344–361.

Garcia, J. and Quintana-Domeque, C. (2005). "Obesity, wages and employment in Europe," Labor and Demography Economic Working Paper Archive No. 0508002, (revised 2006).

Graham, P., Jordan, A., and Lamb, B. (1990). *An Equal Chance? OrNo Chance? A Study of Discrimination Against Disabled People in the Labour Market.* London: The Spastics Society.

Gras, M., Bovenkerk, F., Gorter, K., Kruiswijk, P., and Ramsoedh, D. (1996). *Eenschijn van kans: Twee empirische onderzoekingen naar discriminatie op grond van handicap en etnische afkomst.* Netherlands: Gouda Quint.

Groot, W. and Maassen van den Brink, H. (2007). "The health effects of education," *Economics of Education Review* 26: 186–200.

Hahn, H. (1987). "Advertising the acceptably employable image: Disability and capitalism," *Policy Studies Journal* 15: 551–570.

Hamermesh, D. (2011).*Beauty Pays. Why Attractive People are more Successful?* Princeton: Princeton University Press.

Hammond, C. (2002). "What is it about education that makes us healthy? Exploring the education-health connection," *International Journal of Lifelong Learning* 21: 551–571.

Hanson, A. and Hawley, Z. (2010). "Do landlords discriminate in the rental housing market? Evidence from an internet field experiment in US cities," Syracuse University Unpublished Manuscript.

Harper, B. (2000). "Beauty, stature, and the labour market: A British cohort study," *Oxford Bulletin of Economics and Statistics* 62: 771–800.

Hebl, M., Foster, J. M., Mannix, L. M., and Dovidio, J. F. (2002). "Formal and interpersonal discrimination: A field study bias toward homosexual applicants," *Personalityand Social Psychology Bulletin* 28: 815–825.

Hedegaard, M. and Tyran, J.-R. (2011). "The price of prejudice," The Rockwool Foundation Research Unit, Denmark, Study Paper No. 32.

Heilman, M. E. and Saruwatari, L. R. (1979). "When beauty is beastly: The effects of appearance and sex on evaluations of job applicants for managerial and non-managerial jobs," *Organizational Behavior and Human Performance* 23: 360–372.

Herek, G. M. (2000). "Sexual prejudice and gender: Do heterosexuals' attitudes toward lesbian and gay men differ?," *Journal of Social Issues* 56: 251–266.

Herek, G. M. and Capitanio, J. P. (1996). "Some of my best friends: Intergroup contact, concealable stigma and heterosexuals' attitudes toward gay men and lesbians," *Personality and Social Psychology Bulletin* 22: 412–424.

Hirsch, B. T., Macpherson, D. A., and Hardy, M. A. (2000). "Occupational age structure and access for older workers," *Industrial and Labor Relations Review* 53: 401–418.

Holliday, C. P. (2010). "The age discrimination in Employment Act of 1967: Issueslitigated at the Supreme Court level," *The Florida Bar Journal* 84: 20–34.

Hutchens, R. (1988). "Do job opportunities decline with age?," *Industrial and Labor Relations Review* 42: 89–99.

Iannaccone, L. R. (1998). "Introduction to the economics of religion," *Journal of Economic Literature* 56/36: 1465–1496.

Johnson, R. and Neumark, D. (1997). "Age discrimination, job separations, and the employment status of older workers," *Journal of Human Resources* 32: 779–811.

Kahn, L. M. (1991). "Discrimination in professional sports: A survey of the literature," *Industrial and Labor Relations Review* 44: 395–418.

Kite, M. E. and Whitley, B. E. (1996). "Sex differences in attitudes toward homosexualpersons, behaviors, and civil rights: A meta-analysis," *Personality and Social Psychology Bulletin* 22: 336–353.

Klawitter, M. M. and Flatt, V. (1998). "The effects of state and local antidiscrimination policies for gays and lesbians," *Journal of Policy Analysis and Management* 17: 658–686.

Knowles, J., Persico, N., and Todd, P. (2001). "Racial bias in motor vehicle searches: Theory and evidence," *Journal of Political Economy* 109: 203–229.

Kofi, C. K. and Guryan, J. (2011). "Studying discrimination: Fundamental challenges and recent progress," *Annual Review of Economics* 3: 479–511.

Kruse, D. and Schur, L. (2002). "Employment of people with disabilities following the ADA," *Industrial Relations* 42/1.

Kuhn, P. and Shen, K. (2011). "Gender discrimination in job ads: Theory and evidence," University of California Unpublished Manuscript.

Kuran, T. and McCaffery, E. J. (2004). "Expanding discrimination research: Beyondethnicity and to the web," *Social Science Quarterly* 85: 713–730.

Lahey, J. N. (2005). "Do older workers face discrimination?," Center for Retirement Research, Boston College, Issue Brief No. 33.

Lahey, J. N. (2008). "Age, women, and hiring: An experimental study," *Journal of Human Resources* 43: 30–56.

Levitt, S. D. (2004). "Testing theories of discrimination: Evidence from the weakestlink," *Journal of Law and Economics* 47: 431–452.

List, J. A. (2004). "The nature and extent of discrimination in the market place: Evidence from the field," *Quarterly Journal of Economics* 119: 49–89.

LópezBóo, F., Rossi, M. A., and Urzúa, S. (2012). "Attractive face: Evidence from a field experiment," IZA Discussion Paper No. 6356.

Lundberg, S. J. and Startz, R. (1983). "Private discrimination and social intervention in competitive labor markets," *American Economic Review* 73: 340–347.

Lundborg, P., Nystedt, P., and Rooth, D. (2010). "No country for fat men? Obesity, earnings, skills, and health among 450,000 Swedish men," IZA Discussion Paper No. 4775.

Maestas, N. and Li, X. (2006). "Discouraged workers? Job search outcomes of older Americans," MRRC Working Paper No. 133.

McNeil, J. (1997). "Americans with disabilities: 1994–1995," Bureau of the Census, Washington, DC, Current Population Reports Household Economic Studies, 70–61.

Meyer, B. D. and Mok, W. K. C. (2006). "Disability, earnings, income and consumption," Harris School, University of Chicago Working Paper.

Mobius, M. and Rosenblat, T. (2006). "Why beauty matters," *American Economic Review* 96: 222–235.

Moon, M. and McLean, R. (1980). "Health, obesity and earnings," *American Journal of Public Health* 70: 1006–1009.

Morris, S. (2007). "The impact of obesity on employment," *Labour Economics* 14: 413–433.

Neumark, D. (1996). "Sex discrimination in hiring in the restaurant industry: An auditstudy," *Quarterly Journal of Economics* 111: 915–942.

NHLBI (National Heart, Lung and Blood Institute) (1998). "Clinical guidelines on the identification, evaluation and treatment of overweight and obesity in adults," *NIH Publication* 98: 4083.

Ondrich, J., Stricker, A., and Yinger, J. (1999). "Do landlords discriminate? The incidence and causes of racial discrimination in rental housing markets," *Journal of Housing Economics* 8: 185–204.

Pagan, J. A. and Davila, A. (1997). "Obesity, occupational attainment and earnings," *Social Science Quarterly* 78: 756–770.

Page, M. (1995). "Racial and ethnic discrimination in urban housing markets: Evidence from a recent audit study," *Journal of Urban Economics* 38: 183–206.

Peplau, L. A. and Fingerhut, A. (2004). "The paradox of the lesbian worker," *Journal of Social Issues* 60: 719–735.

Phelps, E. (1972). "The statistical theory of racism and sexism," *American Economic Review* 62: 659–661.

Plug, E. and Berkhout, P. (2004). "Effects of sexual preferences on earnings in the Netherlands," *Journal of Population Economics* 17: 117–131.

Register, C. A. and Williams, D. R. (1990). "Wage effects of obesity among young workers," *Social Science Quarterly* 71: 130–141.

Riach, P. and Rich, J. (2002). "Field experiments of discrimination in the market place," *Economic Journal* 112: 480–518.

Rodriguez, D. and Zavodny, M. (2000). "Explaining changes in the age distribution of workers," Federal Reserve Bank of Atlanta.

Roehling, M. V. (1999). "Weight-based discrimination in employment: Psychological and legal aspects," *Personnel Psychology* 52: 969–1016.

Rooth, D. (2009). "Obesity, attractiveness and differential treatment in hiring: A field experiment," *Journal of Human Resources* 44: 710–735.

Ruffle, B. and Shtudiner, Z. (2010). "Are good-looking people more employable?," Ben-Gurion University of the Negev. Discussion Paper No. 10–06.

Sarlio-Lahteenkorva, S. and Lahelma, E. (1999). "The association of Body Mass Index with social and economic disadvantage in women and men," *International Journal of Epidemiology* 28: 445–449.

US Department of Labor (2008). Report of the Taskforce on the Aging of the American Workforce. Washington, DC: Department of Labor Employment and Training Administration. Wanner, R. and McDonald, L. (1983). "Ageism in the labor market: Estimating earnings discrimination against older workers," *Journal of Gerontology* 38: 738–744.

Webbink, D., Martin, N. G., and Visscher, P. M. (2010). "Does education reduce the probability of being overweight?," *Journal of Health Economics* 29: 29–38.

Weichselbaumer, D. (2003). "Sexual orientation discrimination and hiring," *Labour Economics* 10: 629–642.

Weichselbaumer, D. (2012). "Heteronormativity and discrimination based on sexual orientation," University Linz, mimeo Working Paper.

World Health Organization (1998). *Obesity: Preventing and Managing the Global Epidemic*. Geneva: World Health Organization.

Yang, A. (1997). "Trends: Attitudes toward homosexuality," *Public Opinion Quarterly* 61: 477–507.

Yinger, J. (1986). "Measuring racial discrimination with fair housing audits: Caughtin the act," *American Economic Review* 76: 881–893.

Comments

Alan Manning

The authors of the second part of the book are to be congratulated for opening up a vast unexplored land of unanswered questions. A whole range of research is making us realize that labor market outcomes are correlated not just with our (admittedly limited) measures of human capital but with your physical appearance, your name, your religion, your sexuality, your personality and, it would not be unreasonable to hazard a guess, everything about oneself.

How one interprets these correlations is, as the authors acknowledge, problematic. They may represent discrimination in the sense of prejudice against certain types of people or it may simply be that all agents in the economy spend their time trying to infer relevant information about others from everything they can see about them—that is, they stereotype individuals or, to use economists' jargon, they engage in statistical discrimination. It is very difficult if not impossible to distinguish between these two big explanations.

One possible way to attempt to do that is through a comparison of European countries where one might expect that there are different amounts and types of prejudice in the populations and differences in the strength of government attempts to address discrimination. So Part II of the book does shed some light on these issues; but I think it is fair to say that the results can be no more than suggestive.

The most commonly explored dimensions of discrimination are gender and race. This part of the book does not go over these dimensions instead focusing on sexuality, physical appearance, and religion. This is rather a disparate collection but it is impossible to consider everything.

Are these the most important dimensions of discrimination? Figure 6.1 in Chapter 6 gives an indication of the types of discrimination Europeans perceive to be most widespread. It is interesting that gender, the focus of the most research, records the lowest levels. Sexuality comes "second" behind ethnic origin perhaps justifying the approach of the paper. But it is also clear that there are other sorts of discrimination that are perceived to be

Table 1. Self-reported discrimination by characteristics

	% of Total Population Personally Experiencing Discrimination of this Type	% of Self-Defined Group Personally Experiencing Discrimination
Age	6	–
Gender	3	5
Ethnic origin	2	23
Religion	2	12
Disability	2	31
Sexual orientation	1	12

Source: Eurobarometer, 2008.

widespread, notably age and disability, which are not considered in this part of the book.

There are tricky questions about whether the importance of a particular type of discrimination is determined by how widespread it is or the incidence among the affected group. For example, consider Table 1 with Eurobarometer data.

The difference in the two columns can be easily explained. Women are 50 percent of the population so even though only 5 percent report personally experiencing discrimination, this adds up to a lot of total discriminatory acts. On the other hand, 31 percent of the disabled report experiencing discrimination. I think there is a case for focusing on the second column as the best measure of the extent of a particular form of discrimination and on this dimension, one should be considering disability. I would particularly single out mental health issues as an area where we need to know much more about the treatment of people with those conditions. It is a very difficult area—while it would not be surprising to find that those with mental health problems have lower productivity the question is whether the size of the penalty in the labor market is proportionate or not.

The second part of the book investigates whether the extent of labor market disadvantage varies with government policies, both directly in the discrimination area and also more general labor market policies. Here I think there may be an undue importance attached to the actions of governments. For most people, their experience of discrimination is in the very large number of everyday interactions they have with others and it is the attitudes of others that are probably much more important in influencing the amount of discrimination. Governments try to regulate these interactions but typically can only do so by outlawing the most extreme of discriminatory acts. So I think the authors could have done more, using the wealth of attitudinal information in the Eurobarometer series (and elsewhere) to see whether outcomes are correlated with attitudes. In some earlier research (Azmat et al. 2006) I found that attitudes to women's work were correlated with the gender gap in unemployment rates, so I am perhaps predisposed to this view.

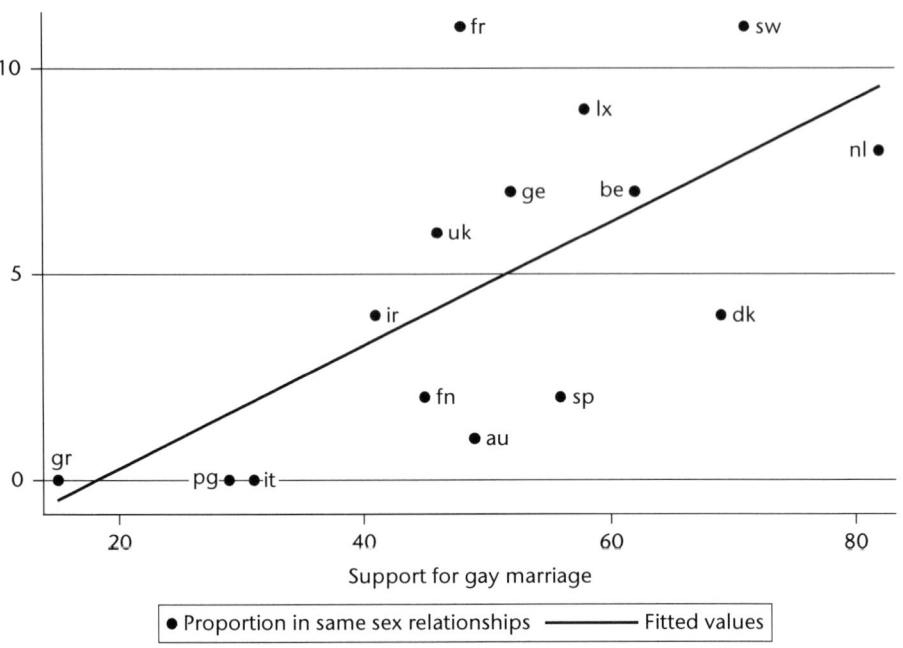

Figure 1 Correlation between proportion in same-sex relationships and support for gay marriage.

I will give one example from the report by Patacchini, Ragusa, and Zenou. As discussed, there is quite a lot of variation in the reported proportions of homosexuals in the different countries. It seems unlikely this reflects variation in the underlying incidence of homosexual inclinations (though Edith Cresson, former French Prime Minister, once opined that she thought 25 percent of British men were gay). In fact, as Figure 1 shows the fraction of the authors' sample who self-identify as gay is strongly correlated with the fraction who support gay marriage. A simple interpretation would be that the fraction of gays who are "out" is related to general attitudes to homosexuality.

In contrast, as Figure 2 shows, the correlation of the proportion in same-sex relationships with the measure of anti-discrimination is much weaker and not statistically significant.

The problems of ascribing all labor market penalties to discrimination is particularly stark when it comes to the poor labor market outcomes of Muslims, something of great importance in many European countries. It could be discrimination but even then it is hard to distinguish whether it is religion or other aspects that makes them a target for discrimination. For example, in the UK although 48 percent of Muslims who have experienced harassment think it was because of their religion (higher than for Christians

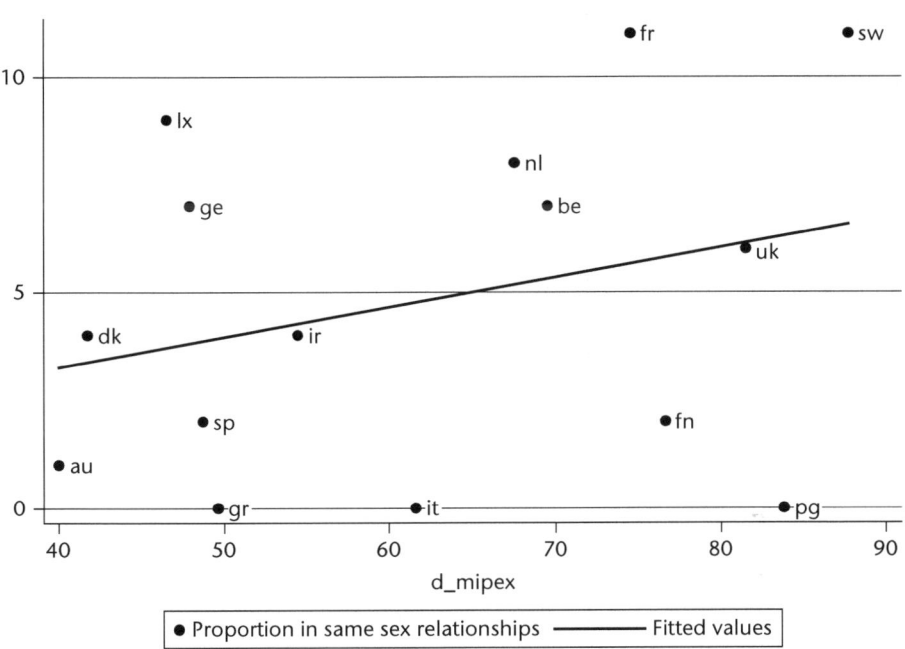

Figure 2 Correlation between proportion in same-sex relationships and anti-discrimination index.

and Hindus), 61 percent of them think it was because of their ethnicity and 41 percent because of their skin color. It is not obvious that religion is the target.

And it is also not obvious that the problem with the first-generation Muslim Europeans is that their parents had very little education and all children from such backgrounds tend to do worse in the labor market. Indeed, Matos (2010) goes so far as to suggest that all the Muslim penalties can be explained using parental characteristics.

It is clear that the low female employment rates among some Muslim communities largely reflects culture so not all employment penalties can be ascribed to discrimination. But it is also important to try to establish the extent of change. For example, Table 2 presents some data from Georgiadis and Manning (2011) that shows how female employment rates in the largest British Muslim communities are changing over time, following a trajectory that most women in Western Europe have followed over the past 50 years as shown by the employment rates for southern Italian women in 1980.

There is a huge amount of interesting information in Part II of the book but the area is so vast that it could not possibly cover anything. In these comments I have tried to outline where I think one could take the analysis further—to look more at cross-country variation, to exploit attitudinal differences across

Alan Manning

Table 2. Female employment rates by country of birth, marital status and presence of dependent children

	Pakistani	Bangladeshi	Indian	Southern Italy 1980
All Women	25%	16%	64%	29%
UK-born				
All	45%	48%	76%	29%
Single	68%	69%	81%	43%
Married	42%	40%	75%	19%
Married—dependent children under 16	36%	34%	69%	20%
Foreign-born				
All	18%	12%	61%	
Single	32%	64%	77%	
Married	19%	12%	61%	
Married—dependent children under 16	16%	11%	62%	

Source: Georgiadis and Manning (2011) and author's own calculations.

countries and to try to say something about trends as these are not static communities, they are constantly evolving.

References

Azmat, Ghazala, Guell, Maia, and Manning, Alan (2006). "The gender gap in unemployment rates in OECD countries," *Journal of Labor Economics* 24: 1–38.

Georgiadis, Andreas and Manning, Alan (2011). "Change and continuity among minority communities in Britain," *Journal of Population Economics* 24: 541–568.

Matos, Ana (2010). "The integration of the children of immigrants in European cities: The importance of parental background." In: *Equal Opportunities? The Labor Market Integration of the Children of Immigrants*. Paris: OECD, pp. 55–77.

Comments

Jan C. van Ours

Differences in labor market position may be related to personal characteristics that affect productivity. Workers with more education and work experience may be more likely to have a job and earn higher wages than workers with less education and work experience. However, not all differences in labor market position are related to productive characteristics. Discrimination refers to valuation of personal characteristics that are unrelated to productivity. Discrimination may occur along various dimensions such as gender, race, ethnicity, sexual orientation, age, and physical appearance.

Chapter 6 by Eleonora Patacchini, Giuseppe Ragusa, and Yves Zenou contributes to the literature on labor market discrimination. It gives a nice overview of previous studies on the impact of labor market discrimination on labor market outcomes. The authors also present an interesting cross-country analysis in which they relate labor market outcomes in Organisation for Economic Co-operation and Development (OECD) countries to a discrimination index. Furthermore, they present analyses based on cross-country individual datasets in which they relate labor market outcomes to measures of religiosity, homosexuality, and obesity. Finally, they present the outcomes of a quasi-experimental analysis of employers' behavior in relation to homosexuality and beauty. For this they sent fake applications to employers in Milan and Rome. In my comments I will shortly summarize and comment each of the empirical findings and then draw some general conclusions with respect to the existence and the labor market effects of discrimination.

1.1 Anti-Discrimination Policy Index

The authors use an interesting policy indicator, the anti-discrimination component of Migrant Integration Policy IndEX. This so-called D-MIPEX consists of scores on 34 items in four areas. First, definitions and concepts of race and ethnicity, religion and belief, and nationality. Second, fields of

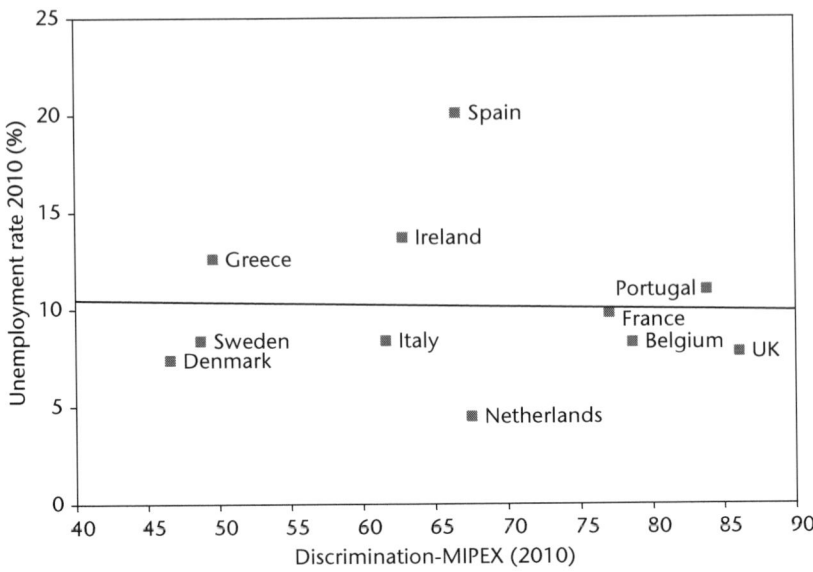

Figure 1 Discrimination index and unemployment rates in 2010.

application distinguishing between training, education, social protection, etcetera. Third, enforcement mechanisms such as judicial, criminal, and administrative procedures. Fourth, equality policies. Figure 1 gives an overview of the cross-country variation in this anti-discrimination index in relation to the unemployment rates, both measured for 2010. The United Kingdom, Portugal, Belgium, and France score relatively high on this index, while Greece, Denmark, and Sweden score relatively low. Unemployment rates in 2010 were relatively low in the Netherlands and high in Spain. At the cross-country level there does not seem to be a relationship between anti-discrimination policies and unemployment rates.

1.2 Religion, Homosexuality, and Obesity

By way of descriptive analysis the authors use the ISSP (International Social Survey Program) database which contains information on labor market outcomes and religion of workers. The authors find that Muslims do poorly in employment and labor force participation. They conclude that there is a "penalty that accrues to Muslims," which "seems to suggest that discrimination might be at work against this group in Southern Europe, in particular against Muslim females." I am not convinced by this analysis as it is not clear to me whether the differences are really related to discrimination.

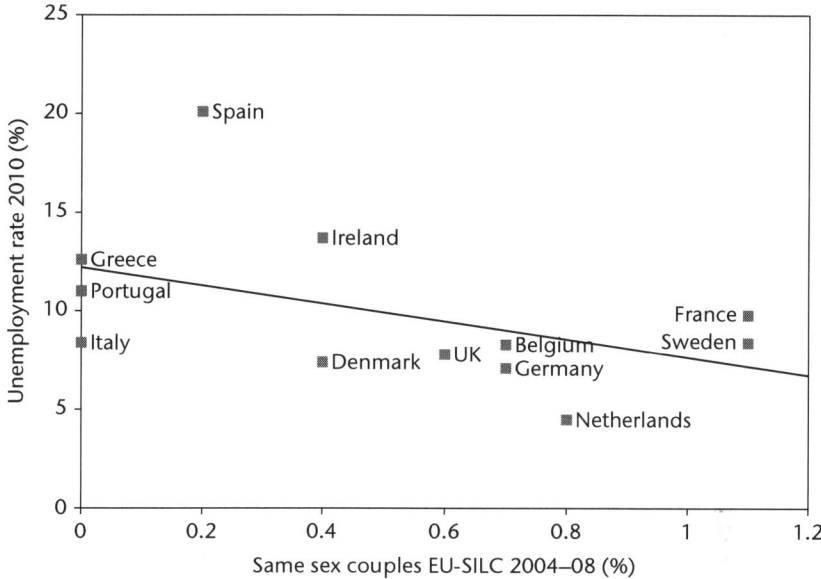

Figure 2 Percentage of same sex couples 2004–08 and unemployment rates in 2010.

There could also be differences between workers in terms of language skills and education that are not accounted for in the analysis.

To study the effect of homosexuality on labor market outcomes the authors use data from EU-SILC (EU-Statistics on Income and Living Conditions). This dataset contains information on self-declared same-sex relationships. Figure 2 gives an overview of cross-country variation in this indicator. As shown, there are no or hardly any same-sex relationships in Italy, Greece, or Portugal. I find this hard to believe. To me, the same-sex relationship is a very coarse measure of homosexuality which generates very small sample sizes for homosexuals in particular in some countries. Indeed, the authors conclude that these results "should be taken with caution." I agree. As is also shown on a cross-country level there is a negative relationship between homosexuality and unemployment rates but needless to say this relationship is not causal.

Finally, by way of descriptive analysis the authors use ECHP (European Community Household Panel) data to study the relationship between obesity and labor market outcomes. Figure 3 gives an overview of cross-country variation in obesity and unemployment. There appears to be a positive relationship which again cannot be interpreted in a causal way. The authors use the well-known BMI (Body Mass Index; the weight in kilograms divided by the square height in meters) as an indicator for obesity where an individual is underweight if the BMI <18.5, overweight if the BMI is 25–30, obese I if the BMI is 30–35 and obese II if the BMI is more than 35. The authors find that

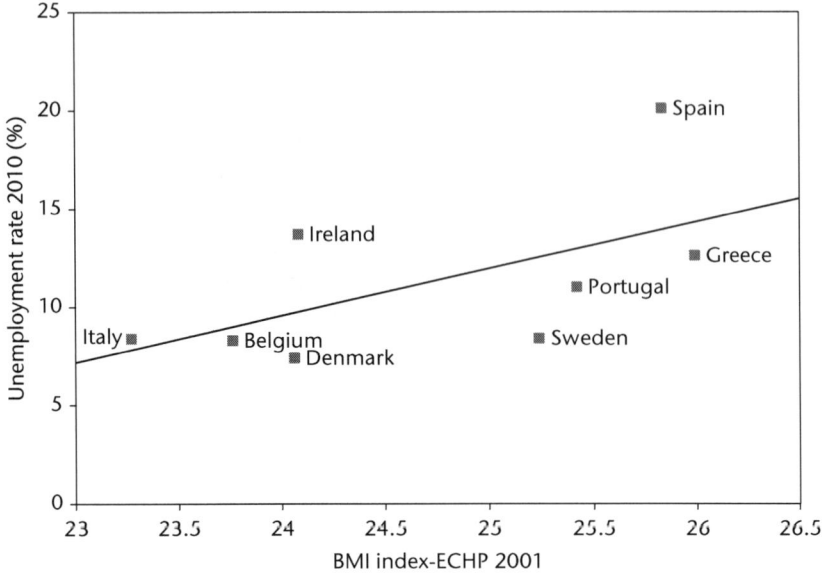

Figure 3 BMI index 2001 and unemployment rates in 2010.

overweight men do best while underweight men do poorest. Normal weight women do best, obese II women do worst. It is not clear to me whether these findings can be interpreted as causal results.

In short, the cross-country analysis of the effect of religiosity, same-sex relationships and BMI on labor market outcomes shows clearly the limitations of such an approach. The outcomes are very hard to interpret. I think it is not possible even to establish whether or not discrimination plays a role at all. Whereas I do not like the cross-country analysis I appreciate the research based on own data collection based on sending out fake applications.

1.3 Studies using Fake Applications

Empirical research on the existence of discrimination is not easy. For some labor market institutions a regression discontinuity can be used or a difference-in-differences approach comparing the situation before and after an intervention and comparing a treatment and control group. This is not possible in discrimination research. An approach which is very common is the estimation of wage equations in which part of the wage differences between groups is attributed to observable characteristics and another part is attributed to differences in returns to specific characteristics. The latter part is then attributed to discrimination. Therefore, discrimination is often equivalent to a "measure of ignorance." The main disadvantage is that the unexplained part of the wage differences depends on the available information on observed characteristics. If more information is available less remains unexplained and thus the magnitude of the discrimination effect is reduced.

Relatively new are quasi-experimental approaches in which fake applications are sent to existing job vacancies. The vacancies are real but the application letters are fake. There is a randomized allocation of stereotypical names to letters and a real response from employers (if any). Studies like this have been carried out along various dimensions of potential discrimination. Booth and Leigh (2010) for example sent application letters to employers with job vacancies in the three largest cities of Australia, Brisbane, Melbourne and Sydney, randomly assigning male and female names to various CV types. The typical female applicant received a callback 32% of the time, while the typical male candidate received a callback 25% of the time. Bertrand and Mullainathan (2004) surveyed all employment ads in the Sunday editions of the *Boston Globe* and the *Chicago Tribune* in the sales, administrative support, and clerical and customer services sections. Then they sent four resumes in response to each ad: two higher-quality and two lower-quality ones. They randomly assigned African American-sounding names and White names to the resumes. The authors find that resumes with White names have a 10% chance of receiving a callback. Equivalent resumes with African-American names have a 6% chance of being called back. Carlsson and Rooth (2007) investigate the presence of discrimination between natives and immigrants in hiring in Sweden. They sent applications to vacancies in twelve occupations and two cities, Gothenburg and Stockholm. Applications with identical skills were randomly assigned Swedish names and Middle Eastern names. They find that on average 29% of the applicants with Swedish sounding names got a callback for an interview, while for only 20% of the applicants with Middle Eastern got such a callback. Ahmed et al. (2011) investigated whether homosexuals experienced discrimination in the hiring process in Sweden. In the fake application letters they indirect labeled applicants as gay, lesbian or heterosexual by showing the gender of the applicants' partner and adding information about doing voluntary work in a homosexual organization or neutral help organization. On average gay men received 4% fewer callbacks than heterosexual men while lesbian women received 6% fewer callbacks than heterosexual women. Finally, Ruffle and Shtudiner (2010) sent out application letters to employers in Israel in pairs, one was without a picture while the second, otherwise almost identical letter contained a picture of either an attractive male/female or a plain-looking male/female. They find that attractive males are much more likely to receive callback than plain males while for females the difference in callbacks rates between attractive and plain applicants was small.

1.4 Discrimination in Milan and Rome

Patacchini, Ragusa, and Zenou sent out fake applications to employers in Milan and Rome to investigate potential discrimination of homosexuality and physical appearance. In randomly assigned letters homosexual preferences were signaled through periods of internship in pro-gay advocacy groups. The physical appearance was indicated by including a photograph to the application letter. The average callback rate was about 11%, but homosexual men received 3.1% age-points fewer callbacks, which was even less if they were highly skilled. Beautiful women received 1.8% age-point more callbacks but this was much lower if they were skilled. The findings are well in the range of findings in earlier studies. The authors conclude that in these Italian cities there is a strong penalty for homosexuals. I agree with the conclusion that there is discrimination of employers in Milan and Rome along the dimension of homosexuality and physical appearance. The question is how these findings should be interpreted. The callback rates are low for everyone. So, many applications have to be made irrespective of whether or not an applicant faces discrimination. How serious is the difference between 9 applications and 12 applications for 1 callback? I don't know but to me measured like this discrimination does not seem to be a major phenomenon. Also, an application is only a first step in a chain a events that might lead to a job. How serious discrimination in the next steps in this process will be remains unknown. Does it matter if some employers discriminate? Well it does from a equity point of view. It probably also does also from an efficiency point of view. If some employers have a reputation of discrimination they will receive fewer applications on their vacancies. Therefore, they may miss out on high-quality applicants. Also, for employers it may be costly not to accept all applications. It makes it more expensive to find the right applicant. As to the physical appearance dimension I find it also hard to assess what the implications are. The authors find a beauty premium for females. Is this discrimination? To the extent that beauty requires an investment it is part of their human capital (Hamermesh 2011).

1.5 What to Conclude on Labor Market Discrimination?

There are several theories that analyze the phenomenon of discrimination by employers. These theories differ in the extent to which they occur in a competitive or a non-competitive labor market. In the setting of a competitive labor market the main theory is the taste-based discrimination based on prejudice of employers. In the setting of a noncompetitive labor market there could be monopsony-based discrimination. Different theories have different implications for anti-discrimination policy. Prejudice of employers leads to smaller profits so a competition-based policy will push discriminating employers from the market. Monopsony-based discrimination occurs if employers have more market power over some groups than they have over other groups. Women and immigrant workers may be more tight to a firm than men and native workers (see for example Hirsch et al. (2010) and Hirsch and Jahn (2012)). As long as this market power exists the discriminated groups will receive a lower pay.

I'm sure discrimination exists but I'm uncertain how important it is for labor market outcomes. Recent socio-psychological research makes it even more difficult to establish whether discrimination exits and to figure out its consequences. This research points to the possibility that workers differ in psychological attributes and preferences (Bertrand 2010). These differences may make some types of jobs more attractive to some group of workers and other jobs more attractive to other groups of workers. If for example women are more risk-averse they will be less likely to accept a risky job with higher earnings but a larger risk of job loss. If this is not accounted for researchers may erroneously conclude that there is discrimination between men and women. Nevertheless, although laboratory based research has documented for example gender differences in personality traits as yet the empirical relevance in real-life data is unclear.

Discrimination is a dark side of labor markets and anti-discrimination policy is important. Patacchini, Ragusa and Zenou provide a nice contribution to the literature in a difficult domain. Much work remains to be done and I am pessimistic about the speed by which research can make progress and research outcomes can contribute to the policy debate.

References

Ahmed, A., Andersson, L., and Hammarstedt, M. (2011), "Are homosexuals discriminated against in the hiring process?", IFAU Discussion Paper 21.

Bertrand, M. (2010). "New perspectives on gender." In: *Handbook of Labor Economics* vol. 4. Amsterdam: Elsevier, pp. 1543–1590.

Bertrand, Marianne and Mullainathan, Sendhil (2004). "Are Emily and Greg more employable than Lakisha and Jamal? A field experiment on labor market discrimination," *The American Economic Review* (Sept.) 94(4): 991–1013.

Booth, A. L. and Leigh, A. (2010). "Do employers discriminate by gender? A field experiment in female-dominated occupations," *Economics Letters* 107: 236–238.

Carlsson, M. and Rooth, D. (2007). "Evidence of ethnic discrimination in the Swedish labor market using experimental data," *Labour Economics* 14: 716–729.

Hamermesh, D. S. (2011). *Beauty Pays: Why Attractive People are More Successful.* Princeton University Press.

Hirsch, B., T. Schank, and C. Schnabel (2010). "Differences in labor supply to monopsonistic firms and the gender pay gap: An empirical analysis using linked employer-employee data from Germany," *Journal of Labor Economics* 28: 291–330.

Hirsch, B. and Jahn, E. J. (2012). "Is there monopsonistic discrimination against immigrants?" First evidence from linked employer-employee data, *mimeo*, paper presented at the third TEMPO Conference on International Migration, Neuremberg, October 4–5, 2012.

Ruffle, B. J. and Shtudiner, Z. (2010). "Are good-looking people more employable?", WP 1006, Beer-Sheva, Israel: Ben-Gurion University of Negev.

Index

Note: page references in *italics* denote figures or tables, page references followed by 'n' denote footnote.

Printed and bound by CPI Group (UK) Ltd, Croydon, CR0 4YY